The Race of Faith

Achieving Spiritual FITNESS in the Christian Life

RANDY DISHAROON

The Race of Faith

Unless otherwise identified, Scripture quotations are taken from the HOLY BIBLE, NEW INTERNATIONAL VERSION®. Copyright © 1973, 1978, 1984 Biblica. Used by permission of Zondervan. All rights reserved.

Scripture quotations identified NASB are from the NEW AMERICAN STANDARD BIBLE®, © Copyright The Lochman Foundation 1960, 1962, 1963, 1968, 1971, 1972, 1973, 1975, 1977, 1995. Used by permission. (www.Lochman.org)

Scripture quotations identified ESV are from the Holy Bible, English Standard Version, copyright © 2001, 2007 by Crossway Bibles, a division of Good News Publishers. Used by permission. All rights reserved.

Printed in the United States of America

Library of Congress Cataloging-in-Publishing Data
Randy Disharoon
The Race of Faith: Achieving Spiritual FITNESS in the Christian Life

Summary: The Race of Faith is a plan, a process, a progression from infant believer to mature follower of Christ. This book is for you. Use it as a tool, as a guide, and as an encouragement to grow in Christ and become all that God has called you to be!

ISBN:-10:147923415X
EAN:-13:9781479234158

To my Dad, whose favorite saying was,
"It isn't where you start, but where you finish, that matters."

The Race of Faith
Course Layout

Foreword

The word *marathon* comes from the legend of Pheidippides, a Greek messenger. The legend states that the Athenian commanders sent him from the battlefield of Marathon to Athens to announce that the Persians had been defeated in the Battle of Marathon (in which he had just fought), which took place in 490 BC. It is said that he ran the entire distance, 26.2 miles, without stopping and burst into the assembly, exclaiming, "νικωμεν" (*nikomen*), which means "We have won!" before collapsing and dying.[1]

Very similarly, the Christian's race of faith is like a marathon, where the Christian is the messenger of the Good News, declaring in his final breath of this life on earth, "We have won!" Paul the apostle, with his death at hand, declared, *I have fought the good fight, I have finished the race, I have kept the faith. Now there is in store for me the crown of righteousness, which the Lord, the righteous Judge, will award to me on that day—and not only to me, but also to all who have longed for his appearing* (2 Timothy 4:7–8).

In our modern Olympic games, the Olympic marathon is traditionally the last event of the Olympic calendar and finishes inside the Olympic stadium, often within hours of, or even incorporated into, the closing ceremonies.

---

1   *Wikipedia*, s.v. "marathon," November 2, 2012, www.theopedia.com/battleofmarathon.

Warm-ups

The Christian life is a journey, a pilgrimage, a race to be run. Along the way, we experience highs and lows, smooth paths and rough patches, tremendous strides and painful setbacks, times when we dig deep inside and press on toward the goal and times when we feel like just giving up. For every Christian, the journey begins with a decision and is marked by many if not all of these experiences.

The same is true for me. I gave my life to Jesus Christ under a large oak tree at the age of seventeen. Since then, I have experienced periods of both tremendous growth and intense disappointment, some of it self-inflicted. There have been times in my life when I was touted as a model Christian and there have been other times when I have been vilified as a hypocrite. With a grateful heart and a hopeful outlook, I know God wanted me to write this book. It is the culmination of all that God has been teaching me during my race of faith.

Throughout my twenty-five years as a Bible student, teacher, pastor, and preacher, I have concluded that many who are running the race of faith have never learned or grasped the deeper truths and disciplines of Christianity. They have not adequately trained for the race. They know about Jesus and have accepted His offer of salvation, but they have never truly learned to follow and obey Him as their Lord. They have merely been exposed to church life and culture, which can be and often is based on traditions of men more than the Word of God. They have never truly experienced the victory of following Jesus Christ.

How can we run the race marked out for us with perseverance? Imagine for a moment what it would take to run a marathon. First, we would have to examine our personal motives for running such a race.

Next, we would have to establish a timeline and a plan to prepare for it. Then, we would have to discipline our body, mind, and spirit for months while training for the race. And on race day, we would need to endure the terrain, obstacles, distractions, and discouragements waiting for us. In order to run a marathon successfully, we would need to be in peak physical and mental fitness.

Similarly, we must be in peak *spiritual* FITNESS to run the race of the Christian faith. After all, every runner wants to experience the runner's high but every runner also hits the wall. Bookstores have shelves of books dedicated to the topic of physical fitness. Yet, there are far fewer books that address spiritual fitness. Some would say that spiritual training is the church's job. If so, how is the church doing? Others would say that it is each individual Christian's job. If so, why are so many languishing in the faith they profess?

Being a follower of Christ is difficult. Throughout my ministry, many Christians have confessed to me that they have not built a strong enough foundation to withstand the storms of life. Many others have admitted readily that they are not as knowledgeable of the Scriptures as they would like to be. Still others who are new to the Christian faith do not know how to develop and strengthen their faith.

The Race of Faith is a plan, a process, and a progression from the infant believer to the mature follower of Christ. This book is based on the motif of running a marathon, which consists of 26.2 miles. The race is broken up into seven legs, comprising the Spiritual FITNESS process.

This book does not presume the runner has any prior understanding of the Christian faith; that way, we all begin the race at the same place. As with a marathon, this book lays the most basic foundation in preparation for the weightier legs of the race. With each successive leg, the process carries us from foundational beliefs and disciplines, to deeper truths, and finally to practical applications of those truths.

Instead of sections and chapters, this book is laid out in legs and miles. Each leg is a one-word descriptor that spells out FITNESS. Each mile consists of questions that are answered with the support of the

Bible. Every Bible reference is fully spelled out so that the runner can easily find the passage for further context and study. I have included personal stories throughout the book to illustrate the teaching. Each mile answers the question, "How can I put feet to my faith?" Finally, each mile ends with a verse or verses from the Bible that speak to that mile's topic; committing these verses to memory will assist you in growing in your faith.

This book is for you. Use it as a tool, as a guide, and as an encouragement to grow in Christ and become all that God has called you to be. The following two verses illustrate the premise of this book:

> *Therefore, since we are surrounded by such a great cloud of witnesses, let us throw off everything that hinders and the sin that so easily entangles, and let us run with perseverance the race marked out for us. Let us fix our eyes on Jesus, the author and perfecter of our faith, who for the joy set before him endured the cross, scorning its shame, and sat down at the right hand of the throne of God.*

(Hebrews 12:1–2)

These verses are so encouraging for every follower of Jesus Christ. There are so many who have run the race before us and have finished well. This is the *great cloud of witnesses:* the faithful ones who have come before us. Our aim, our goal, our guide, and our leader is Jesus Christ, who is the *author* and *perfecter* (or finisher) of our faith. He endured the race, because of the joy that was before Him. In the same way, for the Christian, this life's journey is long and arduous, but it is worth it, because of the joy set before us. Therefore, we are to run our race of faith with steadfast endurance, throwing off the sin and shame of our pasts and pressing on toward the finish line—our home in heaven with God.

Runners, take your marks!

Starting Line

We have warmed up, and now it's time for us to line up on the starting line. The long 26.2-mile trek lies before us. As we mentally prepare for the race, we envision the layout of the course. The diagram below portrays the essence of this book's marathon motif. When a person becomes a follower of Jesus Christ, he or she most likely asks the question, "Now what?" The diagram below answers that question.

- The triangle represents the three-fold mission of every believer and of every church: worship, work and witness.
- Each side of the triangle represents one of the three key imperatives of the Kingdom of God: connection, commitment, and community.
- Each side connects and embodies the relationship between two of the three mission goals.

    ○ Connection: we connect to the church through our worship and the world through our witness.

    ○ Commitment: we express our commitment to God through our worship and our work in God's Kingdom.

    ○ Community: we build community within the church through our work and the world through our witness.

- The interior circle represents the ongoing process of spiritual growth and development for every believer and every church. The seven-leg process toward Spiritual FITNESS follows clockwise along the circle: Follow, Invest, Train, Nurture, Equip, Serve, and Share.

Upon reading and applying the contents of this book, you will have a fuller understanding of God's purpose for your new life in Christ and a pattern for growth and maturity for the rest of your life, as you prepare for the glorious life to come!

Therefore, let us leave the elementary teachings about Christ and go on to maturity...

(Hebrews 6:1a)

Before we begin *The Race of Faith*, it is helpful to see the big picture of God's glory and God's Kingdom. Therefore, as we mentally prepare for the long 26.2 mile trek, let's learn how we can glorify God and manifest His Kingdom on earth.

A. God's Glory

As the marathoner should be able to explain his or her motivation for running a marathon, so too must every person who chooses to follow Jesus explain his or her motivation for following Christ. What is your motivation? Why are you entering the race of faith? The preparation for a marathon is much like the preparation for the new believer. We are to seriously consider the cost of following Jesus. In other words, why are we running, and what is it that our running will accomplish?

As we approach the starting line, we must ask, "What is the mission of all Christians? What are we charged to do?" The Bible declares that the chief purpose of humanity is to glorify God and enjoy Him forever: *So whether you eat or drink or whatever you do, do it all for the glory of God* (1 Corinthians 10:31). There are three ways that every believer and every church brings glory to God.

1. Worship

The top of the triangle and the first way in which we glorify God is worship. Jesus said that we are to be worshipers who worship the Lord "*...in spirit and in truth*" (John 4:24). What is worship then? Worship is the humble response of the Christian to God—who He is, what He has done, what He is doing, and what He will do in the future. As to who God is, the Bible proclaims that God is eternal, spiritual, immortal, invisible, one, unchangeable, independent, all-knowing, all-powerful, ever-present, sovereign, holy, perfect, wrathful, loving, merciful, gracious, just, true, faithful, righteous, patient, compassionate, good, jealous, wise, glorious, and beautiful. We worship God because of who He is.

Furthermore, we worship God because of what He has done, what He is doing, and what He will do in the future. In summary, God created the heavens and the earth and all that is in them. (Genesis 1:1) He created man in His own image (Genesis 1:26-27)

7

and endowed man with freedom of choice (Genesis 2:16). He made a way of redemption when man sinned by coming to earth in the form of a man, Jesus Christ, (John 1:1, 14) to pay the price for sin once and for all (Hebrews 10:9-14), and He is coming again to judge the living and the dead (2 Timothy 4:1-2) and to establish His eternal kingdom. (2 Peter 1:10-11) For those reasons and so many more, we worship God, because He alone is worthy of our worship and praise.

2. Work

The lower right corner of the triangle and the second way of glorifying God is through our work. We are to work out our salvation and to contribute to the larger work of God's Kingdom. Note that we are not saved by our "works" but once we are saved, then we are to get to work. This work transitions us from disciples to disciple-makers. Webster's Dictionary defines "disciple" as "one who accepts and assists in spreading the doctrines of another."[1] A Christian is a fully devoted follower of Jesus Christ. Jesus made it clear that being His disciple would cost one's life. The emphasis was always on suffering and sacrifice. Many in the church today have no idea what it means to suffer and sacrifice for their faith. American church culture is characterized more by consumption than contribution. Too many people attend church to see what they can get out of it, but true followers of Christ present their *bodies as living sacrifices* (Romans 12:1).

Working out our salvation is to progress from infancy in Christ to a mature follower and disciple-maker. This process takes time. It takes discipline. And it takes a plan. Most do not begin because they either don't know where to begin or because the entire process seems too daunting. The fact is that most who give their hearts to Christ

---

1   Merriam-Webster OnLine, s.v. "disciple," November 15, 2012, http://www.merriam-webster.com/dictionary/disciple.

soon become overwhelmed by the distractions of life and the frustration of trying to find time to devote to their newfound faith. Paul encouraged the believers in Philippi to *"work out your salvation with fear and trembling"* (Philippians 2:12) This book was written to serve as a guide for Christians who don't know where to start or for those who have done the Christian/church thing for so long that they feel embarrassed or guilty to ask the simple questions.

In addition to working out our own salvation, Christ commands us to accomplish His greater work in the Kingdom of God. Five times in the Bible, we hear a different version of Christ's Great Commission. (Matthew 28:19–20; Mark 16:15; Luke 24:43–46; John 20:21; Acts 1:8). In every case, Jesus commands His disciples (including us) to make more disciples. In response to this command, we are to baptize and teach. This is the heart of the Great Commission and should therefore be the heart of every Christian and church. Unfortunately, the work of God's Kingdom is not an easy, check-the-box kind of discipline. It is hard. It is messy. It takes time. But if done in accordance with the Word of God, it will bear "much fruit" in the life of the believer and of the church.

3. Witness

The lower left corner of the triangle and the third way of glorifying God is to bear witness. We are to be witnesses to the saving power of Jesus Christ. The word "witness" appears in the Scripture as *marturas* (Greek), from which we get the English word "martyr." That is, we are to testify to the world about Jesus Christ: specifically about His death, burial, and resurrection. This is the action that leads to our "making disciples" and it is the compulsion that drives us to regular, vibrant worship of God.

Another word for witness is "evangelism." The Greek word is *euangelizo*, which literally means "good news." The Good News is the message of the witness. The apostle Paul lays out the witness process:

> *How, then, can they call on the one they have not believed in? And how can they believe in the one of whom they have not heard? And how can they hear without someone preaching to them? And how can they preach unless they are sent? As it is written: How beautiful are the feet of those who bring good news!*

(Romans 10:14–15)

Besides the passages cited above, there are several other passages that speak to Jesus's command to witness (Acts 13:46–47; 1 Corinthians 9:19–22; 2 Corinthians 5:17–21; Colossians 4:2–6; 2 Timothy 1:8–12; 4:2; Philemon 6; 1 Peter 3:15).

The Christian life should be characterized by worshiping, working and witnessing. This is the three-fold purpose of every Christian. While other aspects of the Christian life are important, these three capture the essence of what it means to be a Christian. Our purpose in glorifying God leads us to God's Kingdom and its three imperatives: connection, commitment, and community.

B. God's Kingdom

The word "kingdom" (Greek *basileia*) appears 121 times in the first four books of the New Testament, which are also known as the Four Gospels. By contrast, the word "church" (Greek *ecclesia*) appears only twice. This gives us a healthy perspective on His Kingdom to the world. In fact, the apostle John declared: *The reason the Son of God appeared was to destroy the devil's work* (1 John 3:8b). The devil's work began when he rebelled against God and tempted Eve in the Garden of Eden. This temptation resulted in sin, which broke the holy relationship between God and man. The rest of the Bible, from Genesis 3 to Revelation 22, explains

God's purpose and process in redemption. In fact, we could summarize the Bible in just one word: redemption.

The Kingdom of God is not being built nor is it being grown. Rather, the Kingdom of God is made manifest through the obedience of Christ's followers. It is important to note what Jesus declared at the outset of His earthly ministry: *Repent, for the kingdom of heaven is near* (Matthew 4:17). In other words, Jesus came to establish His kingdom, and He will use the church to manifest it. Now we come right back to the three-fold purpose of the church. Our worship, our work, and our witness all manifest the Kingdom of God. So, the three imperatives of the Kingdom of God are: connection, commitment and community. I will explain each of them below.

1. Connection

The first imperative of God's Kingdom is connection. Connection describes the joining of two entities. In the Bible, the most important connection is the relationship between God and man. When asked, "What is the greatest commandment?" Jesus replied: *"Love the Lord your God with all your heart and with all your soul and with all your mind." This is the first and greatest commandment* (Matthew 22:37–38). This is our vertical relationship. It covers the first four of the Ten Commandments. We connect to God through worship. It is our response to who He is as well as what He has done, is doing, and will do.

We are also called to stay connected to the world—to those who are not in Christ's Kingdom. Jesus stated that the second greatest commandment is: *Love your neighbor as yourself* (Matthew 22:39). This involves our horizontal relationships. It covers the last six of the Ten Commandments. We connect to others through the act of bearing witness. It is our mission to see the world come to Christ.

In fact, the biblical model for the church is the following: they broke bread together, they prayed together, they sang hymns together, and they taught each other from the Scriptures. In a word, they did life together. There was accountability and transparency. They were family. They loved and cared for one another and that love and care spilled over as a beautiful demonstration to the world.

The biblical model for external connection is not isolation from the world, nor is it immersion in the counter-Christian culture of our world. Instead, the biblical model clearly calls for proactive insulation: to be in the world but not of it. We are to be light for those who are in darkness, salt for those who are bitter, and hope for those who feel despair. Our challenge has always been to balance boldness with humility, conviction with compassion, and truth with gentleness. The first imperative of God's Kingdom involves making a connection—first to God and then to others.

2. Commitment

The second imperative of God's Kingdom is commitment. Admittedly, commitment is an overused word. Still, nothing great in life is ever accomplished without commitment. The same is true in the Christian faith. Most who take the step of faith to follow Christ are eager at first to make a difference and become actively involved in their church. Over time, however, many of these new Christians become overwhelmed. They can't seem to connect the dots of doctrine and therefore tend to fall back into their pre-Christian habits. Perhaps they get discouraged by difficult events in their lives, or they become disillusioned because they had an incorrect perception of what the Christian life should be like. The key to avoiding these pitfalls is to resolve to commit for the long haul.

The Christian life is not a sprint—it is a marathon. It is long, it is arduous, and it is painstaking; but it is also rewarding. Each step along the way gives the new Christian a greater capacity to have a tremendous impact on the world around him or her. Commitment results in a greater and deeper worship experience. The Bible says that since Christ died *once for all,* and:

> *Since we have confidence to enter the Most Holy Place by the blood of Jesus, by a new and living way opened for us through the curtain, that is, his body, and since we have a great priest over the house of God, let us draw near to God with a sincere heart in full assurance of faith, having our hearts sprinkled to cleanse us from a guilty conscience and having our bodies washed with pure water. Let us hold unswervingly to the hope we profess, for he who promised is faithful.*

(Hebrews 10:10, 19–23)

Our commitment to worship is based on the truth that Jesus has opened the way to the presence of God.

The second aspect of our commitment is the work we do. We are called by Christ to do His work, beginning with learning about Him. Paul declared: *I want to know Christ, and the power of his resurrection and the fellowship of sharing in his sufferings, becoming like him in his death, and so, somehow, to attain to the resurrection from the dead* (Philippians 3:10–11). True discipleship marries power with suffering. Discipleship means disciplining of the body, mind, and spirit to yield to God's will. As the Christian strives toward knowing Christ more fully, her faith will naturally blossom and grow, which then gives her greater capacity to do God's work and impact the Kingdom of God. The result is that when the storms of life come or tragic circumstances arise, the disciplined Christian's response will be a powerful testimony to the truth of Christianity and the power of the Holy Spirit living inside her.

3. Community

The third imperative of God's Kingdom is community. Community is quintessentially the Kingdom. Ravi Zacharias said: "There is unity and diversity in the community of the Trinity."[2] This is why it was not necessary for God to create either humans or animals. God was not lonely. He was in perfect fellowship with Himself, being the Father, the Son, and the Holy Spirit. We will talk later about the Trinity and how best to think about it, but let it suffice that God chose to create humankind in order to bring glory to Himself, whereby we find our purpose.

We build community within the body of Christ through our work within the Kingdom. Paul explained the essence of this work within the church:

> *It was he who gave some to be apostles, some to be prophets, some to be evangelists, and some to be pastors and teachers, to prepare God's people for works of service, so that the body of Christ may be built up until we all reach unity in the faith and in the knowledge of the Son of God and become mature, attaining to the whole measure of the fullness of Christ. Then we will no longer be infants, tossed back and forth by the waves, and blown here and there by every wind of teaching and by the cunning and craftiness of men in their deceitful scheming. Instead, speaking the truth in love, we will in all things grow up into him who is the Head, that is, Christ. From him the whole body, joined and held together by every supporting ligament, grows and builds itself up in love, as each part does its work.*

> **(Ephesians 4:11–16)**

When the church community is built up, it becomes unified; and when it is unified, it grows to maturity; and when it grows to maturity, it is a powerful witness to the world.

We also build community outside the body of Christ, outside the church, through our witnessing. Interestingly, the testimony of new

---

2   Ravi Zacharias, "The Law of Non-Contradiction and the Trinity," YouTube video, 4:57, from a talk given at Penn State University on February 16, 2005, post by Ravi Zacharias International Ministries on November 27, 2007, http://www.youtube.com/watch?v=kreSbagj_RM.

believers is very palatable and powerful to those outside the church. There are perhaps many reasons for this. One reason is that new believers still have many ties to the non-believing community. Another reason is that new believers have not yet been completely influenced by what some call "churchianity." That is to say, new believers have not yet begun to use the Christian vocabulary, which includes terms like born-again, atonement, transgression, " "Good News, salvation, repentance, and so many more. While all these words are very biblical in their origin and very important for teaching others about Christ, sometimes Christians throw them around in such a way as to alienate outsiders. Even the word outreach means very little to a person who is outside the church!

God has called all Christians and all churches to be salt and light to the world so that they may have a positive influence on the world. We can take a cue from Matthew, the tax collector, who invited sinners to his home to have dinner; he invited Jesus as well. This action, of course, was frowned upon by the religious elite but was welcomed by Jesus, which is another illustration of his purpose on earth (Matthew 9:9–13).

In summary, we glorify God through our worship, work, and witness, and we manifest God's Kingdom through connection, commitment, and community. With God's glory and God's Kingdom as our mission and purpose for running, we can be encouraged by this verse:

Do you not know that in a race all the runners run, but only one gets the prize? Run in such a way as to get the prize. Everyone who competes in the games goes into strict training. They do it to get a crown that will not last; but we do it to get a crown that will last forever.

(1 Corinthians 9:24–25)

Warm-ups are over. The gun sounds. Let *your* race of faith begin!

The Race of Faith

The First Leg: Follow

Becoming a follower of Jesus Christ is the first step on the way toward Spiritual FITNESS. In fact, a Christian disciple is a completely devoted follower of Christ. By following Him, we make a lifelong commitment to His will and His purpose for our lives. No Christian can call himself a disciple without first deciding to *follow* Jesus.

Mile 1: Christianity
Mile 2: The Bible
Mile 3: Core Beliefs
Mile 4: The Church

Christianity

A friend of mine grew up in a Christian home, and his family even went to church most Sundays. To him, church was boring, but it seemed to be what he was supposed to do. He learned a lot of Bible stories, such as Noah and the flood, Jonah and the fish, and Jesus walking on water, but he didn't quite understand how everything fit together. His parents didn't seem to know much more than he did. He went on a couple of pretty cool youth retreats when he was in high school, but when he went away to college, he was a free man, and church was no longer on his radar. Maybe you had a similar experience growing up. This first mile introduces you to what Christianity is and what makes it different from all other religions.

What Is Christianity?

Christianity is not a religion. Christianity is a relationship. All other world religions begin with *man* and involve his desire to reach up to God. By contrast, Christianity begins with *God* and involves His desire to reach down to man. This book will clarify the difference between what Christianity was intended to be and what it has become. That is, many people in the church today call it a religion, but that is not what Jesus came to establish. The following chart shows the various religions in our world today.[3]

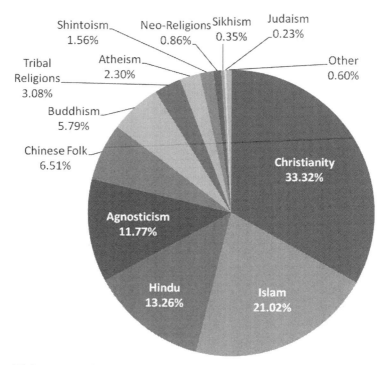

Taken together, those who profess Christianity make up approximately 33 percent of the world's population. How many of these professed Christians have a vibrant, active, and growing relationship

---

3   Charts Bin Statistics Collector Team, "Major Religions of the World Ranked by Number of Adherents," *ChartsBin.com*, 2009, viewed November 20, 2012, http://chartsbin.com/view/3nr.

with God through Jesus Christ? Perhaps you are reading this book to make your faith more active and meaningful.

The God of Christianity desires a relationship with us. He is the one and only true God. He created the world and everything in it. He created you and me. He fashioned us and designed us to be unique: every single person is one of a kind. There never has been nor will there ever be another person like you. The psalm writer declared: *For you created my inmost being; you knit me together in my mother's womb. I praise you because I am fearfully and wonderfully made; your works are wonderful, I know that full well* (Psalm 139:13–14). While God created humans in His own image, the first humans, Adam and Eve, sinned. That is, they disobeyed God's command. The story of the Fall recorded in Genesis 3 describes the first sin. Every single person born thereafter inherited the sin nature. That is, no one born after the Fall is immune from the sin nature. We all have it.

Many people have asked, "Why did God create man knowing they would sin?" This is a great question, but a question of even more importance is, "What joy would there be if man did not have the ability to choose to love God, but instead was coerced to love Him?" The essence of the Christian faith is that God gave men and women the power to choose to obey Him, but with that choice came certain risks and consequences, including spiritual separation from God and both physical and ultimately spiritual death.

The greatest problem with sin is that it separates us from God. Sin is ugly. It is a willful act of disobedience to God's holy commands. The Scriptures declare: *All have sinned and fall short of the glory of God* (Romans 3:23). God created us to glorify Him but our sin separates us from Him.

The penalty of sin is death. The Bible says that there are two deaths. The first death is physical, and because of that initial fall by Adam and Eve, we will all die physically. The second death is spiritual, but not everyone will suffer spiritual death (that is, separation from God forever). The reason for that is simple; it's called Good News but it's really the greatest news any of us could ever hear!

The Good News is that God intervened: *For God so loved the world that he gave his one and only Son, that whoever believes in him shall not perish but have eternal life* (**John 3:16**). Jesus Christ is God's answer to the problem of sin. Jesus was not born naturally—He was conceived and born supernaturally, by the Holy Spirit. He lived the sinless life. He became the only acceptable sacrifice for our sin. He is the Lamb of God. He is the only One who could pay the penalty of sin once and for all. He was crucified, buried, and, by the power of God, was raised on the third day.

All who believe that Jesus Christ is the Son of God—that He was really crucified for our sin, that He was buried, and that He was raised from the dead—will be saved: *That if you confess with your mouth, "Jesus is Lord," and believe in your heart that God raised him from the dead, you will be saved* (Romans 10:9).

We have just summarized the Good News of Christianity. Don't worry if some of the terms or concepts we just used are still a little confusing to you. We will be expounding on these concepts throughout the rest of our journey.

What Is a Christian?

A Christian is a follower of Jesus Christ. The term "Christian" can best be understood as one who strives to be more like Christ every day. The Christian "disciple," having the same root word as the term "discipline," is a completely devoted follower of Jesus Christ. A disciple follows Christ in word and deed by:

- Knowing, adhering to, and proclaiming His commands;
- Knowing, adhering to, and portraying His actions.

Throughout the rest of this book, we will walk through the various Christian disciplines that transform us into completely devoted followers of Christ. The Spiritual FITNESS model will guide us into a more vibrant expression of the faith we profess. The benefits of such discipline are similar to but more powerful and enduring than those of one becoming physically fit.

Benefits of Physical Fitness	Benefits of Spiritual Fitness
Increased Strength	Christ's Power
Increased Endurance	Christ's Perseverance
Increased Flexibility	Christ's Patience
Increased Agility	Christ's Perspective
Increased Ability	Christ's Productivity

What Are the Basic Beliefs of Christianity?

During the first two hundred years of the Christian faith, many different groups or sects added rules or challenged the core beliefs of the early church. Thus it was necessary to establish a set of essential elements that comprised the core of the new faith. The early church established its core faith statement, known today as the Apostle's Creed, which dates back to perhaps as early as ca. AD 215. The following list lays out the basic tenets of the Christian faith. These ten beliefs are agreed upon by all genuine Christians. Those who do not agree to these ten beliefs are not true Christians:

1. God created all that is seen and unseen.
2. Jesus is the Son of God and is one with God.
3. Jesus was conceived by the Holy Spirit and born of the virgin Mary.
4. Jesus suffered and was crucified.
5. Jesus died and was buried.

6. Jesus rose again (the resurrection).
7. Jesus ascended into heaven.
8. Jesus will return to judge the living and the dead.
9. Anyone can receive salvation.
10. Any person who repents of his or her sin and places his or her faith in Jesus Christ will be forgiven and receive eternal life, beginning at the moment of conversion.

We will walk through these beliefs in greater detail as we move through the Spiritual FITNESS model. For now, these basic tenets of Christianity serve as the right foundation for the deeper truths of the faith to be added later.

What Are the Key Teachings (Doctrines) of Christianity?

We can categorize Christianity by the major teachings (or doctrines) of the faith. The major biblical doctrines include: God, Jesus Christ, the Holy Spirit, the Bible, man, sin, salvation, church, and the end of the age. A survey of each of these doctrines in both the Old and New Testaments forms the basis for what unifies all Christians. The doctrines, taken together, answer the fundamental questions of life, including questions about God; man's origins; the meaning of life; truth, ethics, and morality; the afterlife; and the end of the age. The Bible provides substantive answers to all these questions and so many more.

Proper faith and practice are achieved only when each doctrine is developed by the whole counsel of Scripture. Throughout the history of the church, some sects of the church have chosen to place an inappropriate emphasis on one doctrine or another or have developed doctrines that could only be supported by some (and not all) Scriptures. This has resulted in many heretical sects or cults. Therefore, the key to establishing sound doctrine resides in a comprehensive understanding of the Word of God. The Bible reveals God and His will to us.

Once again, it bears repeating that all of these doctrines will be discussed in more detail later, but it is important to understand the big picture and to identify the major categories of Christian doctrine.

Take a few moments now to review the basic tenets of Christianity. Once our review is completed, we can look up and see that the *first* mile marker is just steps away! We can get excited about reaching our first mile marker or we can think to ourselves, "We have such a long way to go." Regardless, we are further along now than when we first started. Let's read on as we introduce the Holy Bible, Christianity's only authoritative source for faith and practice, but first, here is our mile 1 memory verse:

For God so loved the world that he gave his one and only Son, that whoever believes in him shall not perish but have eternal life.

(John 3:16)

The Bible

The aha! moment didn't come for me overnight. When I made the decision to read the Bible for myself, I found that certain topics propelled my exploration. Then, while on a six-month sea training during college, the big picture became clearer to me. Over time, I connected more and more truths from the Old Testament with Jesus and His message in the New Testament. As I saw the connections, I became convinced that the Bible is in fact God's eternal Word to man. Most Christians are still waiting for their aha! moments. This mile establishes the foundation for viewing the Bible as one cohesive message.

What Is the Bible?

The Holy Bible is the written, special revelation of God. While God has revealed Himself to our world through His magnificent creation, design, order, and providence, He has particularly revealed Himself in a number of other ways:

1. First, God spoke His eternal Word to His people directly. He spoke audibly to Adam, Noah, Abraham, Isaac, Jacob, Moses, Joshua, and David, to name a few.

2. Second, God spoke through men by means of the Holy Spirit, and men wrote down His Word. The Holy Spirit's purpose was to ensure God's revelation was perfectly interpreted by the human recorders, thereby giving us the Bible we have today. This is a critical teaching, as the Bible itself declares: *Above all, you must understand that no prophecy of Scripture came about by the prophet's own interpretation. For prophecy never had its origin in the will of man, but men spoke from God as they were carried along by the Holy Spirit* (2 Peter 1:20–21).

3. Third, God became a man. Jesus Christ is God in the flesh accomplishing God's purpose in redemption. Jesus continually taught that He and the Father are one and that if they have seen Him, they have seen the Father. The apostle Philip pointedly challenged Jesus's true identity by saying, *Lord, show us the Father and that will be enough for us* (John 14:8). Jesus replied: *Anyone who has seen me has seen the Father. How can you say, "Show us the Father"? Don't you believe that I am in the Father and that the Father is in me? The words I say to you are not just my own. Rather, it is the Father living in me who is doing his work* (John 14:9–10).

In summary, God has revealed Himself through the spoken word (by God the Father Himself), the living Word (through God the Son), and the written Word (given to us through the Holy Spirit). This chapter introduces you to the written word of God: the Holy Bible.

The Bible is a compilation of sixty-six books, written by over forty different human authors over fifteen hundred years. The word "Bible" comes from the Latin term *biblios*, which means "books." We refer to it more formally as the Holy Bible, acknowledging that it is inspired by the Holy Spirit: *All Scripture is God-breathed and is useful for teaching, rebuking, correcting and training in righteousness, so that the man of God may be thoroughly equipped for every good work* (2 Timothy 3:16–17).

The Bible is also known by other names, such as the Scriptures, the Word of God, and the canon. The word "canon," which means measuring rod or reed, expresses the fact that the Bible is the standard by which we are measured. This is a good way of thinking about the Bible. The Bible tells us that we need to be saved from our sin, and no matter how good we think we are, no amount of goodness will make us acceptable to God. The law of God is a mirror that shows us how unclean we are in the eyes of a holy God: *Therefore, no one will be declared righteous in his sight by observing the law; rather, through the law we become conscious of sin* (Romans 3:20).

While the Bible was written by over forty different human authors from varied walks of life and over such a long period of time, it is simply amazing that the narratives, prophecies, and teachings of the Bible are so congruent and consistent in their revelation of God's plan. Many skeptics have attempted to find inconsistencies or historical inaccuracies within the pages of Scripture, but the Bible remains inerrant and infallible. There is only one reason for that— God wrote it!

Why Should I Believe the Bible Really Comes From God?

This is a crucial question and one that I spent several years investigating. When we are first introduced to Christianity, we immediately have to deal with the question, "Who is Jesus?" Most of what we know about Jesus is found in the Bible. Therefore, we have to ask, "Is the Bible authentic? Is it really what it claims to be—the very Word of God?" Numerous great books have been written that answer these questions, but I will summarize here the top ten proofs that the Bible can be trusted:

1. The Bible claims to be the Word of God. Never in the Bible does it claim to be from any other source than from God Himself (2 Timothy 3:16).

2. The Bible is consistent. After all, it is a compilation of sixty-six books, written over fifteen hundred years by at least forty different authors from every walk of life, and yet it tells a consistent message.

3. The Bible has more manuscript evidence than any other book of history. There are more than 24,000 manuscript copies or portions of the New Testament, while Homer's *Iliad* comes in second place with only 643 copies.

4. The Bible's prophecies have all come true. Every prophecy recorded in the Old Testament has been fulfilled. The prophecies concerning the coming of a messiah were all fulfilled in Christ.

5. The Bible has been confirmed by archaeology. While the Bible is not authenticated by archaeology alone, no discovery made has contradicted the Bible.

6. The Bible is brutally honest about its characters. The authors might have been tempted to exclude some of the failures and flaws of history's heroes, but they did not. Jacob, Moses, David, and Peter are just a few of the examples of fallen men of God.

7. The Bible and external sources record the miraculous change in Jesus's disciples. The Bible clearly portrays His followers as having abandoned Him, yet all of them

would suffer tremendous persecution and even martyrdom as a result of their testimony of His resurrection.

8. The Bible adequately answers all of life's critical questions, including questions about the origins of the universe; humanity's relationship with God; sin; how man can be saved; and what happens when we die.

9. The Bible has miraculously been preserved. Throughout history, evil men (e.g., Adolf Hitler) have tried to destroy this book, and yet it remains the best-selling book of all time!

10. The Bible and its message of hope have changed people throughout history. There are countless testimonies of people enduring trials, tribulations, and temptations because of the Bible's timeless truths. For example, with the exception of John, every apostle was martyred for the faith, and millions since then have given their lives for Christ, knowing that He is the true Savior of the world.

Many people purport that the Bible cannot be trusted because there are errors or contradictions in its pages. If we adopt the motto of the church father Anselm, "faith seeking understanding," we can approach biblical interpretation by trusting the Bible first and then seeking to reconcile any apparent contradictions or errors. In truth, every apparent contradiction drawn from the Bible has a logical and reasonable explanation.

How Is the Bible Organized?

The Bible consists of two parts, known as testaments. The word "testament" means "covenant." The two testaments include the Old Testament and the New Testament. While the two testaments are very different, Jesus Christ ties them together. Each testament can be broken down into five sections:

A. Old Testament (Covenant):

1. Pentateuch, or law: Genesis, Exodus, Leviticus, Numbers, and Deuteronomy
2. History: Joshua, Judges, Ruth, 1–2 Samuel, 1–2 Kings, 1–2 Chronicles, Ezra, Nehemiah, and Esther
3. Writings/poetry: Job, Psalms, Proverbs, Ecclesiastes, and Song of Solomon
4. Major prophets: Isaiah, Jeremiah, Lamentations, Ezekiel, and Daniel
5. Minor prophets: Hosea, Joel, Amos, Obadiah, Jonah, Micah, Nahum, Habakkuk, Zephaniah, Haggai, Zechariah, and Malachi

B. New Testament (Covenant):

1. Gospels (meaning Good News): Matthew, Mark, Luke, and John
2. Acts
3. Paul's Letters: Romans, 1–2 Corinthians, Galatians, Ephesians, Philippians, Colossians, 1–2 Thessalonians, 1–2 Timothy, Titus, and Philemon
4. General Letters: Hebrews, James, 1–2 Peter, 1–3 John, and Jude
5. Revelation

There are several key points to understand when we think about the Bible and how it is organized:

- Some parts are chronological, and some parts are not. For example:
  - Genesis through Esther is historically chronological, but 1–2 Chronicles run parallel to 1–2 Kings.

- ○ Most of Psalms, Proverbs, Ecclesiastes, and the Song of Solomon were written during the lifetimes of David and Solomon, which are detailed in 2 Samuel—2 Kings.
- ○ Most of the prophets wrote during the history recorded in 1–2 Kings.
- ○ While Matthew, Mark and Luke tell a chronological story of Christ's life, John does not. The first three Gospels are therefore known as the synoptic Gospels.
- ○ Acts is a chronological recording of the events of the early church, but the letters (Paul's and the General Letters) do not appear in the Bible in the order they were written. Instead, they are generally organized by author, length, and/or audience.
- ○ Revelation is the last book written and tells of future events that will culminate this age.

- Another way to think about the Old Testament is pre-exile, exile, and post-exile. All history and prophecy recorded prior to 586 BC is known as pre-exile. All history and prophecy recorded between 586—516 BC is known as exile. And all history and prophecy recorded after 516 BC is known as post-exile.
- Some Scripture is told in narrative (or prose); some is told in poetry; and some is didactic (that is, teaching principles). An example of each follows:

  - ○ Narrative: Genesis 6–9 (Noah and the Flood)
  - ○ Poetry: Psalm 23 (The Shepherd's Psalm)
  - ○ Didactic: Philippians 4 (Rejoice in the Midst of Suffering)

- Numerical Bible chapters and verses were added centuries after the books of the Bible were assembled together in order to assist its readers. For example, the reference Psalm 23:4 gives us the Bible book (Psalms), the chapter of that book

(23), and the verse in that chapter (4). Throughout this book, we call out the complete reference for every Bible verse or passage quoted.

How Can We Learn the Bible? Where Do We Start?

One of the key life disciplines to achieving spiritual FITNESS is Bible study. But if we're honest, most new Christians (and even some longer-term Christians) don't know where to begin. Most pastors probably have their own prescribed answer for where to begin a study of the Bible. Genesis is the beginning of the entire Bible (and Old Testament), and Matthew is the beginning of the New Testament, so those might seem like logical choices. While there is no hard-and-fast rule, what follows is a suggested sequence for someone new to the Bible:

1. **Mark** (16 chapters; fast-paced narrative of the life of Christ)
2. **Romans** (16 chapters; clear presentation of the Gospel)
3. **Genesis** (50 chapters; creation, fall and Israel's patriarchs)
4. **John** (21 chapters; depiction of Jesus as God)
5. **Exodus** (40 chapters; Moses, Passover, the Ten Commandments, and the tabernacle)
6. **Acts** (28 chapters; the formation and development of the church)
7. **Hebrews** (13 chapters; Christ's superiority to the Old Testament)

How Do We Study the Bible?

Once we have read through a book, we want to go back and study it. Studying allows us to dive deeper into the truth of each individual passage. The best way to study is to use the headings that are found in most Bibles. For example, in the Gospel of Mark, most translations begin with the heading above Chapter 1, which is titled *John the Baptist Prepares the Way.*

Once we identify the passage, we read it. In the case above, we would read verses 1–8 and then pause. Next, we apply the Seven Cs of Bible Study:

1. **Context:** within what setting is the author writing? In other words, why is this passage here?
2. **Characters:** who are the main characters?
3. **Content:** what is the passage about?
4. **Central proposition:** what is the main spiritual idea being taught?
5. **Christ:** how is Christ related to this passage?
6. **Cross-reference:** what other verses or similar passages are there in the Bible?
7. **Change:** how can I apply this Scripture to my personal, daily life?

These seven steps can be applied to every passage in the Bible. The beauty of this method of studying is that it forces us to think about the passage, understand its meaning, and learn how to apply the truth or principle to our daily life. After a while, the process will become very natural. The more passages we study, the more the pieces of God's plan will fit together, the more confident we will become about the faith we profess, and the more God will open up new doors of understanding for us. It is truly an exciting process!

Ultimately, the entire Bible will come into view, and we will see the common thread of God's redemptive plan in play. Imagine piecing Legos together, a little here and a little there. After a while, we have a completed section of Legos in each hand. Then all of a sudden, we might notice that those two sections fit together perfectly. When we connect them, the object we are building becomes even clearer. That is exactly how daily Bible study works.

Bible Study Practicum: Read Luke 15:11–32.

Now that we have learned the basics of Bible study, it is now time to put it into practice. So, let's look at a great parable of Jesus in the Gospel of Luke. Read Luke 15:11–32, and let's answer the following questions:

1. What is the context of this passage?

    Jesus is accused by the Pharisees of welcoming sinners (15:1–3a).

2. Who are the main characters?

    In the passage, the main characters are Jesus, the sinners and tax collectors, and the Pharisees and teachers of the law. In the parable, the main characters are the father, the younger son, and the older son.

3. Briefly describe the content (what is going on?)

    The younger son wants his inheritance early; the father gives it to him; he squanders it and returns home; the older son gets upset because the father throws a party to welcome home his youngest son; the father explains to his oldest son that he loves both of them.

4. What is the central proposition (main teaching)?

    God loves the whole world.

5. How is Christ or God reflected in this passage?

    Jesus is describing how much the father loves both of his sons, the younger representing the sinners and tax collectors and the older representing the Pharisees and teachers of the law. Jesus is the teacher, and He is describing God's love for all men. Ultimately, by His death on the cross, Jesus made it possible for humankind to be reconciled to God.

6. What other verses/passages are similar?

   Luke 15:3–7; 8–10 and Matthew 18:12–14

7. What change can I make to my spiritual walk?

   We are to acknowledge God's love for all people. We must not condemn sinners but welcome them into a relationship with Jesus. We are to return to God when we sin.

These answers may not have come as easily to you yet, but do not get discouraged. The enemy, Satan, would want you to give up. Just as it is with learning any new skill, practice makes perfect. We will have more opportunities to apply the Seven Cs of Bible Study throughout this book. Read on as we further explore the core beliefs of the Christian faith, but first, here is our next memory verse:

Your word is a lamp to my feet and a light for my path.

(Psalm 119:105)

Core Beliefs

When asked by an agnostic coworker what she believed and why, my friend's heart began to pound inside her chest. In truth, she wasn't really sure if she could put her core beliefs into words. Her first thought was to introduce her coworker to me; after all, she was sure I would be able to answer her questions. My friend thought about looking up Christianity's core beliefs on Google, but she was concerned about trusting the sources. Perhaps you are in the same predicament. This mile lays out the core beliefs that unify all fully devoted followers of Jesus Christ.

What Do Christians Believe about God?

There is one and only one living and true God. This belief is known as monotheism. Monotheism is part of Judaism, Christianity, and Islam. The Christian God is an intelligent, spiritual, and personal Being. He is the Creator of the heavens and the earth and everything in them. He sustains and preserves the universe. He alone redeems man from sin.

He reveals Himself to us as Father, Son, and Holy Spirit, with distinct personal attributes, but without division of nature, essence, or being. This understanding of God is known as the Trinity. The Bible depicts all three persons of the Trinity as coequal and coeternal but distinct in function and manifestation. In fact, throughout the Bible, there are direct references to each of the three persons of the Trinity, both separately and together. For example, Jesus commands us to *Make disciples of all nations, baptizing them in the **name** of the Father and of the Son and of the Holy Spirit* (Matthew 28:19, emphasis mine). Notice that the word "name" is singular, signifying the oneness of the Trinitarian God.

Muslims often dispute the fact that God can be one in essence but three distinct persons. They see this as polytheism (many gods). To be sure, Christians are monotheists, but the power in the Trinity is that God did not have to create man. He was in perfect fellowship within His triune relationship. I have already quoted Ravi Zacharias's description of the Trinity at the Starting Line, but it bears repeating it here: "There is unity and diversity in the community of the Trinity."[4]

God the Father reigns with providential care over His universe and His creatures according to His purposes in grace. God the

---

4   Ravi Zacharias, "The Law of Non-Contradiction and the Trinity," YouTube video, 4:57, from a talk given at Penn State University on February 16, 2005, post by Ravi Zacharias International Ministries on November 27, 2007, http://www.youtube.com/watch?v=kreSbagj_RM.

Father also sets times and seasons according to His divine purposes. He is the author, initiator, and finisher of His redemption plan.

God the Son is eternal and was incarnated as Jesus Christ, conceived by the Holy Spirit and born of the virgin Mary. He lived a sinless life, paid the penalty for man's sin by dying on the cross, and was buried and resurrected on the third day. He is at the right hand of the Father and will return to judge the world and consummate His redemptive mission.

God the Spirit inspired men to write the Scriptures. He convicts men of sin, righteousness, and judgment. He exalts Christ, regenerates and dwells within all believers, reveals the truth of Scripture, and gifts and guides every believer in this life.

What Do Christians Believe about the Bible?

The Bible is God's love letter to mankind. The Bible is God's revelation of Himself to man. The Bible is the story of God redeeming mankind back to Himself. All Scripture is totally true and trustworthy—it is a testimony to Jesus Christ.

It is important to think about the Word of God in three manifestations:

1. **The spoken Word** *(And God said, "Let there be light," and there was light. – Genesis 1:3)*
2. **The written Word** *(This is what the Lord says... - e.g., Isaiah 48:17)*
3. **The living Word** *(The Word became flesh and made his dwelling among us. – John 1:14)*

The Bible must be the ultimate authority for the Christian in both faith and practice. Through the ages, men have considered other authoritative inputs on the same level or even above the Word of God. Such inputs include man's reason, tradition, and experience. To elevate any of these inputs above that of the Bible is dangerous.

Why? These three authoritative inputs have their origin with man and not God. The Bible has its origin with God and is therefore the only truly objective source for faith and morality.

What Do Christians Believe about Humanity?

Mankind is the special creation of God, created in His image. In the beginning, humans were created innocent, but they freely chose to sin, bringing sin into the human race. Did Adam and Eve have to sin? No. They did, however, and, as a result, all people are born with the sin nature. This is known as the doctrine of original sin. Our nature is to disobey authority, which is rooted in self-idolatry. Self-idolatry is placing oneself on a pedestal of greater importance than even God Himself.

All people need to be saved from their sin in order to be reconciled to God. The problem is that there is nothing we can do to be acceptable to God. There never will be enough good works we can do to get ourselves into heaven. This is one of the more common misconceptions in the world today. So many people think they are going to heaven because they are good enough. Many rationalize that they are not murderers or thieves. They build a theology based on the idea that only the really bad people will be consigned to hell. They say that a loving God would never send basically good people to hell.

This may sound rational, but it does not reflect the Bible. The Bible very clearly says: *There is no one righteous, not even one,* and that *all have sinned and fall short of the glory of God* (Romans 3:10, 23). We see the ugliness of our sin when we better understand the holiness of God: *Your eyes are too pure to look on evil; you cannot tolerate wrong* (Habakkuk 1:13).

To the Lord, all sin is intolerable. All sin is an abomination to Him. Different sins have different consequences, but every sin separates us from God. Even one sin separates us from God. We all deserve hell. This is a very unpopular truth, but it is truth, and we must acknowledge it and let it guide our beliefs and actions.

What Do Christians Believe about Salvation?

Jesus Christ is the only Savior from sin. He provided forgiveness for our sins by dying on the cross, shedding His blood (this is known as the atonement, or covering), and rising again to provide eternal life and justification for all who believe in Him. A common myth today is that there is more than one road to heaven. Non-Christians see Christians as intolerant. Pluralism, the belief system that claims there are many ways to heaven or the eternal blessed state, has become the more politically correct option. In essence, this group says, "Don't tell me what to believe, and I won't tell you what to believe."

Unfortunately for the Christian, not telling others what we believe directly disobeys Christ's Great Commission. Many Christians have not gone about spreading the Christian message in the right way. They may have a sense of urgency, but they are offensive when delivering the message of Christ. A friend of mine once said, "Christians don't have to be offensive; the Gospel is offensive enough."

While some Christians have been offensive, this does not negate the fact that we are called and commanded to "Go and tell." To do anything less would be disobedience to the One we follow. The Bible says that Jesus is the only way to God. Jesus said: *I am the way and the truth and the life. No one comes to the Father except through me* (John 14:6).

Salvation is both an event and a process. The moment of conversion is typically signified with a prayer to God, acknowledging Him and accepting the free gift of His grace by trusting in Jesus Christ as our personal Savior and Lord. This prayer typically ends with a commitment to follow Him daily and to tell others of His wonderful love.

The process of salvation includes several phases. We will talk at length about the process of salvation in mile 16, but we will introduce the nine phases here:

1. **Election:** chosen by God
2. **Calling:** pursued by God
3. **Conversion:** trusting in God
4. **Regeneration:** transformed by God
5. **Justification:** declared not guilty by God
6. **Adoption:** becoming a child of God
7. **Sanctification:** progressively growing in Christ
8. **Perseverance:** enduring trials by the strength of Christ
9. **Glorification:** translated by God to dwell in heaven forever with Him

What Do Christians Believe about the Church?

While many people attend worship services at a place called a church, the biblical definition of the church is the body of believers in Jesus Christ in every age. This is known as the universal church. The local church is a body of believers in Christ who have covenanted together to follow the teachings of the Bible in doctrine, worship, and practice. The local church is a self-governed organization served by pastors and lay leaders, all of whom submit to the lordship of Christ and the leadership of the Holy Spirit.

There are two ordinances of the local church expounded in the Bible: believer's baptism by immersion and the Lord's Supper. While the Roman Catholic Church espouses seven sacraments, there is no biblical support for them. They were added as part of the tradition of the Roman Catholic Church. This is one of the primary differences between the Catholic Church and all Protestant churches. The Catholic Church holds the Bible *and* church tradition as equal authorities and the Pope as Christ's infallible substitute on earth, whereas Protestant churches declare the Bible as the only source of authority for faith and practice, and that Christ Himself is the Head of the church, for no man is infallible.

What is the difference between a sacrament and an ordinance? A sacrament is said to be a work that bestows grace to the believer. The Bible clearly disputes that any work of man will obtain salvation: *For it is by grace you have been saved, through faith—and this not from yourselves, it is the gift of God—not by works, so that no one can boast* (Ephesians 2:8–9).

Ordinances, on the other hand, are symbolic representations of the Christian's identification with Christ. A believer's baptism is not to be confused with infant baptism. Infant baptism, espoused by the Roman Catholic Church and many other mainline Protestant churches, can be more accurately likened to a dedication of the infant to the Lord. Believer's baptism is immersion of the new believer *after* he or she has confessed publicly his or her faith in Christ. Baptism symbolizes the death, burial, and resurrection of the new believer in Christ (Romans 6:1–7).

The Lord's Supper is the second ordinance. The Lord's Supper, or communion, symbolizes the union of all believers with Christ in His death. The bread symbolizes His body, and the cup symbolizes His blood. Again, the bread and cup are symbols and are not the actual body and blood of Christ (as taught in the Roman Catholic Church). When the believing community partakes of the Lord's Supper, it remembers Christ's death until He comes again.

Through the ministry of the local church, Christians should become more like Christ every day, both in the knowledge of His truth and in general benevolence toward others. All Christians shall engage regularly in Bible study, prayer, worship, fellowship, evangelism, and stewardship. We will discuss the particulars of these disciplines later.

What Do Christians Believe about the End of This Age?

The Bible clearly teaches the imminent and bodily return of Jesus Christ to the earth. This is known as the Second Coming of

Christ. The dead will rise, and Christ will judge all men: the wicked will be cast into eternal punishment and outer darkness, prepared for the devil and his angels who preceded them. Christians will enter into the eternal state of glory with God and will, in their resurrected and glorified bodies, spend eternity with Him in heaven. Heaven will exist on the New Earth described in Revelation 21–22.

Christians are called to look forward to the return of Christ but to do His work while He is away. One of the more beautiful passages of Scripture that depicts Christ's coming again is found in John 14: *Do not let your hearts be troubled. Trust in God; trust also in me. In my Father's house are many rooms; if it were not so, I would have told you. I am going there to prepare a place for you. And if I go and prepare a place for you, I will come back and take you to be with me that you also may be where I am* (John 14:1–3).

This mile has been a very quick overview of the core beliefs of Christianity. Don't worry if some of it is hard for you to grasp. We will delve more deeply into each belief as we progress through the Spiritual FITNESS model. For now, you have the basics. Next, we need to gain a clearer understanding of the local church, but first, here is our next memory verse:

Jesus answered, I am the way and the truth and the life. No one comes to the Father except through me.

(John 14:6)

The Church

As I write this mile, I am saddened by the number of denominations within Christianity. There are Catholics and Protestants, Eastern Orthodox and Greek Orthodox. Within Protestantism, there are Baptists, Methodists, Lutherans, Presbyterians, Episcopalians, Assemblies of God, and a whole slew of so-called nondenominational churches. The worship wars of the last twenty-five years have only exacerbated the denominational differences of the past five hundred years and confused the honest seeker about how to "be" the church. This mile shuts out all the stereotypes and explains once and for all the biblical model of the Christian church.

What Is the Church?

Most people say that they go to church. However, the Bible clearly teaches that all Christians are the church. Jesus said: *I will build my church...* (Matthew 16:18). We learn from this phrase that Jesus is the builder and owner of the church; notice that He says it is His church.

The Bible teaches that Jesus is both the cornerstone and the capstone of the church. This imagery is instructive to our understanding of the church. The cornerstone of any building is the first stone laid, forms the foundation for the entire building, and establishes the trueness and integrity of the building. All other stones are to be laid in alignment to that one stone in order to ensure the strength and integrity of the structure.

In every aspect, Jesus is the perfect fulfillment of the chief cornerstone (Isaiah 28:16; Zechariah 10:4; Ephesians 2:20; 1 Peter 2:6). Paul paints the picture of the church as the house of God: *You are no longer foreigners and aliens, but fellow citizens with God's people and members of God's household, built on the foundation of the apostles and prophets, with Christ Jesus himself as the chief cornerstone. In him the whole building is joined together and rises to become a holy temple in the Lord* (Ephesians 2:19–21).

The capstone sits at the top of the building. It is the last stone placed and is a fitting finish to the building. Jesus will fulfill His title as the capstone at His Second Coming (Psalm 118:22; Matthew 21:42; Mark 12:10; Luke 20:17; Acts 4:11; 1 Peter 2:7). Peter expresses this truth when he quotes the psalmist: *The stone the builders rejected has become the capstone* (1 Peter 2:7). Jesus Himself declared: *Behold, I am coming soon! My reward is with me, and I will give to everyone according to what he has done. I am the Alpha and the Omega, the First and the Last, the Beginning and the End. Blessed are those who wash their robes, that they may have the right to the tree of life and may go through the gates into the city* (Revelation 22:12–14).

Now that we understand that Jesus Christ is both the foundational and the final stone of the church, we can define the church, both at the macro and micro level. "The Church" is that body of persons who has genuinely confessed that Jesus is Lord and who genuinely believed that God raised Him from the dead (Romans 10:9–13). The church includes all the redeemed of all the ages, since the creation of the world. One day, the church will be assembled together in the presence of God. John, the author of Revelation, saw *a great multitude that no one could count, from every nation, tribe, people and language, standing before the throne and in front of the Lamb. They were wearing white robes and were holding palm branches in their hands* (Revelation 7:9).

To distinguish from "the Church," "a Church" (Greek *ecclesia*), is a local assembly of believers united by covenant in the teaching and practice of the Gospel. The word *ecclesia* is formed from two other Greek words—*ek* and *kaleo*—which together mean "called out." Therefore, a church is a local body of called-out persons. The very first description of what this assembly of "called-out" ones did appears in Acts 2:

> *They devoted themselves to the apostles' teaching and to the fellowship, to the breaking of bread and to prayer. Everyone was filled with awe, and many wonders and miraculous signs were done by the apostles. All the believers were together and had everything in common. Selling their possessions and goods, they gave to anyone as he had need. Every day they continued to meet together in the temple courts. They broke bread in their homes and ate together with glad and sincere hearts, praising God and enjoying the favor of all the people. And the Lord added to their number daily those who were being saved.*

> **(Acts 2:42–47)**

We see several key aspects of the early church in this passage: teaching, fellowship, communion, prayer, wonders and signs, giving, praise, and growth. The teaching (translated from the Greek *didache*) was from the apostles, who were eyewitnesses to the resurrection of Jesus Christ. The word "fellowship" (Greek *koinonia*) connotes an active participation and commitment to the church's mission. The communion, or breaking of bread, continued the ordinance instituted by Jesus during His Passover meal with His apostles. Prayer (Greek *proseuche*) involved the verbal communication with God. The wonders and signs of the apostles served to authenticate their message that Jesus is God to the world. The giving met the needs both inside and outside the assembly. Praise involved the singing of hymns and spiritual songs. And the growth came from God Himself, who through the power of the Holy Spirit's working within the church, drew man to Himself.

What Is the Threefold Mission of the Church?

There have been a lot of very good books written that explain the purpose and mission of the church of Jesus Christ. This book offers three critical components to the mission of the church. We have already defined them during our warm-up section, so we will just reiterate them here:

1. **Worship:** the church's corporate, awe-filled response to the Trinitarian God, His attributes, His providence, His power, and His purpose in redemption.
2. **Work:** the church's purposeful training and sustaining work to root new believers in the faith to grow them to maturity.
3. **Witness:** the church's fulfillment of Christ's Great Commission, to make disciples of *all* nations (people groups).

What Are the Scriptural Offices of the Church?

The Bible speaks of two offices of the church. They are:

1. **Pastor**, also known as elder (Greek *presbuteros*), overseer (Greek *episcopos*), or shepherd (Greek *poimen*): 1 Timothy 3:1–7; 1 Peter 5:1–4
2. **Deacon** (Greek *diakonos*): 1 Timothy 3:8–13

The specific duties and responsibilities of the pastor and deacon are provided in Acts 6:1–7. As the synonyms for pastor (above) would imply, the pastor is responsible to shepherd the flock that God has given him; to oversee the affairs of the church; and to lead in the teaching of and training in God's Word. An easy way to understand the role of pastor is that God has gifted and charged him with the responsibility of praying for, preaching to, and protecting the congregation.

As we see in that passage in Acts, the deacons were tasked with the service-related duties of the ministry. In the early church, they appointed a group of spiritually mature men to distribute food. In today's church, the needs may be quite different, but the principle is that deacons are essentially the serving arm of the church, and, by their service, they are respected as leaders. However, one of the unfortunate misapplications of this office that has crept into many churches is that the body of deacons assumes authority as a "board," conjuring up ideas of some business model that is clearly not biblical. The word "deacon" (Greek *diakonos*) literally means "servant." Thus, those who meet the qualifications of deacon are tasked to sacrificially serve the congregation's needs so that the pastor can focus on prayer and ministry of the Word.

Now, some would hold that there are three offices, thereby separating pastors from elders. The support for this position is found in the fact that the word "elders" is always plural in Scripture. However, if we understand how the early church grew and how each town would have had several "house churches," where new believers in the community would congregate in homes, then we would very easily reason that each house church was led by one pastor/elder, but that Paul often addressed these individual pastors as a group.

What Is Baptism?

The Bible teaches us that baptism is a public and a visible symbol of our heart faith. It is one of the two ordinances of the church. When people place their trust in Jesus Christ and become His disciples, then they are to be baptized. Why are new believers baptized? First of all, the church baptizes in order to follow the example of Jesus, who was baptized Himself (Matthew 3:13–17). Second, we are baptized because that is the biblical model for identifying with Christ and His church. For example, the Ethiopian eunuch in Acts 8:34–39 was baptized immediately after trusting Christ. Also, the Philippian jailer and his whole family were baptized after believing Paul's message. Third, Jesus commanded it! In His Great commission in Matthew 28:19–20, Jesus commanded His disciples to *make disciples of all nations, baptizing them in the name of the Father and of the Son and of the Holy Spirit.*

The sequence is critical. First, there is a cognitive decision to become a disciple. Then there is the obedient action of being baptized. This is exactly how it is presented in Scripture. The mode of baptism is immersion. In fact, the Greek word, *baptizo*, literally means to immerse or plunge beneath the surface of the water. Therefore, while many Christian denominations practice infant baptism, there is no biblical support for it. We could rather view infant baptism, or christening, as a dedication of that baby to be raised in the knowledge of Christ.

As always, the Scriptures dictate why we baptize after the faith decision and by immersion. Romans 6:1–7 teaches that the baptism symbolizes our death, burial, and resurrection to new life. When a person dies, she is buried under the surface of the ground (six feet under!). In the same way, when a person chooses to follow Christ, she dies to her own life, is buried, and then is resurrected to the new life she has found in Christ.

What Is Communion?

The other ordinance of the church is communion, otherwise known as the Lord's Supper or the Eucharist. In this symbolic act of obedience, members of the church take bread, which symbolizes Jesus's body; and the cup, which symbolizes Jesus's blood. This ordinance was instituted the night before Christ was crucified, during the Passover meal. As Jesus shared the bread and cup, He taught His disciples that the cup was the new covenant in His blood and called for them to do it in remembrance of Him. (Matthew 26:26–30). The frequency of the Lord's Supper is not mandated in Scripture. Paul simply instructed the church at Corinth that whenever they take it, they are to *proclaim the Lord's death until He comes* (1 Corinthians 11:23–26).

Some churches require membership in order to participate in the Lord's Supper; this is known as closed communion. Other churches allow participation for all who call themselves disciples, referred to as open communion. Scripture does not address the participation guidelines, but it is clear from Scripture that only professing Christians are to participate, as it is clearly our way of identifying with Christ in His death.

What Characterizes the Church?

The Bible characterizes the church by many different metaphors. There are five such metaphors in the New Testament. They are:

⇨ A bride (2 Corinthians 11:2; Ephesians 5:21–33; Revelation 19:1–10)

⇨ A body (1 Corinthians 12; Ephesians 4:7–16)

- ➪ A family (Galatians 6:10; Ephesians 3:15; 1 Peter 4:17)
- ➪ A building (Ephesians 2:19–22; 1 Peter 2:1–12)
- ➪ An army (Philippians 2:25; 2 Timothy 2:1–5; Revelation 19:19)

Each of these metaphors adequately portrays the relationship between God and His people. We are the bride of Christ, adorned by His righteous act to be made holy and blameless. We are the building of God, with Jesus Christ as our chief cornerstone and the apostles as the foundation on which the church is built. We are a body, with many members all working together to accomplish God's purposes. We are an army, soldiers of the cross of Christ with Jesus Himself as our great commander. And we are a family, God's children adopted by Him when we first trusted in His Son, Jesus Christ.

This mile has been a very quick overview of the church. The key to this whole discussion is to dispel the myth that we simply "go to church." Truly, all believers make up the church. Therefore, on Sunday mornings, the church gathers to worship the one, true God!

Congratulations! You have just completed the first leg in the marathon of becoming a mature follower of Christ—*Follow*. Now that you understand what it means to follow Christ, let's take the next step in learning how to invest. But first, here is our next memory verse:

And I tell you that you are Peter, and on this rock I will build my church, and the gates of Hades will not overcome it.

(Matthew 16:18)

The Second Leg: Invest

When we invest in something, we sacrifice our time, our money, and our will to it. In the Christian life, we acknowledge that we no longer live for ourselves, but instead we live for Him. Therefore, we invest each and every day to doing His will in our lives by applying certain disciplines to our faith journey.

Mile 5: Bible Study

Mile 6: Prayer

Mile 7: Stewardship

Mile 8: Spiritual Disciplines

Bible Study

I have been an avid student of the Bible for most of my adult life. Yet I am convinced that I will never get to the bottom of its hidden treasures. When a member of our church experienced a lot of pain and loss over an extended period of time, the Psalms and the promises of Jesus comforted her. I have gone through plenty of my own storms in life, and each time, I have sought the wisdom and counsel of Scripture to help me make it through. The encouragement, correction, comfort, and advice I am able to offer others is not my own, but the natural by-product of a life spent feeding on God's Word. Most Christians would say they haven't taken the time to truly study the Bible. This mile lays out a step-by-step plan to develop the crucial discipline of Bible study.

What Are the Prerequisites to Bible Study?

Bible Study is perhaps one of the toughest disciplines for most Christians. The Bible is so long, and the stories seem so far removed. Depending on the version you are using, it can seem impossible to understand. The Bible can be described as God's love letter to man. Many believers simply don't know where to start. A few miles ago, we gave a broad overview of the Bible, but at this stage in the journey, we want to delve a little more deeply and make a few commitments along the way. So, first of all, let's agree to this list of initial actions:

1. **Make a commitment to daily Bible study.** You wouldn't think of going a day without food to feed your physical body. In the same way, the Word of God is your daily bread for nourishing and sustaining your spirit.

2. **Dedicate a block of time each day.** If you don't schedule it, it won't happen. You must make this a priority and eliminate other mundane activities from your calendar in order to make room. I believe that devotionals are good, but they are not (and hopefully all the writers of them would agree) a substitute for the Scriptures. The Bible is *living and active, sharper than any two-edged sword* (Hebrews 4:12). The time of day is completely up to you, but many choose the first part of the day. By choosing the morning, you demonstrate that this study is a priority and a great foundation for the rest of the day. Of course, the point is not to do Bible study in order to check it off your spiritual to-do list but instead to draw nearer to God.

3. **Choose a translation** (New International Version, or NIV; English Standard Version, or ESV; New King James Version, or NKJV; or New American Standard Bible, or NASB). I list these four translations because they offer a word-by-word or thought-by-thought translation of the original languages (Hebrew in the Old Testament and Greek in the

New Testament). Avoid paraphrase Bibles like the Open Book, the Message or the New Living Translation (NLT). Paraphrase Bibles can be used for general reading, but due to their loose translation of the original text, they are not appropriate for forming biblical doctrine.

4. **Choose a type of Bible** (study, life application, devotion). There are so many types of Bibles out there that choosing one can be quite overwhelming. One rule of thumb is to make sure you remember that only the Bible's words are inspired by God. Study notes, principles, and historical comments are all helpful but are merely man's words and sometimes can be a distraction from the actual study of God's Word. We will say more about this later.

5. **Gather your study materials in one place.** It's a waste of time to try to locate all your materials each day. Keep them safe in the place you have chosen to study.
   a. Bible
   b. Journal or notebook
   c. Pens and highlighters
   d. Study aids

What Are the Steps to Studying the Bible?

As you can imagine, choosing where to start is not easy. Most Christians find it challenging to maintain the discipline. I have heard the sob stories of too many well-meaning Christians who started eagerly in Genesis, trudged through the first half of Exodus, and then petered out in the midst of all the gory details of the tabernacle construction. If they made it to Leviticus, they were lost before they ever really got started!

This is not uncommon, and you should take some solace in the fact that you are certainly not alone. However, when you see the plan of God from the thirty-thousand-foot level unfold before your very eyes, and when you see the ways the Israelites' journey parallels and foreshadows the Christian journey, you will get excited; making this type of connection will most assuredly drive your faith to the next level. So, here are the steps that you can follow to get started:

a. **Choose a book.** In mile 2, I suggested a sequence of the Bible books to study, beginning with Mark. There is one simple reason for it: It is a quick-paced book that covers the life, death, and resurrection of Jesus Christ. Mark writes to the non-Jewish world and portrays Jesus as the suffering servant. It also happens to be the shortest of the four Gospels.

b. **Begin with prayer.** Since the Bible was inspired by the Holy Spirit, and since the Holy Spirit lives in the believer (more detail about this later), then the Bible student should begin with a prayer, asking the Holy Spirit to illumine the truth of God's Word so that the heart and mind of the reader might gain greater understanding and wisdom.

c. **Read the entire book a couple of times.** This may seem like a chore, but doing it allows one to see the overall flow of the book, and the major themes seem to be more evident to the reader. Too many times, we dive into a passage and lose the context or the flow of the book. This can lead to a lot of unsound conclusions or beliefs. The Bible has been used too often for proof-texting, which is the act of combing the Scriptures for a verse that supports one's stated belief. This is a dangerous way to use the Bible. Reading a book through at least twice before zooming into individual passages/sections is a good way to gain context, perspective, and propositional emphases.

d. **Zoom in verse-by-verse.** Once you have read the entire book at least twice, then you can zoom in on each section.

Most Bibles have headings throughout each book, at logical breaks in the narrative. This is a good way to break a book down into bite-size pieces. It is at this time you would use the Seven Cs of Bible Study (introduced in mile 2 and reviewed in the next section of this chapter).

e. **Consult Bible study aids.** Bible study aids include the notes within the Bible itself or other books, such as commentaries, Bible dictionaries, and Bible handbooks. There are a lot of online sources to use as well, such as Biblegateway.com. These aids do not replace the reading and studying of the Word, but they assist in giving context to the reader. Please resist the temptation to depend solely on the aids at the expense of thinking about each verse. Remember, the Holy Spirit that lives in you is the same as the Holy Spirit who wrote the Bible, so He will guide you into all truth.

f. **Think of ways to apply the Word.** This is where the rubber meets the road. James, the half-brother of Jesus, said, *"Faith without deeds is dead."* (James 2:26) He had a way of giving it to us straight! Anyway, his point is valid. We don't read to gain knowledge. We read and study to gain understanding, and we are called to put feet to our faith in order to apply God's truth to our lives. This applied truth is manifested through our worship and our witness.

g. **Use the Seven Cs of Bible Study.** These seven steps were introduced in mile 2 and are now repeated here. In the Bible, the repetition of a word or concept indicates its importance. The same is true here. If you train your mind to study the Bible this way, I promise you will get it more and more, and it will cause you to hunger and thirst more and more for the glorious riches found in Christ.

What Are the Seven Cs of Bible Study?

You know the Seven Cs of Bible Study, so let's tackle a passage right now. Let's look at Genesis 22:1–19. Read that passage right now and then come back to complete the Seven Cs together.

1. **Context:** Isaac, the son God promised to Abraham and Sarah, was born. Sarah became upset that Ishmael, the son Abraham had with Hagar, his servant girl, began to mock Isaac. Sarah demanded that Hagar and Ishmael be sent away. This distressed Abraham, but God told him that it would be through Isaac that his offspring would be reckoned. Abraham then sent Hagar and Ishmael away, but God comforted Hagar and confirmed to her that her son would become a great nation. Abraham then made a treaty with Abimelech, the King of Gerar (the Philistines). It was some time later (probably six years), that God tested Abraham's faith.

2. **Characters:** Abraham, Isaac, two servants, God, and the ram caught in a thicket.

3. **Content:** God tests Abraham's faith by telling him to sacrifice his one and only son. Now that we know the context, and the fact that Abraham no longer had Ishmael, we see the measure of faith required by Abraham. Interestingly, God refers to Isaac as Abraham's "one and only son," signifying that he is the son of promise. But how is that possible if God is now ordering his sacrifice? Abraham gets up early the next morning and, accompanied by two servants, takes Isaac to the place called Moriah. He instructs the two servants that they will worship and then return. On the way, Isaac asks his father where the lamb is, and Abraham replies that *God himself will provide the lamb*. Abraham tied Isaac to the altar, raised his arm to slay him, and then heard God's voice, commanding him not to slay his son. God knew that

Abraham truly feared him. Abraham then saw a ram caught in a thicket by its horns and sacrificed the ram instead of his son. The two of them worshiped on the mountain. Abraham called that place, "God will provide." The angel of the Lord then reminded Abraham of God's covenant with him, that God would bless Abraham and make his descendents as numerous as the stars in the sky, and that through his off-spring (Isaac's line), all nations on earth would be blessed. Abraham and Isaac then returned to the servants and traveled back home.

4. **Central proposition:** Trust God, no matter the circumstances. Abraham had every reason in the world to question or to disobey God, but he chose to trust Him instead. *Without faith it is impossible to please God...* (Hebrews 11:6).

5. **Christ:** Jesus Christ is all over this passage! Mount Moriah is the same mountain range where Christ was crucified at Calvary. The ram would be sacrificed instead of Isaac, just as Jesus was sacrificed for us. God provided the ram as a sacrifice, and God the Father provided the Lamb of God, Jesus Christ.

6. **Cross-references:** John 3:16; Heb. 11:17–19

7. **Change:** This passage should cause us to have complete and unquestionable faith in God, no matter how difficult our circumstances or even how crazy the call of God may seem to us. God is going to use every means possible for us to see His mighty works. This is as true today as it was in Abraham's lifetime.

What Are the Various Bible Study Aids?

The following Bible study aids are available in most stores or even in your Bible. For example, the Bible Book Index, concordance, and maps are found in most Bibles. The index helps you to find the book you are looking for by page number. For example, Mark begins on page 985 in my Bible. A concordance is a list of key words, normally in the back of the Bible, with their locations throughout Scripture. For example, the word "righteous" appears in Psalm 37:25, Proverbs 11:30, Matthew 5:45, and Romans 1:17, as well as in numerous other verses. The maps section typically includes the geography during the patriarchal age (Abraham to Joseph), the Exodus from Egypt and conquest, the land of the twelve tribes, the kingdoms of David and Solomon, Jesus's ministry, and Paul's missionary journeys.

There are also other aids, outside the Bible. They are listed below:

⇨ **Biblical dictionary:** definitions of all terms, persons, and places in the Bible.

⇨ **Biblical handbook:** a broad-brush overview of each book of the Bible.

⇨ **Bible commentaries:** in-depth interpretation of each book of the Bible.

⇨ **Hebrew and Greek lexicons:** explanations of the Hebrew and Greek vocabulary of the Bible.

⇨ **Systematic theology:** an orderly account of the beliefs of the Christian faith.

We have taken our first step in investing in our relationship with Jesus Christ, and we have just completed the fifth mile! Now, here is our next memory verse:

For the word of God is living and active. Sharper than any double-edged sword, it penetrates even to dividing soul and spirit, joints and marrow; it judges the thoughts and attitudes of the heart.

(Hebrews 4:12)

Prayer

A good friend of mine knows the power of prayer. He has a dynamic, personal relationship with his heavenly Father. While he is awed by the truth that he has direct access to the Creator of the universe, he readily and regularly calls upon God with a childlike faith. Prayer is the lifeblood of his relationship with God. Throughout his life, he has seen God answer his prayers in ways that can only be described as miraculous. Such acts of God only fuel his passion to know God more fully and to serve as His witness here on earth. Perhaps you struggle to maintain prayer as a regular discipline. This mile defines and describes prayer in a way that brings life to your communication with your Creator.

What Is Prayer?

Simply put, prayer is communication with God. It includes two components: us talking to God and God speaking to us. Prayer is a very difficult discipline. There are a number of reasons for this. First, we are praying to God, whom we cannot see or hear. Second, we don't dedicate time to it. Third, we become so distracted with other activities during our attempts to pray. And fourth, we aren't always sure of what we ought to say. In addition, many are deathly afraid to pray out loud. Most of the time, we call out to God only when we feel we need Him.

A better way to view prayer is as a father talking to his child and a child talking to his father. This view implies an intimate relationship, one characterized by trust and love. This is the image of prayer painted for us in the Bible. God is our heavenly Father, and He created us to be in relationship with Him. While prayer is a discipline whereby our intimacy with God is developed over our lifetime, prayer should eventually become as natural to the Christian as breathing is to the runner.

Why Should We Pray?

There are three primary reasons why we should pray. First, Jesus modeled it. In the Bible, we see Jesus praying to the Father (Matthew 14:23; 26:36; Mark 1:35; 6:46; Luke 3:21, 5:16; 6:12; 9:18, 28; 11:1). Jesus is our example in everything, and His life of prayer demonstrates how to increase our intimacy with our heavenly Father.

The second reason we should pray is to demonstrate our faith in God. Our relationship with God ultimately comes down to trust. Do you trust Him to do what He says He will do? When Jesus told His disciples, *You may ask me for anything in my name, and I will do it,* He essentially told us to test His faithfulness and power to work through us (John 14:14). Now, so many miss the caveat that our prayers need to be in alignment with God's will. All selfish requests go out the window immediately. For example, Jesus also said: *If you remain in me and my words remain in you, ask whatever you wish, and it will be given you* (John 15:7, emphasis mine). The point is that we are to pray to God because we believe in Him and His ability to move in our lives.

Third, we pray in order to align our will to His will. This is the most important purpose of prayer. The goal of any prayer is to align ourselves with God's will. The question we must answer for ourselves is this: Do we pray to God for what he can do for us, or do we pray to God because we want to be with Him? In the Bible, there are a couple of great illustrations of that truth. Enoch walked so closely with the Lord that God took him (Genesis 5:24; Hebrews 11:5). In other words, Enoch didn't die; God just called him to His side. There is also the story that contrasts two women, Martha and Mary. Martha was busy getting everything prepared for serving Jesus while Mary was sitting at His feet. Jesus gave us great insight into the contrast by saying that *Mary has chosen what is better* (Luke 11:41–42). Being at the feet of Jesus is better than being busy for Jesus.

How Should We Pray?

As we said earlier, prayer includes two parts: listening to God and speaking to God. When we are listening, it is critical to shut out all distractions. This includes radio, television, even our family. It requires us to go to a quiet place and to be still before God. If you are like me, this oftentimes results in your mind racing with all the things you have to do, which then agitates you to action and right on out of your listening mode. This may sound weird to you, but it takes a tremendous amount of discipline to just sit and listen; often, silence can be deafening!

We are to listen for that still, small voice of God. That is, if we clear our minds and yield to the Holy Spirit who lives within us, then He will bring us thoughts, ideas, convictions, and direction. He will also help us to reflect on God's working in our lives and to accept, peacefully, that God is in control. The end result is that through prayer, we enter the day with a greater sense of purpose and a healthier perspective on life.

The second component to prayer is speaking to God. So many don't know what to say when they bow their heads to pray, so I have learned an old acrostic that really works well. It is the acrostic for ACTS:

Adoration: Praise God for who He is.
Confession: Admit your sins to God.
Thanksgiving: Tell God how grateful you are.
Supplication: Make specific requests for you/others.

If we are studying the Bible, we will know the attributes of God and call them out to Him to open our prayer; for example, we can acknowledge God's sovereignty, love, comfort, mercy and power when praying for a sick friend. If we are honest with ourselves and know God's commandments, we will be able to confess our sins of the past day. If we understand the power of the Gospel and the blessings we have in this life, we will be able to utter words of thanksgiving and praise. And when we are aligned with His will, we will be able to boldly approach God with our requests.

What Is the Model Prayer?

The model prayer given to us in the Bible is taken from Matthew 6:9–14 and Luke 11:2–4. This is Jesus's answer to His disciples' request to teach them how to pray. Obviously, they saw Jesus pray numerous times, and it was clear to them that Jesus had such an intimate relationship with the Father that they too wanted to know how to relate to God through prayer. His answer is a model for all of us:

1. Address God personally: *Our Father in heaven…*

2. Show respect for God's name: *Hallowed be your name.*

3. Commit yourself to God's plan: *Your kingdom come, your will be done, on earth as it is in heaven.*

4. Ask God to provide for your needs: *Give us today our daily bread.*

5. Ask God for forgiveness: *Forgive us our debts, as we also have forgiven our debtors.*

6. Ask God for conviction and protection: *And lead us not into temptation, but deliver us from the evil one…*

When we recite the Lord's Prayer today, we often include the following doxology at the end: "For Thine is the kingdom and the power and the glory, forever and ever. Amen." The word "Amen" means "So be it" or "Let it be so!"

How Often Should We Pray?

We are called to pray continually. Paul challenged the believers in Thessalonica: *Be joyful always; pray continually; give thanks in all circumstances, for this is God's will for you in Christ Jesus* (1 Thessalonians 5:16–18). Since Jesus is the best friend of every believer, then the relationship should be a continual one, meaning that prayer is both communication with God during a specific time each day as well as an ongoing conversation with God throughout each day. Most Christians would say they pray all the time, but that normally means that they pray before meals or while driving in the car. The key to a devotional life of prayer is to set aside time each day for dedicated prayer, both listening and making requests to our Father.

For example, if you are going through a drive-through window for lunch, stop and utter a prayer for the person working at the window (or for all the workers!) while you wait. When you see a newscast talking about the unrest in the Middle East, intercede on behalf of those people. One such prayer might go like this, "Lord, I know that you created each of those people that just appeared on my television screen, and I know that many of them may not have any relationship with you. I ask that you may show Yourself to them as the one, true God. I pray this prayer in the Name of Jesus. Amen." When we end our prayers with "in Jesus's name," we are claiming Christ's promise when He told His disciples: *If you remain in me and my words remain in you, ask whatever you wish, and it will be given you* (John 15:7). This act of praying in Jesus's name gives glory to Christ.

What Is the Correct Posture for Prayer?

There is no correct posture for prayer. In fact, nowhere in the Bible does it command us to close our eyes or bow our heads! So why do we do that? Well, I would suggest that closing our eyes allows us to shut out potential distractions and helps us to focus. I believe that bowing our heads reflects our humility before the Lord. Even so, there is no mandate in God's Word to be in any particular posture.

Jesus did prohibit public, look-at-me prayers and encouraged individual prayer to be done privately. For example, Jesus told His followers during His famous Sermon on the Mount: *And when you pray, do not be like the hypocrites, for they love to pray standing in the synagogues and on the street corners to be seen by men. I tell you the truth, they have received their reward in full. But when you pray, go into your room, close the door and pray to your Father, who is unseen. Then your Father, who sees what is done in secret, will reward you* (Matthew 6:5–6).

However, when the church or a group of believers is assembled, verbal prayers offered to God are very appropriate. Other Bible prayer postures include:

- Kneeling (1 Kings 8:45)

- Bowing (Exodus 4:31)

- Prostrate (2 Chronicles 20:18; Matthew 26:39)

- Standing (1 Kings 8:22)

So, we see that God wants us to communicate with Him and for us to give ear to Him. Jesus said, *He who has an ear, let him hear what the Spirit says to the churches* (Revelation 2:7, 11, 17, 29; 3:6, 13, 22). It was so important that Jesus repeated it seven times!

Now that we have been introduced to the topic of prayer, let's keep up the pace as we approach the next mile marker, stewardship. But first, here is our next memory verse:

Do not be anxious about anything, but in everything, by prayer and petition, with thanksgiving, present your requests to God. And the peace of God, which transcends all understanding, will guard your hearts and your minds in Christ Jesus.

(Philippians 4:6–7)

Stewardship

With only $17 left to his name, a visitor sat next to me in church, literally at the end of his rope. When the offering plate came by, in a moment of final surrender, he pulled the $17 out of his wallet, dropped his head in prayer, and placed it all in the plate. He was strapped with both a monthly mortgage on a home that hadn't sold for six months and the rent on his apartment in a new city where he'd relocated for a new job. He'd depleted his savings, and he was reduced to eating popcorn for dinner. This man's surrender represents the core meaning of stewardship. Some may call it a coincidence, but when he received a call from his real estate agent the next morning telling him his house had sold, he knew it was God's work. This mile defines stewardship and why every Christian is called to a stewardship lifestyle.

What Does the Term "Stewardship" Mean?

The word "stewardship" can be defined as the use of God-given resources for the accomplishment of God-given purposes. Stewardship is founded on the truth that everything belongs to God. The Bible begins with these words: *"In the beginning God created the heavens and the earth."* (Genesis 1:1) Everything is from God and ultimately belongs to God. The psalmist declared, *"The earth is the LORD's, and everything in it, the world, and all who live in it* (Psalm 24:1).

Furthermore, God made man and woman stewards over all creation. In fact, the first command to human beings in Scripture is: *"Be fruitful and increase in number; fill the earth and subdue it. Rule over the fish of the sea and the birds of the air and over every living creature that moves on the ground."* (Genesis 1:28) What a tremendous privilege and responsibility! As the highest order of God's creation, human beings are called to tend and keep the earth, to be good stewards of the world which God has given us.

Our current generation has elevated the necessity of being environmentally responsible to protect our planet. We have a day dedicated to this awareness called Earth Day. On this day, we celebrate our huge strides in recycling programs, and most communities and companies today have enacted green and sustainability initiatives. While this may seem like a new movement, the truth is that God instituted a planet protection program when He created the world and put human beings in charge.

What Are the Different Aspects of Stewardship?

There are three primary resources that God has given humanity and for which God has made us responsible to use for His divine purposes: time, money, and ability. Time is one of the most precious commodities, because once it is gone, you can't get it back. Money is the taboo topic in the church and, frankly, one of the most contentious topics as well. Money is needed to do the work God has called us to do. Ability is one of those areas for which we often give God little mention, except when the football player is having his postgame press conference and says, "I thank God for giving me the ability to run as fast as I do." If we look at each one of these three resources, the question needs to center on how each can be used for God's glory.

1. How Are We to Use Our Time for God's Glory?

The average person lives more than seventy years upon this earth. We all have fifty-two weeks a year. We all have exactly one hundred and sixty-eight hours per week. How we use every hour matters to God. Since our charge is to be a worshiper, a worker, and a witness, then we must be proactive in dedicating time to that charge. If we were to evaluate the use of our time on a daily/weekly basis, we would have a good idea of what we consider to be important.

Now, most of us sleep or rest about eight hours a day, and most of us work or go to school between forty and fifty hours a week. That leaves us about sixty-two hours per week for other activities, such as eating, house chores, time with family and friends, and personal time. How many of those hours are dedicated to your relationship with God?

If we were to devote just 10 percent of our waking hours each week to God, including regular worshiping, working, and witnessing, that would be eleven hours per week. If we set aside forty-five minutes each day for quiet time and Bible study, two hours each week for worship at our church, then we would have another four hours each week to work and witness on behalf of Christ's Kingdom. When we look at it in this light, the commitment is not too great, but it does take planning and resolve to make it happen.

A word of caution about this way of thinking: we should not compartmentalize our faith. The overarching theme of the Christian journey is that our faith is active in every moment of our existence. We are to be in a continuous and never-ending mode of working out our faith—whether we are at work, at the gym, having dinner, or just resting in our chair late at night, drifting off to sleep. We are ever before our Lord: *So whether you eat or drink or whatever you do, do it all for the glory of God* (**1 Corinthians 10:31**).

2. How Are We to Use Our Money for God's Glory?

Money is a hot topic in our world—how to make it, how to invest it, and how to spend it. There is little doubt that money was a big deal in Jesus's day as well, for most of His parables had some component of money tied to them. In fact, nineteen of Jesus's parables were about work and wages. Certainly, Jesus knows that money can be our master or our slave. Which is it for you?

The biblical model of financial stewardship is defined by tithes and offerings. Tithing is returning to God a portion of what He has given to us, and offerings include anything we give that is above and beyond the tithe. For example, when Abraham returned from rescuing his nephew Lot, he met Melchizedek, king of Salem, and gave him a tenth of all the spoils from war (Genesis 15:18–20). We get the word "tithe" from this tenth given by Abraham to Melchizedek. Notice too that this tithe came *before* the law, and therefore was not abolished with the law. Every Christian's tithe is 10 percent of our gross income. Our tithe is based on our gross income and not our net income because we prioritize our return to God over our payment to the government.

Tithing is based off the principle of "first fruits." When Abel and Cain presented their offerings before God in Genesis 4, the key distinction between the two offerings was that Cain brought "some of the fruits" of the land and Abel sacrificed the "firstborn" of his flock (Genesis 4:3–4). God accepted the sacrifice of Abel for two reasons. First, Abel's offering was the firstborn of the flock, honoring God with his first and best. Second, Abel's offering required the shedding of blood. This event marks the first sacrifice recorded in Scripture and is a picture of faith, as we learn in Hebrews 11:4: *By faith Abel offered God a better sacrifice than Cain did. By faith he was commended as a righteous man, when God spoke well of his offerings. And by faith he still speaks, even though he is dead.* So, we see that tithing is a matter of faith.

We also learn from Scripture that tithing is a matter of testing God and His faithfulness. The Lord explained that withholding the tithe is in fact robbing Him, so He issued a test to His people: *Bring the whole tithe into the storehouse, that there may be food in my house. Test me in this," says the LORD Almighty, "and see if I will not throw open the floodgates of heaven and pour out so much blessing that you will not have room enough for it"* (Malachi 3:10). God commands us to tithe and then issues a promise to bless us. We must be careful not to use this Scripture to justify an expectation of material blessing. God's blessing can take many forms; it is not always monetary. Too many have falsely preached that kind of gospel, and it is simply not biblical.

Tithing demonstrates our love for God and our faith in God. If I might be so bold, I believe that the tithe is one of the most tangible demonstrations of our heart faith. It separates those who say they have faith from those who actually live it out. But many would say that the New Testament does not command tithing. This is where adherence to the "whole counsel of God" is most important. In His rebuke of the Pharisees (a religious sect of Jesus's day), Jesus states, *Woe to you, teachers of the law and Pharisees, you hypocrites! You give a tenth of your spices—mint, dill and cummin. But you have neglected the more important matters of the law—justice, mercy and faithfulness. You should have practiced the latter, without neglecting the former* (Matthew 23:23). Notice that His rebuke lends credence to the tithe and commands that they keep practicing that aspect of their faith.

3. How Are We to Use Our Abilities for God's Glory?

When we become Christians, God gives us His Holy Spirit to guide, teach, comfort, and convict us. The Holy Spirit also endows every believer with one or more spiritual gifts. We will discuss spiritual gifts later, but at this point, we need to draw a distinction between human talents, abilities, and spiritual gifts. The talents we possess, whether athletic, artistic, or academic, are truly God-given, because God created each and every person on the earth.

We are called to use our God-given talents and abilities for His glory. Churches need singers, musicians, sound board technicians, multimedia gurus, computer operators, administrators, coordinators, construction workers, interior decorators, landscapers, planners, children's workers, maintenance persons, etc. to do the work of the church.

God also wants us to use our talents and abilities *outside* the church. Letting our Christian identity pervade our life is perhaps one of the biggest shifts that must happen in our Christian paradigm. That is to say, God never commands us to compartmentalize our faith to be worked out only within the church environment. In fact, we are called to invest in the world around us, to influence it, and to make such an impact that it brings victorious, eternal results.

While every person on this earth has certain God-given talents, every believer is also gifted by the Holy Spirit to minister to the church. Paul likens the church to the body, where *the body is a unit, though it is made up of many parts; and though all the parts are many, they form one body. So it is with Christ* (1 Corinthians 12:12). He goes on to say that the church is the body of Christ and that every member of the body has a function and a purpose in order to build up and edify the rest of the body.

Church leaders often ask themselves why they are ineffective at accomplishing their God-given mission, but it should be no surprise since most church bodies do not all function as units. In fact, many church members never use their gift for the common good, and, worse, many don't even try to discover their gifts. Imagine the body missing a leg or an arm. It may still function, but it is not nearly as capable of running and serving as it would have been if it had both arms and both legs. As a member of a church, one of our first duties is to discover our spiritual gifts and then to use them for God's glory.

To be sure, there are different gifts, but none is any better than the other. For example, the preacher is out in front of everyone, and everyone can see him use his gift, but preaching is no more important in God's eyes than the person who sits with a struggling friend over coffee on Wednesday morning, using her gift of mercy. Also, the body (the church) depends on each one of us to use our gift to minister to the rest of the body. Finally, all gifts are to be used to glorify God and not to draw any attention to ourselves. When the body functions according to the biblical mandate, then it will have a positive impact on the church and the community in which God planted it.

How Should We Apply the Stewardship Command to Our Life?

The best way to think about stewardship and to place it as a priority in our Christian journey is to ask ourselves these four questions:

1. Does Jesus have the first part of our day?
2. Does Jesus have the first part of our pay?
3. Does Jesus have the first part of our say?
4. Does Jesus have the first part of our way?

So, as we finish up this mile in our race of faith, we are called to be good stewards of all that God has given us. We are to use our time, our money, and our talents and gifts for His glory. Now, before we move on to investing in all the spiritual disciplines called out in Scripture, let's pause to memorize our next memory verse:

Remember this: Whoever sows sparingly will also reap sparingly, and whoever sows generously will also reap generously.

(2 Corinthians 9:6)

Spiritual Disciplines

For those who know my mother-in-law, they see her as a woman who walks with God. How does she do it? At an early age, she dedicated herself to drawing closer to her Savior in every aspect of her faith journey; she was sensitive to His leading and prompting. She applied discipline both in her vertical relationship with God and her horizontal relationships with others. Because she fully relied on God when He called her to early childhood ministry, she literally had a spiritual and practical impact on thousands of families in her community over the next forty-four years. Every Christian is called to a life of spiritual discipline. This mile explains many of these disciplines and how to apply them to daily life.

What Is Spiritual Discipline?

Since the Christian life is a journey, a pilgrimage, a race to be run, we must exercise our bodies, minds, and spirits to contend with the terrain and the obstacles along the way. Spiritual discipline prepares the Christian for the unknown and the unforeseen. Paul encouraged his young protégé Timothy with these words: *discipline yourself for the purpose of godliness* (1 Timothy 4:7b, NASB). The Greek word for "discipline" (also translated as exercise or training) is *gumnasa*. It means to train, to exercise, or to discipline. We get our modern-day word, "gymnasium," from this Greek word.

The Bible commands all Christians to train themselves for the purpose of godliness. There is only one catalyst for transforming the Christian—the Holy Spirit. However, He uses three influences by which to accomplish such transformation: people, circumstances, and spiritual disciplines. We are all affected by the relationships we have with others, the events of our lives, and the preparations we make on a daily basis. The heart of spiritual discipline is training and preparation for the journey called life.

Let's take a quick survey of the various spiritual disciplines called out in the Word of God. This may seem overwhelming at first, but, again, most of these activities are to be woven into the daily routines of life; they're not intended to be add-ons to our already busy schedules.

What Are the Spiritual Disciplines?

1. Learning

The first spiritual discipline is learning about God, specifically through the Bible's teachings. The mere fact that this is God's Word to man should be motivation enough for us to dedicate our time and energy to this discipline. The Bible challenges and realigns our preconceptions about our faith. It also encourages and comforts us in our struggles and frustrations. It further empowers us with the one weapon we have to fight the spiritual battles in this world—His Word. Jesus quoted Old Testament Scripture in response to each of Satan's three temptations. For example, when Satan tempted Jesus to turn stones into bread, Jesus replied by saying: *It is written, 'Man does not live on bread alone, but on every word that comes from the mouth of God.'* (Matthew 4:4) Jesus is our example in everything! With that said, here are seven keys to knowing God's will through His Word. Just remember the acrostic: **BE SMART!**

1. **B**elieve God's Word – Trusting that what God commands is truly best for us and that we can rely on His presence and His promises: *Consequently, faith comes from hearing the message, and the message is heard through the word of Christ* (Romans 10:17).

2. **E**ngage God's Word – Engaging the Bible and using it for training during church and dedicated Bible studies: *All Scripture is God-breathed and is useful for teaching, rebuking, correcting and training in righteousness* (2 Timothy 3:16).

3. **S**tudy God's Word – Applying the Seven Cs of Bible Study (Context, Characters, Content, Central proposition, Christ, Cross-references and Change): *Now the Bereans were of more noble character than the Thessalonians, for they received the message with great eagerness and examined the Scriptures every day to see if what Paul said was true* (Acts 17:11).

4. **M**editate on God's Word – Proactively thinking about key verses or biblical concepts throughout each day; delving into a particular doctrine and determining one's position based on biblical evidence. The psalmist declared: *May my meditation be pleasing to him, as I rejoice in the LORD* (Psalm 104:34).

5. **A**pply God's Word – Looking for practical ways to live out the commands of Scripture or to embody the fruit of the Spirit in our daily interactions with others. James exhorts us: *Do not*

merely listen to the word, and so deceive yourselves. Do what it says (James 1:22).

6. **R**emember God's Word – Memorizing key stories, verses and principles of God's Word to bolster our faith, works and witness. The psalmist declared: *I have hidden your word in my heart that I might not sin against you* (Psalm 119:11).

7. **T**each God's Word – Teaching it first to ourselves, then to our children, and then to others. God instructed the Israelites in this way: *These commandments that I give you today are to be upon your hearts. Impress them on your children. Talk about them when you sit at home and when you walk along the road, when you lie down and when you get up* (Deuteronomy 6:6–7).

2. **Praying**

As mentioned in our previous mile on prayer, the spiritual discipline of prayer must be an ongoing exercise for the fully devoted follower of Jesus Christ. Prayer is the two-way communication between God and man. There are three biblical truths about prayer. First, prayer is expected. That is, Jesus constantly modeled and commanded a life of persistent prayer: *Then Jesus told his disciples a parable to show them that they should always pray and not give up* (Luke 18:1).

Secondly, prayer is learned. Remember that the disciples asked Jesus to teach them how to pray. From a practical standpoint, we all have to learn how to pray. We begin as children, reciting simple pre-meal prayers, such as:

> God is great. God is good.
> Let us thank Him for our food.
> By His hands we are fed.
> Give us Lord our daily bread. Amen.

The first time we are asked to pray out loud can create a lot of anxiety, but remembering the parts to Jesus's model prayer or using the acrostic ACTS (Adoration, Confession, Thanksgiving, and Supplication) will help us to organize our thoughts as we pray. There are two important encouragements for us as we pray out loud:

1. What we say or how we say it is not as important as *saying* it.
2. We get good at what we do; we will feel more comfortable the more we pray.

Thirdly, prayer is answered. Smith Wigglesworth said this about God's desire to answer our prayers: "God is more anxious to answer than we are to ask."[5] Because God is faithful, we can trust that He not only hears our prayers but that He answers them as well—in His time and in His way. We must never give up praying to God, whether it is about a person, an issue, or a decision. Ultimately, God will answer our prayers, even if His answer is "no" or "wait."

3. **Worshiping**

God seeks true worshipers. The spiritual discipline of worship will be covered in more detail in the next chapter, but at this time we can define worship as the humble response of the Christian to God, who He is, and what He does. Jesus told the Samaritan woman that God seeks worshipers who worship Him *in spirit and in truth* (John 4:23–24).

These two components to worship are critical. First, we are to worship God in spirit. The Holy Spirit who lives in us is the One who guides us in our worship. There is an experiential feeling that comes over us as we sing praises, offer prayers, take communion, and hear the Word. This is the ethereal component to worship. Since true worship is brought about by the Holy Spirit, it follows that only true believers can truly worship God fully. This is why it is so important for worship planners to plan worship for the believing community

5   Smith Wigglesworth, *On Prayer, Power and Miracles*, compiled by Roberts Liardon (www. servantofmessiah.org), page 18.

instead of the non-believing community, or seekers. Obviously, our worship service should be welcoming to all people, but the focus should be to unify and edify the church.

The second component to worship is truth. If worshiping in spirit lifts us up, then worshiping in truth keeps us grounded. The truth component demands that every song that is sung, every prayer that is offered, and every sermon that is preached must come from the Word of God. In fact, the best part of any sermon is when the preacher reads from the Bible, because it is the only part of his sermon that is infallible. Every aspect of the worship service should teach the worshiping body biblical truth, and the sermon should exposit biblical truth such that the hearer is convicted, convinced, and changed as a result. In summary, the weekly worship service should encourage, exhort, educate, and equip the church to go out and evangelize the world.

4. Witnessing

Witnessing, or evangelism, is a natural by-product of our worship, as well as all the other spiritual disciplines. Five times in the first five books of the New Testament, Jesus issued some form of His Great Commission. Paul answered God's call to be a *light for the Gentiles* (Acts 13:47). Gentiles include everyone who is not Jewish. Jesus calls every one of His disciples to be salt and light to the world (Matthew 5:13-16). Paul referenced the salt motif when he encouraged the Colossian church to lead a life of witnessing: *Be wise in the way you act toward outsiders; make the most of every opportunity. Let your conversation be always full of grace, seasoned with salt, so that you may know how to answer everyone* (Colossians 4:5–6).

We will spend a lot of time later talking about how to share our faith, but for now, let's just brainstorm a few simple ideas. For example, when you go to a restaurant, ask your server how you can pray for him or her. When a coworker approaches you on Monday morning and asks you how your weekend was, share the specifics of that Sunday's sermon and how it spoke to you. While your child is practicing with his or her sports team, take it upon yourself to get to know the other parents.

The bottom line is that we are to be on the lookout for every opportunity that God may place in our paths. Witnessing is simply bearing testimony to our new life in Christ. Too many in the world are under the false impression that Christianity is boring or restrictive, but the more Christians exercise the spiritual discipline of witnessing, the more the world will learn about the fulfillment and purpose that results from a life devoted to Christ.

5. Serving

Serving others is the fifth spiritual discipline. Our culture feeds the human desire to take care of ourselves first, sometimes to the exclusion of all others. Serving others certainly does not come naturally to us, so this is a discipline every Christian must intentionally practice.

There are three aspects of serving—motivation, method, and message. The first aspect of our serving is our motivation. Jesus is our example in everything. On the night He was betrayed, Jesus showed His disciples the essence of serving others by washing their feet. In Jesus's day, this was the lowliest of duties, done by someone who occupied the lowest position in society. After Jesus finished washing His disciples's feet, He asked them: *Do you understand what I have done for you? You call me "Teacher" and "Lord," and rightly so, for that is what I am...I have set you an example, that you should do as I have done for you* (John 13:12b–13, 15). Therefore, our motivation is to obey Jesus by doing what He has shown us to do, namely, to serve.

The second aspect of serving is the method. There are many ways we can serve others with the love of Jesus Christ. A few examples include buying someone a cup of coffee; providing roadside assistance; mowing your neighbor's lawn; inviting someone over to dinner; sending a note of encouragement to a friend who is going through a difficult time; and picking up trash in your neighborhood, park, or shopping center. Jesus said: *Whoever wants to become great among you must be your servant* (Matthew 20:26). All Christians are gifted by the Holy Spirit to serve, and while service can be hard work, it is also rewarding.

The third aspect of serving is the message. When we are asked about our motivation for serving others, this is our opportunity to talk about Jesus. Most people are not offended if you give them the reason for your service. The fact is we are being obedient to God. This is why Peter encouraged the church with these words: *If anyone speaks, he should do it as one speaking the very words of God. If anyone serves, he should do it with the strength God provides, so that in all things God may be praised through Jesus Christ. To him be the glory and the power forever and ever. Amen* (**1 Peter 4:11**).

6. Giving

Paul quoted Jesus as saying, *It is more blessed to give than to receive* (Acts 20:35). This is so true! The word "give" appears over 1,400 times in the Bible. Based solely on the number of times it is used, we can surmise that giving is a significant principle in Scripture. Jesus commands us: *Give, and it will be given to you. A good measure, pressed down, shaken together and running over, will be poured into your lap. For with the measure you use, it will be measured to you* (Luke 6:38). This verse echoes God's promise to the Israelites through the prophet Malachi (Malachi 3:10), which we discussed in mile 7 on stewardship.

While we have already covered giving our time, money, and abilities to the glory of God, it is also important to give of ourselves in service to others. When we take the initiative to give someone else our ears and our hearts, we are essentially investing in that person. We are not only called to invest into our relationship with Jesus, but Jesus calls us to invest in others as well, in order to lead them into a saving relationship with Him.

7. **Fasting**

Fasting is a discipline that is not practiced very often in our society and is not understood that well either. Fasting is biblical and is assumed as a necessary spiritual discipline by Jesus. He taught His disciples, *When you fast, do not look somber as the hypocrites do, for they disfigure their faces to show men they are fasting* (Matthew 6:16). Note that He said: *When you fast…*and not "If you fast."

The primary purpose of fasting is described best by Ezra: *I proclaimed a fast, so that we might humble ourselves before our God and ask him for a safe journey for us and our children, with all our possessions* (Ezra 8:21). Fasting necessarily causes us to humble ourselves and to focus on God and His guidance, direction, and protection. Fasting can be a way to gain greater clarity from God on an important decision we have to make. We should pray through any cravings we experience while fasting.

There are three kinds of fasts: the normal fast, the partial fast, and the absolute fast. The normal fast is when we abstain from all food and only drink water. The partial fast is when we abstain from certain foods or drinks. The absolute fast is when we abstain from both food and drink. Obviously, for health reasons, most today do not enter an absolute fast, but we find this type of fast called for in Ezra 10:6, Esther 4:16, and Acts 9:9.

There is nothing in Scripture that mandates fasting for a specific period of time. Normal and partial fasts can last anywhere from several hours to several days, weeks, or even months. Many in the Christian faith participate in Lent, which is a tradition of prayer and fasting for forty days leading up to Easter. The forty days represent the forty days and nights Jesus fasted during his time in the wilderness, where Satan tempted him (Matthew 4:1–11; Luke 4:1–13). While this activity is not mandated in Scripture, fasting during Lent is an appropriate motivation for tangible sacrifice leading up to the most holy event of the Christian calendar, Easter.

8. Journaling

Journaling can be defined as recording the works and ways of the Lord in our life. How is God working in our lives? What prayers have been answered? What new biblical truth has become clearer to us? The answer to these questions can be captured when we journal. The biblical purpose for journaling is to reflect on God's Word and God's working in our lives. As Paul instructed Timothy, *Reflect on what I am saying, for the Lord will give you insight into all this* (2 Timothy 2:7).

While journaling may seem like a chore to us, there are at least two tangible benefits. The first is that it will lead us to a greater understanding of the deeper truths of God's Word. For example, organizing our observations on paper helps us to think more critically about a particular doctrine. Also, when we write down memory verses, we can usually memorize them faster. Finally, we record specific prayer requests from others and use our journal as a way to remember to pray for them.

The second tangible benefit of journaling comes later in our journey when we look back on how God has worked in our lives. When we reflect on what God has done in our past, we can forge ahead through a current crisis with greater confidence and boldness. This is true when we think about the Christian life as a race to be run. After we have been running for some time, we may feel like we have not progressed very far, but when we look back over the path we have taken, we can celebrate how far we have really come. This kind of reflection increases our faith and propels us forward in our journey.

9. Meditating

In our world of multimedia, it seems almost impossible to get away from all the noise and distractions. Many of us enter our home or get in our car and immediately turn on the radio, the television, or some other background noise. Spending time in meditation, in a place and time of silence or solitude, takes planning and discipline. But even

Jesus found time to be alone with His Father: *Very early in the morning, while it was still dark, Jesus got up, left the house and went off to a solitary place, where he prayed* (Mark 1:35). Solitude provides a time to think, pray, meditate, and plan.

Without planning, meditation will never happen. There are at least three ways of getting away to meditate. I call them minute moments, daily quiet times, and regular retreats. During a minute moment, sit in silence for a short length of time and clear your mind of all the clutter and noise. Pause and think about God. Daily quiet times (otherwise known as a DQT) offer a more extended time to get away, study God's Word, pray, and perhaps journal alone. Finally, there are times when we can go away for the specific purpose of rejuvenating our spirits, setting spiritual goals, and refocusing our priorities. This can happen annually, quarterly, or even monthly.

When we spend time in silence, we gain a greater sense of perspective on life and our calling as a Christian. Time is of such great value, and yet in God's economy, much like the spiritual discipline of giving, we find that our productivity actually increases as we set aside time to be alone. This is a very healthy discipline, and it manifests itself in greater growth as a follower of Christ.

10. Mentoring

The final spiritual discipline is mentoring. God desires every Christian to move from being a disciple to being a disciple-maker. Who are you mentoring? Most of the time, we carry little self-confidence in being able to teach anything to others, much less the Christian faith. The apostle Paul instructed Timothy to pass on the torch of the faith when he said, *And the things you have heard me say in the presence of many witnesses entrust to reliable men who will also be qualified to teach others* (2 Timothy 2:2). Notice the four generations in this one verse: Paul, Timothy, reliable men, and others. This is the pattern of perpetuity in realizing the Kingdom's inhabitants in every generation.

When we take the step to teach, we have to accept that we don't have everything figured out ourselves. That is not the qualification of a mentor. Later in our race, we will examine the qualifications of being a mentor, but for now, we need to be willing to devote time and patience to this discipline. Jesus spent three-and-a-half-years mentoring His apostles. They did life together, and He taught them through His words, His actions, and His example.

Discipleship doesn't just happen. It takes a lot of time and a lot of patience. Not every person we mentor will respond in the same way or grow at the same pace. This book was written in part to get the Christian community refocused on the basics of our faith. When we get back to the basics, we will then become the light that the author of our faith, Jesus Christ, called us to be. For the individual Christian, it all begins with committing to the spiritual disciplines.

Now, let's pause to recap our run. We have completed the first two legs of our race: *Follow* and *Invest*. We have learned what it means to be a follower of Christ and we have learned how to invest in Him. Next, we enter the third leg of our race, appropriately titled *Train*. But first, here is our next memory verse:

Trust in the Lord with all your heart and lean not on your own understanding; in all your ways acknowledge him, and he will make your paths straight.

(Proverbs 3:5–6)

The Race of Faith

The Third Leg: Train

Training is a significant activity in any endeavor. We train for our careers. We train in sports. We train for the arts. We must also train for godliness. God desires that we become spiritually fit for the battles of this life. Spiritual training is imperative for success in the Christian life.

Mile 9: Worship

Mile 10: Witness

Mile 11: Old Testament Overview

Mile 12: New Testament Overview

Worship

Having struggled with addiction for many years, a friend of mine still can't get over how far God reached down to pull him up out of the pit and set him on a solid rock. So, when he worships God, he is responding to how wide, long, high, and deep Christ's love is. When my friend plays his instrument during worship, he is not playing for himself; instead, he worships God with all that he has, and he uses his talent for God's glory. When a fellow believer asked him why he gets so emotional when singing songs of praise, he pointed out that the lyrics reveal biblical truths that take him back to his day of salvation. Worship is the core response of every Christian. This mile teaches us why and how we are to worship God.

What Is the Purpose of Worship?

As we mentioned earlier, worship is one component of the three-fold mission of the church and the Christian, and it is also one of the key spiritual disciplines. Worship is our humble response to God—who He is, what He has done, what He is doing, and what He will do in the future. This definition takes into account the eternal nature of God—past, present, and future.

We worship God to glorify, honor, praise, exalt, and please Him. The psalmist declared, *May the words of my mouth and the meditation of my heart be pleasing in your sight, O LORD, my Rock and my Redeemer* (Psalm 19:13–14). God takes great pleasure in our worship. We have already learned that God seeks worshipers who worship in spirit and in truth. Some churches have a lot of spirit but have little truth, and other churches have a lot of truth and very little spirit. This is a conundrum for many modern-day churches.

Many churches today wrestle with the idea of being relevant to a culture that is increasingly disinterested in church. The worship wars began a couple of decades ago, with the megachurch movement taking on a life of its own and the emerging church movement quickly following. So here we are today with a smorgasbord of church denominations and styles. Attendants have as many choices as television channels. Regardless of the church we choose, the Bible should be our guide for worshiping God.

Therefore, we can surmise from Scripture a couple of critical corollaries that characterize biblical worship. First, all worshipers are to be active participants and not spectators. By definition, worshiping is responding to God's character, whether in the form of singing, praying, reading God's Word, taking communion, or giving. One of the more unfortunate developments in recent years is that many attend church simply to check it off their to-do list, as if it were some obligation or chore. This is not what God intended when He created us for the purpose of worshiping Him.

Second, we do not assemble for worship to be entertained. Paul defines worship as such: *I urge you, brothers, in view of God's mercy, to offer our bodies as living sacrifices, holy and pleasing to God—this is your spiritual act of worship* (Romans 12:1). In reality, we are not to attend a worship service to see what we can get out of it. We are to attend a worship service to present our whole being as a living sacrifice to the Lord. How many people leave church service on Sunday morning and think (or say out loud), "I didn't get much out of that service today," or "That sermon didn't meet my needs." Let's agree that neither of those comments represents the right attitude in worship.

What does it mean to present our body as a living sacrifice? David confessed: *You do not delight in sacrifice, or I would bring it; you do not take pleasure in burnt offerings. The sacrifices of God are a broken spirit; a broken and contrite heart* (Psalm 51:16–17a). When you worship with that kind of heart, then you will get more than you ever gave, for Jesus said, *It is more blessed to give than to receive* (Acts 20:35). This truth is always true.

What Are the Different Kinds of Worship?

There are two kinds of worship: personal worship and corporate worship. Personal worship is based on the general revelation of God. Even the casual observer can take in the world around her and come to the conclusion that some transcendent force or Being brought it all into existence.

For the Christian, that transcendent Being is God, and He created the heavens and earth and everything in them. Under the inspiration of the Holy Spirit, the psalmist declared: *The heavens declare the glory of God; the skies proclaim the work of His hands. Day after day they pour forth speech; night after night they display knowledge* (Psalm 19:1–2). Personal worship acknowledges the beauty and power of God's creation.

How do we engage in personal worship? When you witness a beautiful sunset, a majestic mountain range, a colorful rainbow in the sky, or the birth of a baby, pause and worship God. When you wake up in the morning and feel completely refreshed, healthy, and happy, take a moment to worship God. When God answers one of our prayers or causes us to reflect on our salvation and our security in Christ, respond in worship.

Corporate worship happens when the people of God assemble in one place to worship God. The Christian family responds to God: who He is and what He has done in the life and finished work of Jesus Christ. All three persons of the Trinity are involved in the worship experience. The Father presides over our worship; the Son is the object of our worship; and the Holy Spirit leads us in our worship.

What Are the Elements of Corporate Worship?

Most worship services incorporate most or all of the following elements: prayer, singing, Scripture reading, preaching, giving, communion, and commitment. The Scriptural example is found in Acts: *They devoted themselves to the apostle's teaching and to the fellowship, to the breaking of bread and to prayer* (Acts 2:42). In this same passage, it says that they praised God. Further, Paul instructed the churches in Corinth about giving: *On the first day of every week, each one of you should set aside a sum of money in keeping with his income...* (1 Corinthians 16:2).

Most worship services begin with a prayer or a song. This first prayer is called an invocation. The purpose of this prayer is to invoke the Holy Spirit to come and direct our worship. Other prayers offered during the service express our relationship as an assembly to our God—the One who redeemed us. The final prayer offered is often called the benediction, or good word. It is a proper way to close the worship service.

Songs offered serve to prepare our hearts for the preaching of His Word and also to teach us biblical truth. Every song should reflect the truth of God's Word and the key doctrines of the faith. There has been a tremendous change in the music of worship over the last several decades. Traditional services have included organ and/or piano accompaniment, but contemporary worship includes more musical instruments—from guitars to keyboards to drums, even various woodwind and brass instruments.

Many traditional services still sing songs out of a hymnal while many contemporary services project the lyrics onto a screen or screens in the front of the worship center. The lyrics are important, as they should teach biblical truth. There are a lot of songs that churches sing today that fall far short of that imperative. Some churches even sing secular songs! This kind of worship is directed to the outsider, but since worship is for those who are part of the Kingdom of God, singing secular music does not build the vertical relationship between God and His redeemed.

Scripture reading and preaching are designed to educate, exhort, and encourage the assembly. Make sure to partner with a church that preaches *from* God's Word, otherwise known as expository preaching. Expository preaching is the effective conveyance of biblical truth and proposition directly from the Bible. Because the Bible is infallible, faithful preaching of its truth results in the hearer's real transformation.

Tithing is another act of corporate worship. It is a great expression of sacrifice. We are to give a tenth of our income toward the work and mission of the church. It costs money to pay for our pastors and other full/part-time ministers, mission work resources, ministry resources, meeting space expenses, utilities, maintenance, and other numerous administrative expenses.

Communion is another important aspect of corporate worship. Communion is the body's remembrance of Christ's death until He comes again. This is a symbolic ordinance that identifies those who follow Christ and binds them into a unified family of faith.

Another component of worship is commitment, which is typically the appeal made at the end of each service, whether it is in the form of a challenge to the assembly to apply God's truth that week, or an opportunity for worshipers to respond with some commitment. That commitment can come in the form of a decision to become a follower of Christ, a decision to renew one's commitment to Christ, or some other decision that leads the follower to take the next step in his or her faith journey.

What Should Result from Our Worship?

Genuine biblical worship brings a fresh encounter with God, an exaltation of Jesus Christ, an engagement with the Holy Spirit, an exhortation to the Christian, an encouragement to the non-Christian, a biblical education for all worshipers, the equipping of the body for service, and an evangelistic zeal. This zeal compels followers to go out and be such shining witnesses that the world will want to come and join us in our worship of God. For most who attend worship each Sunday, the experience ends at the end of the service. However, that's where the real work begins.

One final outcome of genuine worship is the healthy and holy fear of the Lord. As the writer of Hebrews closes his convincing argument of the supremacy of Christ, he concludes: *Therefore, since we are receiving a kingdom that cannot be shaken, let us be thankful, and so worship God acceptably with reverence and awe, for our "God is a consuming fire"* (Hebrews 12:28–29). Worship is the ultimate expression of our love for and thankfulness to God.

Another mile marker is just ahead, and we are making solid progress. Worship is about giving honor and glory to God. Before we begin the next mile on our journey to maturity, here is our next memory verse:

Therefore, I urge you, brothers and sisters, in view of God's mercy, to offer your bodies as a living sacrifice, holy and pleasing to God—this is your true and proper worship. Do not conform to the pattern of this world, but be transformed by the renewing of your mind. Then you will be able to test and approve what God's will is—his good, pleasing and perfect will.

(Romans 12:1–2)

Witness

From an early age, my son's friend has had a heart for people who did not yet know Jesus. He is unashamed of his faith, and, just as importantly, he continually prays for opportunities to witness to his friends. In a word, he takes the Great Commission of Jesus Christ very seriously. He not only has a sense of urgency about others trusting Jesus, but he also acknowledges that he is only a vessel that God has chosen, so he doesn't ever worry about rejection. Most Christians are afraid to share their faith, but this mile lays out simple approaches to being a powerful witness for Jesus, regardless of your personality.

What Are the Three Elements to Your Story?

Toward the end of his ministry, Paul had the opportunity to defend himself before King Agrippa. He had shared his story many times before, but in this final appeal, he laid out for all of us the three elements of his and every Christian's story. Paul's example is found in Acts 26. If you evaluate Paul's testimony, he describes his conversion.

1. **Before Christ** (verses 4–11): Paul was a persecutor of the church.
2. **Encounter with Christ** (verses 12–18): Paul was confronted by Jesus Christ with the truth of his sin and challenged to answer God's call on his life.
3. **After Christ** (verses 19–23): Paul has been a faithful missionary to share the light of the Gospel with the gentiles.

Why Is Your Story Important?

Our story is important for many reasons. First, other people are normally interested in hearing about major events in our lives. Whether the major event is a graduation, wedding, the birth of a baby, a promotion, or some other event, none of these events is as eternally important as our salvation. We would never shy away from telling others about our wedding or the birth of our baby, so why do we shy away from telling our salvation story?

Second, other people can relate to our stories. When we are clear about describing our sin nature, including specific sins that we have committed, most would agree that they too have been sinful. One of the most difficult parts of telling our stories is to relate how our sin nature separates us from holy God. One of the biggest lies in our culture is that most people think they are basically good and, as a result, will go to heaven when they die. This idea contradicts what the Bible teaches. Paul declared: *For all have sinned and fall short of the glory of God* (Romans 3:23).

They may also be able to relate to aspects of our journey of faith as well. Many who made a decision to follow Jesus at an early age fell away in some measure during their teenage or college years. It is important to be honest when talking about our faith journey, including those times in our race of faith when we seem to be wandering in the wilderness and those times when we feel like we have reached the mountaintop.

Third, other people cannot argue with our stories. Our stories are unique to each of us; this uniqueness cannot be denied. We should be clear, concise, and confident that our stories can be used by the Holy Spirit to speak to the hearts of those who hear them. We each need to know our own story and be able to share it anytime, anyplace, and with anyone.

What Is Your Story?

Take a moment and think about your story. Maybe you are still in the before-Christ phase. Maybe you are seriously considering becoming a follower of Jesus Christ as you read this book. Maybe you have been a follower for a long time but haven't shared your story with others. Today is the day to put pen to paper and recount your story. It is important to incorporate all three elements of your story (i.e., before Christ, encounter with Christ, and after Christ) if in fact you are a Christian. Keep it concise and practice telling it to a Christian friend you can trust. The biblical mandate is this: *Always be prepared to give an answer to everyone who asks you to give the reason for the hope that you have; but do this with gentleness and respect* (1 Peter 3:15). Before today is over, take some time to write down your story and then practice reciting it.

What Are the Elements of His Story?

Our stories are important and deeply personal, but they would be worthless without God's story. We have stories to tell because

God created a way for us to be reconciled to Him. Therefore, let's make sure we have a simple, concise understanding of His Story that we can share with others. There are four parts to His story, and it begins with God.

1. **God**
   a. He is love (1 John 4:16).
   b. He is holy (1 Peter 1:16).
   c. He is just (2 Thessalonians 1:6).

2. **Man**
   a. We are sinful from birth (Romans 3:23).
   b. We deserve death (Romans 6:23).
   c. We are spiritually helpless (Isaiah 64:6).

3. **Jesus**
   a. He is God, who also became man (John 1:1, 14).
   b. He died as our substitute (1 Peter 2:24).
   c. He offers forgiveness as a free gift (Ephesians 2:8–9; Romans 6:23).

4. **You**
   a. You must respond to God's offer (John 1:12; Romans 10:13).
   b. You must trust Christ for salvation and make Him Lord of your life (Romans 10:9–10; 1 Peter 3:15).
   c. You will be transformed and gifted by the Holy Spirit (2 Corinthians 5:17; 1 Corinthians 12).

There are a number of ways to tell God's story, but this outline helps us to focus on what God has done and is a logical sequence that anyone can understand. Just as we are to write down and practice telling our story, we should also write down and practice telling God's story. One strategy for doing this is to insert the outline above into your Bible or notebook. It will guide you as you share the Good News with others.

What are the Different Styles of Evangelism?

It is important to realize at this point that there is not just one way to share the Good News with others. Because each of us is unique, God has given each of us a certain personality and style that suits our life. In the Bible, we see at least six styles of sharing the Gospel with others. Let's take a quick survey of them, and hopefully we will gain some insight into how to apply each style to our specific situations.

1. **Confrontational (Example: Peter in Acts 2)**: Peter stands up during the feast of Pentecost and boldly lays out how Jesus Christ is the Messiah prophesied in the Old Testament. He goes on to challenge his audience with these words: *God has made this Jesus, whom you crucified, both Lord and Christ* (Acts 2:36). Peter did not mince words; he gave it to the people straight. In other words, he confronted them with the truth. When they asked him what they should do, he commanded them, *Repent and be baptized, every one of you, in the name of Jesus Christ for the forgiveness of your sins. And you will receive the gift of the Holy Spirit* (Acts 2:38). This passage serves as a great support for an invitation to be offered at the end of worship services.

2. **Intellectual (Example: Paul in Acts 17)**: Paul enters Athens and gives a three-step Gospel presentation. First, he establishes common ground when he says, *I see that in every way you are very religious* (Acts 17:22). Second, he makes the transition statement: *I even found an altar with this inscription: To An Unknown God. Now what you worship as something unknown I am going to proclaim to you* (Acts 17:23). Third, he presents the Good News in a clear, concise manner in verses 24–31. We also find the three responses to his Gospel presentation in verses 32–34. Some sneered, some wanted more information, and some believed.

3. **Testimonial (Example: blind man in John 9):** Jesus heals a man born blind, and the Pharisees question the man's parents and then the man himself. As the narrative progresses, we learn that the healed man refers to Jesus as "the man," "a prophet," "from God," "the Son of Man," and "Lord" (John 9:11, 17, 33, 35, 38). When the Pharisees call Jesus a sinner, the man confessed: *Whether he is a sinner or not, I don't know. One thing I do know. I was blind but now I see* (John 9:25).

4. **Interpersonal (Example: Matthew in Luke 5:27–32):** Matthew invites a group of his friends to his house for a dinner. The key to this story is that the religious people took issue with Jesus hanging out with sinners. His reply is a good verse to remember: *It is not the healthy who need a doctor, but the sick. I have not come to call the righteous, but sinners to repentance* (Luke 5:31–32).

5. **Invitational (Example: woman at the well in John 4):** Jesus meets a Samaritan woman at a well and engages her in conversation. This was taboo in His day. He converses with a woman who is not a Jew. However, He invites her to everlasting life when He declares: *whoever drinks the water I give him will never thirst. Indeed, the water I give him will become in him a spring of water welling up to eternal life* (John 4:14). Jesus's invitation to her compels her, a publicly shamed sinner, to go tell the whole town about Jesus.

6. **Miraculous (Example: Dorcas in Acts 9:36–43):** Dorcas, otherwise known as Tabitha, was a servant. She is described as one *who was always doing good and helping the poor* (Acts 9:36). She becomes sick and dies, but Peter prays for her, and God raises her from the dead. The news of this miracle spreads throughout the region and *many people believed in the Lord* (Acts 9:42).

As we see from these biblical examples, there are at least six ways we can share the Good News of Jesus Christ with others. The key is to always be able to explain an answer for the hope that we have. When we fully understand the glorious truth of the Gospel, we will be so compelled to share it that we will proactively invest in other peoples' lives and invite them into a life-changing relationship with Jesus Christ!

We have rounded the bend in the road and completed yet another mile. Now, we will press on as we see the path take a gradual incline ahead. But first, here is our next memory verse:

I am not ashamed of the gospel, because it is the power of God for the salvation of everyone who believes, first for the Jew, then for the Gentile.

(Romans 1:16)

.

Old Testament Overview

For many people, the Old Testament is, well, old! When they read it, the stories seem so far removed from our modern culture. But I have engaged the Old Testament enough to see the big picture of God's redemption plan throughout history. Every time I read about Noah, Abraham, Moses, David, or any other Old Testament character, I see the promise of God's deliverance for His people ultimately fulfilled in the person and work of Jesus Christ. Christians cannot fully understand the New Testament message unless they grasp the Old Testament message. This mile sets the foundation for the Good News of Jesus Christ.

How is the Old Testament Organized?

The Old Testament consists of thirty-nine books. While Genesis through 2 Kings are for the most part historically sequential, the remaining books consist of either additional information about the kings of Israel (Chronicles), are poetic writings (Job through the Song of Solomon), or are prophetic books addressed to the nation of Israel (Isaiah through Malachi). Therefore, the books of the Old Testament can be organized according to major categories:

Section	Books	Dates
Law	Genesis - Deuteronomy	Creation – 1445 BC
History	Joshua - Esther	1445 – 539 BC
Poetry	Job – Song of Solomon	1010 – 930 BC
Major Prophets	Isaiah - Daniel	739 – 539 BC
Minor Prophets	Hosea - Malachi	930 – 425 BC

The Law section consists of the first five books of the Old Testament, and they are historically sequential. Genesis begins with the creation story and runs through the patriarch Joseph. Exodus begins with the descendents of Jacob, the 12 tribes of Israel, enslaved in Egypt and records Moses' leading their exodus out of Egypt; God's giving of the law at Mount Sinai; and the construction of the tabernacle. Leviticus records other civil laws and the seven festivals the nation of Israel are to observe. Numbers records the census, the sending of the twelve spies, and the wandering in the wilderness for forty years. Deuteronomy records the re-giving of the Law by Moses to the next generation on the plains of Moab.

The History section is, for the most part, sequential. Joshua recounts the conquest of the land God gave to the Israelites (modern-day Israel). Judges covers the next three hundred and fifty years, during which a series of judges rule the nation of Israel. The story of Ruth takes place during the period of the judges. First and second Samuel describe the reigns of Saul and David. First and second Kings describe the reign of Solomon, followed by the division of the kingdom of Israel into North and South, beginning in 930 BC, and the reigns of their successive kings. First and second Chronicles retell much of the history covered in Samuel and Kings. Ezra, Nehemiah, and Esther give an account of the exile, the return of the Israelites from exile, and the rebuilding of the temple.

The Poetry section begins with Job, but the actual date of its writing is unknown. Many place its writing during the patriarchal period (2100–1700 BC). The book of Psalms was mostly written by David and fits in with the reign of David (1010–970 BC). Proverbs, Ecclesiastes, and the Song of Solomon were all written primarily by Solomon and discuss events that occurred during his reign (970–930 BC).

The Major Prophets section is so named due to the size of the books. Isaiah, Jeremiah, and Lamentations (authored also by Jeremiah) were written during the Divided Kingdom era (739–586 BC). Ezekiel and Daniel were both written during the exile (586–516 BC) and focus on the future restoration of Israel, as well as the so-called times of the gentiles, leading up to the final days and Christ's Second Coming.

The Minor Prophets section consists of twelve prophets. The first nine of those books, Hosea through Zephaniah, were written during the reigns of the various kings of the Northern Kingdom (Israel) and the Southern Kingdom (Judah) between 930–586 BC. The last three books—Haggai, Zechariah, and Malachi—were written during the restoration of the city and the rebuilding of the temple (539–445 BC), historically chronicled in both Ezra and Nehemiah.

What Are the Major Periods of the Old Testament?

Another way to think about the Old Testament history is to divide it into major periods. The following seven periods, along with the books that belong to each period, are captured in the following table:

Historical Period	Books	Dates
1. Creation	Genesis 1 – 11	Creation – 2100 BC
2. Patriarchs	Genesis 12 – 50	2100 – 1500 BC
3. Exodus & Conquest	Exodus – 1 Samuel 9	1500 – 1050 BC
4. United Kingdom	1 Samuel 10 – 1 Kings 11; 1 Chronicles 1 – 2 Chronicles 9; Job – Song of Solomon	1050 – 930 BC
5. Divided Kingdom	1 Kings 12 – 2 Kings 25; 2 Chronicles 10 – 36; Isaiah – Lamentations; Hosea - Zephaniah	930 – 586 BC
6. Exile	Ezekiel, Daniel	586 – 539 BC
7. Restoration	Ezra – Esther; Haggai - Malachi	539 – 425 BC

There are a few key points to make relative to the table above. First, a lot of historical time is covered in only the first eleven chapters of Genesis. Second, there are four patriarchs whose lives are recorded in Genesis 12–50: Abraham, Isaac, Jacob, and Joseph. Third, the Israelites left Egypt but wandered for forty years. So, the book of Exodus describes Moses, the Ten Commandments and the construction of the tabernacle. Leviticus records the additional laws decreed at Mount Sinai, where the Israelites stayed for about a year.

Numbers records the census taken (thus the name Numbers) and the wandering in the desert for forty years because of their rebellion at Kadesh-Barnea, when the Israelites decided not to trust God to give them the land He promised them through Abraham. Deuteronomy records Moses's passing on the law to the next generation prior to their entering the Promised Land. The book of Joshua records the conquest of the land and the division of the land among the twelve tribes of Israel. Judges and Ruth describe the three hundred and fifty years after the death of Joshua, where God raised up judges to lead Israel away from pagan influences. The final judge was Samuel, whose story begins in 1 Samuel.

The United Kingdom includes the reigns of Saul, David, and Solomon (in succession). After Solomon's death, his rightful heir,

Rehoboam, chose to increase his control over the people and they rebelled, making Jeroboam their king. Therefore, the kingdom split into the Northern Kingdom (Israel) under Jeroboam and the Southern Kingdom (Judah) under Rehoboam (1 Kings 12). Most of the prophets wrote their books during the reigns of the kings in these two kingdoms.

The exile lasted seventy years, as prophesied by Jeremiah (Jeremiah 25), and both Ezekiel and Daniel, who prophesied to the Israelite captives in Babylon. Daniel describes a series of visions and dreams where God shows him the rise and fall of successive empires— Babylon, Media-Persia, Greece, Rome, and even the empire during the end-time—to oppose God's people. Under the Persian King Cyrus, the Israelites were allowed to return to Israel around 539 BC. Ezra and Nehemiah record the return to the law, the rebuilding of the city, the wall, and the temple, all encouraged by the last three prophets of the Old Testament—Haggai, Zechariah, and Malachi.

Who Are the Key People in the Old Testament?

There are literally hundreds of people whose stories we could follow in the Old Testament. However, there are a handful that God specifically used to bring about His plan and purpose in redemption. A brief overview of seven key people in the Old Testament follows:

1. **Abraham (Genesis 12–26)**: The first patriarch and the man called a *friend of God,* (James 2:23). Abram answered God's call to relocate to Canaan, to become the father of many nations (at which point God changed his name from Abram to Abraham), and to serve as the ultimate example of faith for God's chosen people. At a very old age, Abraham would have a son, Isaac, who would become the second patriarch and the father of Jacob (later

renamed by God to Israel), who would have twelve sons, from whom the names of the twelve tribes of Israel came.

2. **Joseph (Genesis 37, 39–50):** The eleventh son of Jacob and the ultimate example of God's providence, Joseph was a dreamer who believed his dreams. His brothers sold him to Egyptian slave traders. However, despite a series of seemingly unfortunate events, God providentially enabled Joseph to interpret Pharaoh's dreams. As a reward for Joseph's service, Pharaoh elevated him to a powerful position in Egypt. When a severe famine swept over the land, Joseph was able to preserve God's people by providing for his family. Ironically, Joseph saved the very brothers who had sold him into slavery.

3. **Moses (Exodus–Deuteronomy):** The prophet leader of the Israelite people, Moses, born in the tribe of Levi (the priestly tribe), would preside over the ten plagues God rained down on Egypt; the night of Passover; the exodus; the parting of the Red Sea; the Ten Commandments at Mount Sinai; the construction of the tabernacle; the institution of the sacrificial system; the wandering in the desert for forty years; and the handing down of the law to the new generation on the plains of Moab. Moses's brother Aaron would serve as the first High Priest, but neither of them would accompany the rest of Israel into the Promised Land. That task was given to Joshua.

4. **Joshua (Joshua):** One of the twelve men sent by Moses to spy on the land God would give them, Joshua was one of two (Caleb being the other) to trust that God would give them victory. Joshua would lead the Israelite people across the Jordan River into the Promised Land and would lead the conquest of many pagan peoples and their cities. At his death, Israel had become one nation under God.

5. **David (1 Samuel–1 Kings 3; 1 Chronicles; Psalms):** After the period of the judges, the people wanted a king, because all the other nations had a king. God gave them a king, King Saul, but he disobeyed God, so God had Samuel anoint young David. David defeated Goliath; gained the people's popularity; was hunted by the jealous king Saul; ascended to the throne; ushered in a time of conquest and stability for Israel; fell into sin with Bathsheba; endured the betrayal of his son, Absalom; and died as a man denied by God to build His temple. However, the Bible describes him as *a man after God's own heart* and the greatest king of Israel, reigning from 1010 to 970 BC (Acts 13:22). Bethlehem, where Jesus was born, was known as the City of David.

6. **Solomon (1 Kings 3–11; 2 Chronicles 1–9; Proverbs, Ecclesiastes, Song of Solomon):** David's son and the wise king of Israel, Solomon ruled from 970 to 930 BC, presiding over the nation of Israel during times of great peace and prosperity. Instead of asking for wealth or power, Solomon asked God for wisdom, and God granted him wisdom and everything else as well. He was perhaps the richest and wisest man to have ever lived. He built the glorious temple of God, and his wealth and wisdom became known all over the world.

7. **Isaiah (Isaiah):** The greatest prophet of the Old Testament, Isaiah prophesied during the reigns of four kings. He is known as the messianic prophet, because his book contains some of the most specific prophecies concerning Jesus Christ. These include: the messiah would be *born of a virgin* and would reign as the *Wonderful Counselor, Mighty God, Everlasting Father, and Prince of Peace.* Isaiah further prophesied the Messiah would be the *Root of Jesse;* the *precious cornerstone;* God's *chosen*

one; a light for the Gentiles; the *suffering servant;* and the *anointed one* (Isaiah 7:14; 9:6;11; 28:16; 42:1–9; 49:6; 52:13–53:12; 61:1–2).

What Are the Key Events of the Old Testament?

There is no way to describe the entire Old Testament and what it teaches in this mile, even though there *is* so much to teach. However, since we are only in the third leg of our journey, it would suffice to highlight just sixteen key events:

1. **Creation and fall (Genesis 1–3):** establishes God's eternal nature and sovereignty as creator and sustainer; describes the creation of Adam and Eve. When tempted by the serpent (Satan), Adam and Eve disobey God's command not to eat of the tree of knowledge. As a consequence, they are subject to death and expelled from the Garden of Eden.

2. **Flood (Genesis 6–9):** portrays God's justice, mercy, and faithfulness as He judges man's wickedness by means of a flood, but He saves Noah's family as a faithful remnant, promising by the sign of a rainbow to never flood the earth again.

3. **Abraham and Isaac (Genesis 22):** God tests Abraham's faith in order to demonstrate that God is the provider of the atoning (covering) sacrifice for man's sin.

4. **Passover and Exodus (Exodus 12–14):** deliverance of Israel from four hundred years of slavery in Egypt and crossing of the Red Sea to a new life of freedom; foreshadows Jesus Christ as our deliverer from sin and as our Passover Lamb; the Red Sea crossing is a type of baptism.

5. **The Ten Commandments (Exodus 20):** establishes God's holiness and righteousness as Moses serves as mediator between God and man; Jesus, the fulfillment of the law,

became the perfect mediator between God and man, reconciling man back to God.

6. **Walls of Jericho (Joshua 6):** demonstrates God's power and faithfulness, as the Israelite people finally enter the land God had promised to them forty years earlier.

7. **Gideon (Judges 6–8):** accentuates the truth that God fights for us against our enemies and that we need only trust Him at His word.

8. **Samson and Delilah (Judges 13–16):** a story of tragedy and triumph, highlighting man's misplaced confidence and vulnerability to temptation; God is seen as the ultimate victor.

9. **David and Goliath (1 Samuel 16–17):** a historical account of a turning point in Israel's history, where God demonstrates His power and provision to a pagan world.

10. **David and Bathsheba (2 Samuel 11):** a raw look at the life of *a man after God's own heart*, but who was still susceptible to sin and its consequences.

11. **Solomon's wisdom (1 Kings 3):** an event early in Solomon's reign causes him to display the wisdom that God had given him; his fame spreads all over the world as a result of this one wise decision.

12. **Elijah's God versus Baal (1 Kings 18):** demonstrates that there is only one, true God; he responds to Elijah's contest with the Baal worshipers.

13. **The suffering servant (Isaiah 52–53):** graphic portrayal of the coming Messiah's suffering, depicting specific details of the Crucifixion.

14. **The valley of dry bones (Ezekiel 37):** captivating story of God's power to make the dead live again, as Ezekiel prophesies Israel's resurrection and restoration.

15. **Daniel in the lion's den (Daniel 6):** God shows his faithfulness. Daniel continues to pray to God despite the warning

that those who pray to anyone but the king would be thrown to the lions. Daniel is thrown into the lion's den, but God protects him.

16. **Jonah and the big fish (Jonah 1–4):** God disciplines Jonah for being disobedient to His call to tell sinful Nineveh to repent; this story shows the mercy God has for all people, even the most wicked.

That was a quick overview of the Old Testament, but hopefully it has helped us get our bearings relative to its key dates, people, and events. We are beginning to see how the Old Testament narrative points us to the coming of God's Promised One. The New Testament picks up with that Promised One, the Messiah, Jesus Christ, and we will move to our New Testament overview next, but first, let's review this mile's memory verse:

Keep this Book of the Law always on your lips; meditate on it day and night, so that you may be careful to do everything written in it. Then you will be prosperous and successful. Have I not commanded you? Be strong and courageous. Do not be afraid; do not be discouraged, for the LORD your God will be with you wherever you go.

(Joshua 1:9)

New Testament Overview

Some of the most powerful proclamations and principles ever recorded are contained in the New Testament. My friend had been exposed to the teachings of Jesus at church, but she had a lukewarm faith until she finally read Christ's words for herself. Jesus claimed to be God. He claimed to be the world's Savior from sin. He accepted worship. And He promised eternal life to all who placed their trust in Him. Confronted by those claims, my friend knew she had to make a decision. Jesus does not allow anyone to straddle the fence, so she jumped in with a full commitment to Christ. This mile teaches that the New Testament first emphasizes who we are in Christ and then what we are to do for Christ.

How Is the New Testament Organized?

The New Testament consists of twenty-seven books. They are not chronological. Instead, they are categorized according to content or author:

Section	Books	Dates
Gospels	Matthew - John	AD 60 – 65
Early Church	Acts	AD 65
Paul's Letters	Romans - Philemon	AD 53 -66
General Letters	Hebrews - Jude	AD 60 - 70
Prophecy	Revelation	AD 90 – 95

The Gospels account for the first four books of the New Testament. They recount the life, death, and resurrection of Jesus Christ. Matthew portrays Jesus as the king who was prophesied to come; his audience consisted of Jewish people living in Israel. Mark portrays Jesus as the suffering servant; his audience consisted primarily of gentiles. Luke portrays Jesus as the Son of Man and his audience was specifically a man named Theophilus, but more broadly the inhabitants of the entire Roman Empire. Finally, John portrays Jesus as the Son of God; his audience was the entire Roman Empire. The first three are called the synoptic Gospels, due to their parallel depictions of the life of Christ. John wrote much later, probably around AD 85, and does not necessarily follow the historical sequence of the life of Christ.

Luke also wrote the book of Acts. Acts records the actions of the apostles and early church. Beginning with the replacement of Judas Iscariot with Matthias and the pouring out of the Holy Spirit at Pentecost, the narrative then follows the preaching and teaching of Peter and John; the stoning of Stephen, the conversion of Saul (Paul); Paul's subsequent missionary journeys; and the planting of churches throughout the Roman Empire.

Paul's letters (thirteen in all) address various doctrines (teachings), issues, and concerns to several of the churches he planted or to individuals he mentored. As a general rule, Paul began each of his letters with biblical doctrine followed by practical ways of living out those beliefs. For example, the first eleven chapters of the book of Romans contains the most comprehensive explanation of the Gospel, using numerous Old Testament quotes as support, whereas chapters twelve through sixteen offer practical guidelines for living out the Gospel.

The General Letters include letters written by other authors besides Paul. Some scholars credit Paul with writing Hebrews, but it is not certain, so Hebrews is most often included in this section. The other authors include James (the half-brother of Jesus), Peter, John, and Jude (another half-brother of Jesus). These letters are addressed to different audiences and are comprised of varying doctrinal themes, but all of them encourage their readers to hold fast to the faith and to the teachings of Christ.

Revelation is the final book of the Bible and is the culmination of the special revelation of God. Written by the apostle John while he was exiled by the Roman Emperor to the Isle of Patmos, it contains a series of visions that most scholars understand to show the events immediately leading up to the Second Coming of Christ, the final judgment of all men, and the eternal abiding destiny of all men, whether in heaven or hell. Just as Genesis explains the beginning, Revelation prophesies the end.

What Are the Major Sections of the Gospels?

When we study the four Gospels—Matthew, Mark, Luke, and John—we can quickly break each of them down into four major sections. Those sections and the corresponding references appear in the table below:

Section	Book References
Birth Narratives	Matthew 1 – 2; Luke 1 – 2
Jesus' Baptism/Early Ministry	Matthew 3 – 11; Mark 1 – 6; Luke 3 – 7; John 1 – 2
Road to Jerusalem	Matthew 12 – 20; Mark 7 – 10; Luke 8 – 19:27; John 3 – 12:11
Jesus' Crucifixion & Resurrection	Matthew 21 – 28; Mark 11 -16; Luke 19:28 – Luke 24; John 12:12 – John 21

The birth narratives recount the prophecies concerning the birth of the messiah, Jesus Christ. Matthew and Luke each use genealogies to support the fact that Jesus is the Messiah promised to His forefathers in the Old Testament. Matthew's genealogy traces Joseph's ancestry while Luke's genealogy traces Mary's ancestry. Matthew includes the visit of the Magi (wise men) and the family's escape to Egypt. Luke describes the birth of John the Baptist, the angel Gabriel's visit to Mary, the birth announcement of the angels to the shepherds, and Jesus's presentation at the temple. Most scholars agree that Jesus was born 6–4 BC, even though the calendar would have us to believe that he was born in AD 1.

Jesus's baptism is recorded in the first three Gospels, and John alludes to it as part of John the Baptist's testimony. Jesus spent the majority of His early ministry in Galilee, the region north of Jerusalem and Samaria. Much of His early ministry consisted of sermons and miracles, including physical healings and authority over the natural world. Most scholars agree that Jesus's earthly ministry, beginning with His baptism, lasted about three-and-a-half years. Luke tells us that Jesus began His ministry when he was thirty years old, the age when Jewish priests first entered service (Luke 3:23). Therefore, we can surmise that Jesus began His public ministry in the fall of AD 26.

The Road to Jerusalem section records Jesus's final year on earth and his approaching passion. During this period, His teachings carry a stronger message; His miracles are more incredible; and His parables are more specifically focused on the kingdom of God. Luke records some of the more well-known parables on Jesus's approach to Jerusalem, including the Good Samaritan, the Great Banquet and the Prodigal Son.

Fully one-third of all the Gospel narratives are devoted to the final section: Jesus's crucifixion and resurrection. Every one of the Gospels prioritizes the final week of Jesus's life, beginning with His triumphal entry into Jerusalem. Matthew devotes seven chapters to this period; Mark, six; Luke, six; and John, ten. There is tremendous corroboration among all four Gospels about the Last Supper, the garden of Gethsemane, the betrayal, the arrest, the trials, and the Crucifixion. Further, every one of the Gospels affirms the resurrection on the third day. The fact that Jesus remained on earth for a period of forty days prior to His ascension is recorded in the first chapter in Acts (Acts 1:3). Since we can estimate that Jesus's ministry began in the fall of AD 26, then we can estimate that His death and resurrection occurred in the spring of AD 30.

What are the Six Key Components of the Gospels?

As we evaluate the Gospels, we can identify six key components that comprise the majority of the narratives. They are sermons, parables, healings, miracles, Old Testament references and answers to questions.

1. **Jesus's sermons.** Jesus preached to crowds throughout His ministry. The most popular sermon is known as the Sermon on the Mount, which he delivered at the Mount of Olives (Matthew 5–7; Luke 6:17–49). Other sermons include the sending of the twelve, the sending of the seventy-two, the upper room discourse (John 13–17), and the end-time prophecy (Matthew 24–25; Mark 13; Luke 21).

2. **Jesus's parables.** These are short stories that teach spiritual truths. Throughout His ministry, Jesus taught spiritual truth to His followers. He explained to them that parables can reveal truth to those who are open to it: *The knowledge of the secrets of the kingdom of heaven has been given to you, but not to them* (Matthew 13:11). He quoted Isaiah's prophecy that the religious elite would not recognize the coming of the Messiah because their hearts were calloused. Jesus used parables to teach the common people about the kingdom of heaven. In fact, Matthew 13 alone records seven of Jesus's parables related to the kingdom of heaven. Some of the most popular parables, besides those just mentioned earlier, include: The Sower (Matthew 13:3–23); The Unmerciful Servant (Matthew 18:21–35); Workers in the Vineyard (Matthew 20:1–16); The Wedding Banquet (Matthew 22:1–14); The Tenants (Mark 12:1–11); The Rich Fool (Luke 12:13–21); and The Ten Minas (Luke 19:11–27).

3. **Jesus's healings.** Jesus healed people to give them hope and to establish His authority over the natural world. Truly, His healings gave Him a hearing among those who followed Him. When John the Baptist was in prison, he sent his followers to ask Jesus if He was in fact the Messiah they had been waiting for. Jesus replied, *Go back and report to John what you hear and see: The blind receive sight, the lame walk, those who have leprosy are cleansed, the deaf hear, the dead are raised, and the good news is proclaimed to the poor* (Matthew 11:4–5). His healings included the centurion's servant (Matthew 8:5–13); the paralytic (Mark 2:1–12); the deaf and mute man (Mark 7:32–35); Jarius's daughter (Luke 8:51–55); the man born blind (John 9); and Lazarus (John 11).

4. **Jesus's miracles.** Separate from His healings, His miracles demonstrated power over nature. Jesus told His disciples to

believe that He and the Father were one: *Believe me when I say that I am in the Father and the Father is in me; or at least believe on the evidence of the miracles themselves* (John 14:11). Some of Jesus's miracles include: walking on water (Matthew 14:22–33); calming the stormy sea (Mark 4:35–41); feeding of five thousand people (John 6:5–14); and catching a great number of fish (John 21:4–11).

5. **Old Testament references.** Jesus confirmed the authority of the Old Testament's history and prophecy. In fact, Jesus leant credibility to some of the more unbelievable Old Testament accounts, even those that many Christians find difficult to believe. For example, he referenced the marriage relationship between Adam and Eve (Matthew 19:4–6); Noah's flood (Matthew 24:36–39); Daniel's seventy-week prophecy (Matthew 24:15); and Jonah's three-day stay in the belly of a huge fish (Matthew 12:39–41).

6. **Jesus's answers to questions.** The longest recorded answer Jesus gave to His disciples was in response to the question: *What will be the sign of your coming and of the end of the age?* (Matthew 24:3). His answer runs for the next ninety-three verses (Matthew 24:4–25:46). Jesus explained why His disciples did not fast (Matthew 9:41); by what authority He taught and performed miracles (Matthew 21:23); about paying taxes to Caesar (Matthew 22:17); about marriage at the resurrection (Matthew 22:23–27); about the greatest commandment (Matthew 22:34–36); and about whose son is the Christ (Matthew 22:41–42). Jesus's responses teach and confirm His authority as the Son of God.

Who Are the Key People in Acts?

There are many key people in the book of Acts, but for the sake of brevity, we will only mention five here. These five individuals dominate the narrative and are briefly introduced below in the order in which they appear in Acts.

1. **Peter (Acts 2–5, 10–12, 15)**: The impetuous, passionate, eldest apostle of Jesus Christ, Peter, a fisherman by trade, was a prominent follower of Jesus during His earthly ministry. Known for his divergent responses to Jesus, Peter on the one hand confessed to Jesus that He was the Christ (that is, the Messiah), and on the other hand denied Him three times. After His resurrection, Jesus reinstated Peter by asking him three times if he loved Him. Ten days after Jesus's ascension, Peter stood up on the Day of Pentecost and gave the first public sermon about the salvation offered in Christ (Acts 2:14–41). After that sermon, or perhaps because of it, Peter became the leader of the early church, healing the crippled beggar; rebuking Ananias and Sapphira; converting the first gentile, Cornelius; and miraculously escaping from prison.

2. **John (Acts 3–5)**: Perhaps the youngest of the apostles, and also a fisherman by trade, John demonstrated a quiet faith and a continual devotion to Jesus. He was the only apostle who was present at the Crucifixion, and while Peter entered the empty tomb asking questions, John entered the empty tomb and believed (John 20:1–9). John was instrumental in the early church as well, taking a bold stand with Peter before the Sanhedrin (the Jewish religious ruling body in Jerusalem); participating in the believers' prayer that invoked the Holy Spirit's power; and enduring the persecution of the Sadducees, a religious sect of Jesus's day.

3. **Stephen (Acts 6–7)**: Stephen is first mentioned when the apostles chose seven men to assist with the service within the early church. This role was a precursor to the office of deacon. However, religious leaders accused Stephen of blasphemy before the Sanhedrin. Stephen's answer to that

charge is one of the most compelling explanations of God's redemptive plan, which is laid out in the Old Testament and points to Jesus Christ as the Messiah. Stephen used nine references from the Old Testament to buttress his argument. Nevertheless, Stephen was stoned, and it was Saul (later known as Paul) who witnessed this first Christian martyr's death.

4. **Philip (Acts 8)**: As persecution broke out against the church, Philip, one of the first deacons with Stephen (Acts 6:5), went to Samaria to preach the Gospel. While he had great success there, God nevertheless sent an angel to tell him to go south toward Gaza. He obeyed and met an Ethiopian eunuch on his way back to Africa, who inquired about a prophecy in the book of Isaiah. Philip started with that very Scripture (Isaiah 53:7–8) and told Him the Good News of Jesus Christ. Philip baptized the eunuch as a new believer in Christ. Because Philip obeyed God, the Gospel was opened up to all of Africa. Philip had four daughters who were prophetesses (Acts 21:9).

5. **Paul (Acts 9, 13–28)**: Half of the book of Acts and half of the New Testament books are attributed to the apostle Paul. A devout Jew by birth and training, Paul vehemently persecuted the early Christians. However, during his travel to Damascus, Jesus converted him and commissioned him to serve as His missionary to the gentile nations. Thus, God used the one who most vehemently persecuted the church to spread the Gospel throughout the entire Roman Empire. Commissioned in Antioch with Barnabas, Paul would make four missionary journeys, sharing the Gospel in the synagogues of every city he visited and planting churches to offer salvation to Jews and gentiles alike. Paul had many traveling companions, including Barnabas, John Mark (the writer of the Gospel of Mark), Silas, Timothy, and Luke. Most of his

letters served to correct those churches on doctrinal issues or practical applications of their new faith. Paul would ultimately be accused of stirring up a revolt against the Jewish laws. He was tried three times before Jewish officials sent him, by ship, to Rome to appeal to Caesar. Acts ends with Paul's imprisonment in Rome, where he awaited trial. Tradition says he was beheaded.

What Are the Major Themes in the Letters?

The table below lists each of the letters in the New Testament and the major themes addressed in each letter. This table will serve as a guide for you in choosing books to study.

Letter	Major Themes
Romans	Sin, Salvation, God's Sovereignty
1 Corinthians	Unity, Purity
2 Corinthians	Faith, Hope, Generosity
Galatians	Faith, Freedom, Fruitfulness
Ephesians	God's Purpose, Unity
Philippians	Humility, Unity, Joy
Colossians	Holiness, Witness
1 Thessalonians	Hope, Preparation
2 Thessalonians	Last Days, Perseverance
1 Timothy	Worship, Leadership, Discipline
2 Timothy	Boldness, Faithfulness, Truth
Titus	Character, Leadership
Philemon	Forgiveness, Freedom
Hebrews	Sacrifice, Maturity, Faith, Endurance
James	Works, Wisdom
1 Peter	Salvation, Unity, Judgment
2 Peter	Diligence, Last Days
1,2, 3 John	Love, Truth, Faithfulness
Jude	Truth, Judgment

What Is the Key to Interpreting Revelation?

Revelation is the final book of the Bible and describes in graphic detail the final days leading up to and including the Second Coming of Christ, His final judgment, and the final destinies for all people of all time. Many who read Revelation are confused by its symbolic language and don't believe it can be understood. However, the very name of the book is "Revelation," which means to reveal, disclose, or uncover what was once hidden. If that is true, then this apocalyptic book *can* be understood.

In fact, there is a clue early in the book about how to interpret its contents. The book sequentially records the visions that unfold for John, its writer. The angel gives John the following command: *Write, therefore, what you have seen, what is now and what will take place later* (Revelation 1:19). In this one sentence, we see the three major divisions of the book:

1. Write what you have seen (chapter 1)
2. What is now (chapters 2–3)
3. And what will take place later (chapters 4–22)

When we conduct an overview of the book, we see that John saw Jesus Christ in chapter 1, the church in chapters 2–3 (representing seven types of churches as well as the seven periods of the church age), and the world in chapters 4–22. The "revelation" of Jesus Christ is that He was in fact the promised Messiah during His First Coming and that He will come again as the conquering *King of Kings* (Revelation 19:16) to establish His eternal Kingdom at His Second Coming. Revelation is a fitting culmination of God's redemptive plan, as it closes with these beautiful words of comfort:

Now the dwelling of God is with men, and he will live with them. They will be his people, and God himself will be with them and

131

be their God. He will wipe every tear from their eyes. There will be no more death or mourning or crying or pain, for the old order of things has passed away.

(Revelation 21:3–4)

We have now completed our training on worship, the spiritual disciplines, and the overviews of both the Old and New Testaments. Having finished this third leg of our journey, we can see the next several miles are a steep climb, but we take comfort in knowing that we do not run it alone. Let's continue the race as we learn to *Nurture* our faith to maturity, but first, here is our next memory verse:

In the same way, let your light shine before men, that they may see your good deeds and praise your Father in heaven.

(Matthew 5:16)

The Race of Faith

The Fourth Leg: Nurture

To nurture is to feed and educate for the purpose of sustained growth. In the same way, every Christian must nurture his or her faith in order to achieve the ultimate goal of becoming more like Christ. Many Christians give up in this leg of the race, but if they were to press on, they would develop such a greater understanding of the deeper truths of the faith and make a greater impact for Christ.

Mile 13: The Doctrine of God
Mile 14: The Doctrines of Christ and the Holy Spirit
Mile 15: The Doctrine of Mankind
Mile 16: The Doctrine of Salvation

The Doctrine of God

An atheist is someone who believes that God does not exist. Our "seeing-is-believing" world culture challenges the notion of an invisible, all powerful Being presiding over our universe. That said, the vast majority of humans believe in a Supreme Being commonly called God. My faith journey was a process of discovery, first resulting in an acknowledgement that God does exist and second that God is defined perfectly within the pages of the Bible and more specifically in the person and work of Jesus Christ. Maybe you have never doubted God's existence, but it is a healthy exercise to know what you believe about God and why. This mile argues for the existence of God and explains God the Father's attributes and functions.

Does God Exist?

While the Bible and Christianity assume the eternal existence of God, the first question that any honest inquirer should ask as we delve into what we believe is: does God exist? The answer to that question establishes a baseline for all other doctrine. We should not rely solely on what we have been taught. We should always be of the mind-set to work out our faith. Therefore, let us begin this mile by considering carefully the question of God's existence.

There are four arguments that we can use to conclude that there is a God and that He is both transcendent (completely removed from and beyond this world) and immanent (completely personal and involved in this world).

The first argument for the existence of God is based on the evidence of both nature and Scripture. The fingerprints of an intelligent, transcendent Being are obvious when we observe the awesome creation around us and when we consider how best to explain the origin of all of creation, including life. Further, God has revealed Himself through Holy Scripture. The Bible never questions the existence of God; the first sentence of Genesis assumes His existence and then goes on to explain that He created the heavens and the earth. Throughout the entire Bible, God is portrayed as the Creator and Sustainer of the universe.

The second argument is that God is the first cause. This is known as the cosmological argument. The question of origins is at the heart of the discussion of God's existence. Everything that exists has a cause. The universe exists and therefore was caused by someone or something. That someone or something must be greater than the universe. Over the last forty years, science has attained sufficient evidence to conclude that the universe is not eternal and has had an absolute beginning. Some scientists call this the big bang theory. Interestingly, the big bang theory presupposes the existence of matter, time, and space. So the question remains: From where did that matter, time, and space come? Astrophysicist Robert Jastrow, noted agnostic, is quoted as saying, "The Universe flashed into being, and we cannot find out what caused that to happen."[6] God is the most logical answer to that question.

The third argument is that God is the intelligent designer. This is known as the teleological argument. There is much evidence that the universe was designed by an intelligent Being. First, the earth is the perfect size and perfect distance from the sun. Even a fractional variance of the earth's position to the sun or away from the sun would make life on earth impossible. Second, this intelligent Being created water, without which no living thing could survive; in fact, two-thirds of the human body is composed of water. Evaporation takes ocean water and leaves the salt behind while forming clouds in the sky, which are moved by the wind to disperse that water, creating the perfect environment to support life.

The marvels of the human body also serve as evidence of the existence of an intelligent designer. For example, the human brain processes more than a million messages per second. The theory of evolution does not explain the irreducible complexity of the eye or the brain. Charles Darwin himself confessed, "If it could be demonstrated that any complex organ existed which could not possibly have been formed by numerous, successive, slight modifications, my theory would absolutely break down."[7] It has been proven that the human eyeball and brain are both irreducibly complex. This breaks down the theory of evolution, which is one of many reasons that evolution remains only a theory.

Just think about the relatively recent discovery of the DNA code. Every cell in our body has a unique code that tells it what to do. Scientists have assigned four letters, ATGC (nucleotides), to

---

6   Robert Jastrow, "Message from Robert Jastrow," *Leader U.com*, 2002, http://www.leaderu. com/truth/1truth18b.html.

7   Charles Darwin, *The Origin of Species* (New York, NY: P. F. Collier & Son, 1909), Page 194.

every cell, so that a single cell may look like this random pattern: CGTGTGACTCGCT, and so on. Keep in mind that there are three billion nucleotides in every cell![8] The complexity of the simple cell is itself a marvel and virtually unexplainable without a perfectly intelligent and creative designer. For Christians, this perfectly intelligent and creative Designer is God.

The fourth argument is that God is the author of right and wrong. This is known as the moral argument. Moral values cannot be objective if God does not exist. In the world, there is a gradation of values: better, truer, and nobler. Comparatives lead us to superlatives, such as best, truest, and noblest, etc. There must be some objective moral agent that *is* the most, and Christians believe this agent is God. Relativism is the result of a world without absolute morals. For example, if someone stole money from you to give to someone else less fortunate, who is to say whether that is right or wrong? How can a changeable human have authority over all the people in the world? The answer is that only an objective authority can establish right and wrong. That objective authority is God.

The Bible says that we can pursue God and find Him. James encourages us with these words, *Come near to God and He will come near to you* (James 4:8). In addition, Jeremiah quotes God with this wonderful promise:

> *For I know the plans I have for you, declares the LORD, plans to prosper you and not to harm you, plans to give you hope and a future. Then you will call upon me and come and pray to me; and I will listen to you. You will seek me and find me when you seek me with all your heart. I will be found by you.*

(Jeremiah 29:11–14a)

---

8   R. Webster Kehr, "DNA and RNA" in *Introduction to the Mathematics of Evolution*, (March 2009), http://www.mathematicsofevolution.com/ChaptersMath/Chapter_090__DNA_and_RNA__.html.

God pursues us because He desires to have a relationship with us. The writer of Hebrews declares, *Without faith it is impossible to please God, because anyone who comes to him must believe that he exists and that he rewards those who earnestly seek him* (Hebrews 11:6). Truly, God exists, and our belief in Him pleases Him.

What Are God's Attributes?

The Bible is God's special revelation of Himself to the world. We only listed God's attributes at the starting line, but now we will look at them in a bit more detail. To review, the Bible teaches us that God is: eternal, spiritual, immortal, invisible, one, unchangeable, independent, all-knowing, all-powerful, ever-present, sovereign, holy, perfect, wrathful, loving, merciful, gracious, just, true, faithful, righteous, patient, compassionate, good, jealous, wise, glorious, and beautiful.

Each attribute is equally important; they work together in perfect tension. For example, we know that God is both loving and just. Our challenge is to never elevate any one attribute of God above the others; this is a critical teaching to maintaining the biblical view of God. I will define each attribute and give a few biblical references below. Please take your time in reviewing and meditating on these twenty-eight attributes. Your faith and your worship will be greatly enhanced as you take time to truly seek to know God!

1. **God is eternal** (Genesis 21:33; Psalm 90:2; Revelation 1:8): God's existence has no beginning and no ending. He is ever-abiding in the present.
2. **God is spiritual** (John 4:24; 2 Corinthians 3:17): God has no physical form, though He has manifested Himself in physical form, most significantly in the form of Jesus Christ.
3. **God is immortal** (1 Timothy 1:17; 6:16): God has always existed and will always exist. He will never die, and he confers immortality to the human spirit.

4. **God is invisible** (John 1:18; 1 Timothy 1:17): God cannot be seen or discerned by any other senses. He alone makes Himself known to those He chooses to reveal Himself.

5. **God is one** (Deuteronomy 6:4; Isaiah 45:5; Galatians 3:20): God is one in number and in unity. He is one in essence and three in person. Each of the Persons is coeternal, coequal, and co-essential.

6. **God is unchangeable** (Psalm 102:25–27; Malachi 3:6; James 1:17): God does not change His essence, purposes, will, mind, or promises, for He is perfect.

7. **God is independent** (Exodus 3:14; Acts 17:24–25): God is self-sufficient and requires nothing to sustain His existence or remain completely perfect.

8. **God is all-knowing** (Job 37:16; 1 John 3:20): God knows all things perfectly, whether they occur in the past, present, or future.

9. **God is all-powerful** (Genesis 17:1; Psalm 24:8; Matthew 19:26): God is able to do whatever His will dictates; nothing is impossible for Him.

10. **God is ever-present** (1 Kings 8:27; Psalm 139:7–10; Jeremiah 23:23–24): God fills the entire universe, and He is present everywhere at once. He is not restricted by time or space.

11. **God is sovereign** (Daniel 4:37; Romans 9:20–21; Revelation 19:16): God is the supreme ruler of the universe and everything in it. He is in complete control of all events and history.

12. **God is holy** (Leviticus 19:2; Isaiah 6:3; 1 Peter 1:16): God is purely sinless and is completely and forever separated from evil.

13. **God is perfect** (Psalm 18:30; Matthew 5:48): God does not sin, and He does not make mistakes. He lacks nothing in His qualities and ways.

14. **God is wrathful** (Jeremiah 10:10; Romans 1:26–28): God's righteous anger at human sinfulness demonstrates His divine judgment. Because He is perfectly holy, He hates evil.

15. **God is loving** (Psalm 59:10; Romans 5:8; 1 John 4:8–10): God places no conditions on His love for His creation; nothing we do will make Him love us any more or any less.

16. **God is merciful** (Exodus 34:6; Psalm 103:8; Ephesians 2:4–5): God withholds His wrath for our sin, and does not give humanity what it deserves.

17. **God is gracious** (Isaiah 30:18; Romans 3:23–24; Ephesians 2:7): God freely offers His gift of eternal life to all who would receive it. His gift is essentially unmerited favor bestowed upon humanity.

18. **God is just** (Deuteronomy 32:4; 2 Thessalonians 1:6; 1 John 1:9): God is fair in the administration of His law and punishments. His judgments are true and right.

19. **God is true** (Jeremiah 10:10; John 17:3; Romans 1:25): God is the only true God, and His words and actions are absolutely right and perfect.

20. **God is faithful** (Psalm 145:13; Lamentations 3:21–23; 1 Corinthians 10:13): God is trustworthy, and He always does what He says He will do.

21. **God is righteous** (Psalm 119:137; Daniel 9:14; Romans 3:24–25): God continually adheres to the mandates of His own law. He never acts in contradiction to His truth.

22. **God is patient** (Nahum 1:3; Romans 9:22; 2 Peter 3:9): God is slow to anger and shows great restraint in bringing to judgment those whom he loves.

23. **God is compassionate** (Psalm 145:8; Matthew 14:14; 2 Corinthians 1:3): God actively desires to free mankind from the suffering and pain of this life.

24. **God is good** (1 Chronicles 16:34; Psalm 119:68; Luke 18:19): God has never done anything wrong nor does He cause anyone to do any wrong. He brings about good in spite of our sin.

25. **God is jealous** (Exodus 34:13–14; 2 Corinthians 11:2): While jealousy has a negative connotation in our minds, God's jealousy is a righteous desire to guard and foster His possession.

26. **God is wise** (Psalm 104:24; Romans 16:27; Ephesians 3:10): God applies His knowledge perfectly in accomplishing His purposes.

27. **God is glorious** (Psalm 24:10; Luke 2:9; Revelation 21:23): God is supremely radiant in His revelation of Himself to humanity.

28. **God is beautiful** (Psalms 27:4; 50:2; Revelation 4:2–3): God is the sum of every desirable quality. He possesses an attractiveness that draws us to Him.

There are probably many more attributes we could list, but suffice it to say that there are countless ways in which we can describe God in all His splendor and majesty.

How Does God Reveal Himself?

God reveals Himself as Father, Son, and Holy Spirit, each with distinct personal attributes but without division of nature, essence, or being. Because God is one, all three persons are in perfect unity of fellowship and purpose. In fact, Jesus told His disciples: *Anyone who has seen me has seen the Father* (John 14:8).

God the Father's functions include: creator, ruler, and preserver. Jesus is the member of the Trinity who created the universe (John 1:1–3; Colossians 1:15–16). However, it is the Father who spoke His will in creation: *And God said, "Let there be light, and there was light"* (Genesis 1:3). God's question to Job was: *Where were you when I laid the earth's foundation?* (Job 38:4). God is the creator of the heavens and the earth and everything in them.

God the Father is also the sovereign ruler of the universe. He sees everything, hears every prayer, and knows everything before it happens. In this way, He uses the choices we make to accomplish His will and purpose. He is ever seated on His throne, and nothing we can do will thwart God's purposes or surprise Him. The prophet Isaiah declared: *For the LORD Almighty has purposed, and who can thwart him? His hand is stretched out, and who can turn it back?* (Isaiah 14:27).

Finally, God the Father is the preserver of the universe. He established the earth and everything in it, and now He maintains the earth. In an instant, God could cause cataclysmic change to the world we live in, but He chooses to sustain His creation. He preserves life and the balance needed to hold the whole universe together. This is the power of God in continuous display, though often we never even think about it. God gives us each day as a gift. Even the greatest and most devoted aspects of our praise and worship are but a feeble response to that truth.

In this mile, we have answered the question, "Does God exist?" We have also listed and explained many of God's attributes. Finally, we have learned how God has chosen to reveal Himself to man. Now, we turn our attention to the doctrines of Jesus Christ and the Holy Spirit, but first, here is our next memory verse:

For I know the plans I have for you, declares the Lord, plans to prosper you and not to harm you, plans to give you hope and a future. Then you will call upon me and come and pray to me, and I will listen to you. You will seek me and find me when you seek me with all your heart.

(Jeremiah 29:11–13)

The Doctrines of Christ and the Holy Spirit

A neighbor of mine, a Hindu, once told me, "I believe in many gods, but Jesus is my favorite!" I answered, "He's my favorite too!" She did not know how to reply. Most people in the world today have no issue with Jesus, but they have relegated Him to a historical figure who was a great moral teacher. In that role, he is a safe deity. However, the Jesus of the Bible does not allow a casual respect; He demands total commitment. The Holy Spirit points to Christ and is oftentimes misunderstood, even within the church. Many Christians struggle with the concept of the Trinity and their respective functions. This mile explains the distinctive roles of Jesus Christ and the Holy Spirit.

How is Jesus Fully God and Fully Man?

While man only has a human nature, Jesus uniquely has two natures—a human nature *and* a divine nature. Therefore, Jesus is fully human *and* fully God. The Bible teaches us that the historical Jesus was fully human and there are at least three pieces of evidence to support that fact.

1. **Jesus was born of woman.** Matthew and Luke both record the details related to Jesus's birth. Matthew recounts: *After Jesus was born in Bethlehem in Judea, during the time of King Herod, Magi from the east came to Jerusalem* (Matthew 2:1). What made His birth unique, however, was that He was born of a virgin: *All this took place to fulfill what the Lord had said through the prophet: "The virgin will be with child and will give birth to a son, and they will call him Immanuel"—which means, "God with us"* (Matthew 1:22–23).

2. **Jesus had human attributes.** He had a physical body and emotions. He used all of His senses. As a human, He was limited by space and time. He experienced hunger, thirst, and exhaustion. He experienced joy, temptation, sorrow, pain, anguish, and even death. In every possible way, Jesus was human. He cried when Lazarus died. He anguished in the garden of Gethsemane. He thirsted as He hung on the cross. What made Jesus unique in His human nature was that He never sinned. It was possible for Him to have sinned, but because He was also fully God, He never sinned, since that would have been contrary to His divine nature and attributes. Paul would declare this truth to the church in Corinth: *God made him who had no sin to be sin for us, so that in him we might become the righteousness of God* (2 Corinthians 5:21). The writer of Hebrews confirms this

truth and affirms that Jesus can sympathize with our human weakness: *For we do not have a high priest who is unable to sympathize with our weaknesses, but we have one who has been tempted in every way, just as we are—yet was without sin* (Hebrews 4:15). The apostle Peter referred to Jesus as *a lamb without blemish or defect* (1 Peter 1:19).

3. **Jesus experienced physical death.** All four Gospels and virtually every other book of the New Testament confirm that Jesus died by crucifixion. God's curse as a result of man's fall in the Garden of Eden included physical death. The Bible confirms this truth: *Just as man is destined to die once, and after that to face judgment, so Christ was sacrificed once to take away the sins of many people; and he will appear a second time, not to bear sin, but to bring salvation to those who are waiting for him* (Hebrews 9:27–28). Everyone is appointed to die physically, but Jesus will come again. This passage prophesies His Second Coming, which we will cover in detail later. While there are two men in the Bible who might not have experienced physical death (Enoch and Elijah), some Scriptures point to a day when perhaps these two men will return to the earth and face the physical deaths appointed for them (Revelation 11:1–12).

Jesus is not only fully man, but He is fully God as well. Four proofs support His divinity:

1. **Jesus claimed to be God.** Throughout His public ministry, Jesus declared Himself to be the Messiah and to be coequal with God. He confirmed to the Samaritan woman that He was the Messiah (John 4:25–26). In addition, John records that Jesus *was even calling God his own Father, making himself equal with God* (John 5:18). Furthermore, He told His disciples, *I and the Father are one* (John 10:30).

When He said this, the religious leaders picked up stones to stone Him, saying: *We are stoning you…for blasphemy, because you, a mere man, claim to be God* (John 10:33). The New Testament writers all refer to Jesus Christ as God. For example, Paul exhorts the church at Rome: *from them [the patriarchs] is traced the human ancestry of Christ, who is God over all, forever praised! Amen* (Romans 9:5). Also, the Bible says that *In Christ all the fullness of the Deity lives in bodily form* (Colossians 2:9).

2. **Jesus possessed the attributes of God.** In His human form, Jesus laid aside His divine privilege in order to be fully human. This truth is powerfully described in Philippians 2: *Your attitude should be the same as that of Jesus Christ: Who, being in the very nature God, did not consider equality with God something to be grasped, but made himself nothing, taking the very nature of a servant, being made in human likeness. And being found in appearance as a man, he humbled himself and became obedient to death—even death on a cross!* (Philippians 2:5–8) That said, we see divine power displayed in Christ. His miracles, healings, and divine knowledge all point to His divinity. God called Jesus His Son at His baptism and enabled him to calm the storm, walk on water, multiply food, give sight to the blind, and raise the dead. Jesus was also omniscient. There are several examples in Scripture of Jesus knowing others' thoughts (Matthew 9:3–4; Mark 2:8; Luke 9:46–47).

3. **Jesus forgave sins.** The Jewish teachers rebuked Jesus when He told the paralytic: *Son, your sins are forgiven* (Mark 2:5). The teachers' reply is yet another example of Jesus's claim to divinity: *Why does this fellow talk like that? He's blaspheming! Who can forgive sins but God alone?* (Mark 2:7). Jesus not only forgave the paralytic but Jesus also healed him to

prove His power over the physical nature of man. Jesus also forgave the sinful woman who anointed Him with perfume (Luke 7:36–50). On the day of Pentecost, Peter told the people how to be saved: *Repent and be baptized, every one of you, in the name of Jesus Christ for the forgiveness of your sins* (Acts 2:38). Jesus, God in the flesh, forgave sins. His death on the cross made it possible for all of us to be forgiven.

4. **Jesus accepted worship.** Worship of Jesus began almost immediately at His birth, when the wise men came to bring Him gifts in worship. At that time He was a baby and would not have been able to refuse worship. However, during His three-and-a-half year ministry, He accepted worship numerous times. For example, after he walked on water, the disciples worshiped Him, saying, *Truly you are the Son of God* (Matthew 14:33). Jesus also accepted the worship of the man whose sight He restored (John 9:38). Furthermore, after His resurrection and prior to His Great Commission, His disciples worshiped Him (Matthew 28:17). At no time did Jesus refuse their worship. By contrast, Peter refused worship (Acts 10:25–26). So did the angel that showed John the vision of the wedding of the Lamb: *At this I fell at his feet to worship him. But he said to me, "Do not do it! I am a fellow servant with you and with your brothers who hold to the testimony of Jesus. Worship God!"* (Revelation 19:10).

Was it Necessary for Jesus to Die?

Was it necessary for Jesus to die? There are two answers to this very important question. According to God's justice, the answer is no, but according to God's love, the answer is yes. In other words, God would have been perfectly just to let our punishment stand:

death and hell. However, because of God's love for humanity, He chose to do for us what we could not do for ourselves—offer a sinless sacrifice to atone for our sin.

Jesus Christ atoned for our sin with His blood. Therefore, His crucifixion both appeased God's wrath and demonstrated His love. An important group of terms comes into play when we talk about Jesus Christ's atoning sacrifice. First, the term "sacrifice" means the object of the penalty of sin. In the Old Testament, God instructed the Israelites to sacrifice animals to serve as a substitute death for the sins of the nation. The Bible says that *without the shedding of blood there is no forgiveness* (Hebrews 9:22).

The second term is "propitiation," which means to satisfy God's wrath. Because God hates sin, and because the punishment for sin is death, God's wrath had to be alleviated in concert with His justice and love. God's wrath was alleviated when sin's penalty was placed on Christ: *He is the propitiation for our sins…* (1 John 2:2, ESV).

The third term is "reconciliation," which means to bring back into fellowship or to settle a dispute. Paul explained: *All this is from God, who reconciled us to himself through Christ and gave us the ministry of reconciliation: that God was reconciling the world to himself in Christ, not counting men's sins against them. And he has committed to us the message of reconciliation* (2 Corinthians 5:18–19). The wonderful fact is that we don't reconcile ourselves to God; instead, He reconciles us to Himself. What a beautiful act of love!

The fourth term is "redemption," which means to be recovered or purchased back. Sin separates us from God, and He redeems us by paying the price for our sin. Paul encouraged the church in Ephesus by telling them that Jesus Christ had redeemed those who believed in Him: *In him we have redemption through his blood, the forgiveness of sins, in accordance with the riches of God's grace* (Ephesians 1:7). The entire Bible can be summed up in the word "redemption," for the entire premise of the Bible is God's plan to redeem humanity.

Was Jesus Resurrected and Will He Return?

All four Gospels describe the resurrection in great detail, and the entire New Testament points to it as the basis for belief. In fact, Jesus's resurrection is the linchpin of our faith. Paul even postulated the ultimate consequences if Jesus were not raised from the dead:

> *And if Christ has not been raised, our preaching is useless and so is your faith. More than that, we are then found to be false witnesses about God, for we have testified about God that he raised Christ from the dead. But he did not raise him if in fact the dead are not raised. For if the dead are not raised, then Christ has not been raised either. And if Christ has not been raised, your faith is futile; you are still in your sins. Then those also who have fallen asleep in Christ are lost. If only for this life we have hope in Christ, we are to be pitied more than all men.*

> **(1 Corinthians 15:14–19)**

There is a very serious distinction that must be made between the Jesus presented in Scripture and the Jesus presented in modern-day society. Many want to equate Christianity's beliefs with other belief systems, claiming that all religions teach essentially the same thing. Such thinking reduces Jesus to a great moral teacher, but that is *not* what He claimed to be. Ravi Zacharias said, "Jesus did not come to make the bad good; He came to make the dead live."[9] Jesus told Martha, *I am the resurrection and the life. He who believes in me will live, even though he dies; and whoever lives and believes in me will never die* (John 11:25–26). Jesus Christ defeated sin with His death, and He defeated death with His resurrection.

Jesus talked at length about His Second Coming. In the first three Gospels, Jesus answered His disciples' question about the sign

---

9   Ravi Zacharias, "Born to be good or born to be evil," YouTube video, 3:05, from a Question and Answer Session, post by askizim, July 6, 2010, http://www.youtube.com/watch?v =Dkp88KxhkG0&feature=related.

of His return: Matthew 24–25; Mark 13; Luke 21. In John, Jesus comforted His disciples with these words:

> *Do not let your hearts be troubled. Trust in God; trust also in me. In my Father's house are many rooms; if it were not so, I would have told you. I am going there to prepare a place for you. And if I go and prepare a place for you, I will come back and take you to be with me that you also may be where I am.*

(John 14:1–3)

His coming is not only signaled by certain events on earth, but also by His preparations in heaven.

Since His ascension, Christians have believed that the Second Coming of Christ is imminent and will consummate His redemptive mission. The moment after He ascended in full view of His disciples, two angels explained, *This same Jesus, who has been taken from you into heaven, will come back in the same way you have seen him go into heaven* (Acts 1:11). The rest of the New Testament describes the expectation of Jesus Christ's return. Titus calls for his readers to *live self-controlled, upright and godly lives in the present age, while we wait for the blessed hope—the glorious appearing of our great God and Savior, Jesus Christ* (Titus 2:12–13). We should be living in such a way that our hope is grounded in the imminent, bodily return of Jesus Christ.

What Are Christ's Three Offices?

As we examine the person and life of Jesus Christ, we are introduced to the three offices that He occupies as part of His anointing as God's Son.

1. **Jesus is Prophet.** This office carries the function of declaring God's Word to man. The Old Testament prophets foreshadowed the coming of the ultimate prophet. Jesus

declared Himself to be a prophet (Matthew 13:57; Luke 13:33). On His walk with the two disciples after His resurrection, the disciples described Him this way: *"About Jesus of Nazareth," they replied. "He was a prophet, powerful in word and deed before God and all the people."* (Luke 24:19). In the book of Deuteronomy, Moses recorded the word of God concerning a special prophet: *I will raise up for them a prophet like you from among their brothers; I will put my words in his mouth, and he will tell them everything I command him. If anyone does not listen to my words that the prophet speaks in my name, I myself will call him to account* (Deuteronomy 18:18–19). Jesus is this special prophet from God and He claimed to be the Word from God.

2. **Jesus is Priest.** This function is to be God's sacrifice for man's sin. The first High Priest was Aaron, Moses's brother, but the Bible teaches that Christ's priesthood is *in the order of Melchizedek* (Hebrews 7:11). Melchizedek is the priest who appeared to Abraham in Genesis 14, but many biblical scholars identify this mysterious figure as a pre-figuration of Jesus Christ. The psalmist asserts: *You are a priest forever, in the order of Melchizedek* (Psalm 110:4). We learn in the book of Hebrews that this "priest forever" is Jesus Christ. He is the ultimate fulfillment of the High Priest office, as He meets all requirements of God's holy law: *Such a high priest meets our need—one who is holy, blameless, pure, set apart from sinners, exalted above the heavens. Unlike the other high priests, he does not need to offer sacrifices day after day, first for his own sins, and then for the sins of the people. He sacrificed for their sins once for all when he offered himself* (Hebrews 7:26–27). Jesus was the final, perfect sacrifice that paid for man's sin once and for all.

3. **Jesus is King**. This function is God's eternal rule over man. The Magi came seeking Jesus, referring to Him as the King of the Jews (Matthew 2:2). He began His earthly ministry by declaring that *the kingdom of heaven is near* (Matthew 4:17). His triumphal entry into Jerusalem on Palm Sunday declared Him as King (Matthew 21:5). Jesus Himself accepted the title when Pilate questioned Him: *Jesus stood before the governor, and the governor asked Him, "Are You the King of the Jews?" "Yes, it is as you say" Jesus replied* (Matthew 27:11). Furthermore, His official title when He returns will be *King of Kings and Lord of Lords* (Revelation 19:16). The Bible says that we who are Christians will be *priests of God and of Christ and will reign with him for a thousand years* (Revelation 20:6). This is the millennial kingdom of Christ, which will occur in the future.

In summary, we can think of these three offices in this way: Jesus is the Word of God (prophet), who completed the work of God (priest) to usher in the eternal worship of God (king). His fulfillment of these three offices also helps us to understand how God has revealed Himself to the world—God the Father spoke the verbal Word, the Holy Spirit inspired the written Word, and the Son of God became the living Word.

What Is the Work of the Holy Spirit?

As the third member of the Trinity, the Holy Spirit manifests God's active presence in the world, and especially in the church. Like the Father and the Son, the Holy Spirit is coeternal, coequal, and co-essential. The biblical words for "Spirit" are *ruach* (Hebrew) and *pneuma* (Greek). The Spirit of God is first seen as *hovering over the waters* (Genesis 1:2). Throughout history, the Holy Spirit has functioned and continues to function in numerous ways to bring about

God's purposes. We will list and describe ten of the Holy Spirit's functions now.

1. **The Holy Spirit inspires.** The Holy Spirit inspired the writers of God's Word. In fact, His inspiration is described as carrying them along: *Above all, you must understand that no prophecy of Scripture came about by the prophet's own interpretation. For prophecy never had its origin in the will of man, but men spoke from God as they were carried along by the Holy Spirit* (2 Peter 1:20–21). There are also many other Scriptures which affirm that the Holy Spirit spoke through David (Matthew 22:43; Mark 12:36; Acts 1:16, 4:25). Moreover, Jesus told His apostles that the Holy Spirit would give them remembrance of all they had witnessed as they walked with Jesus: *But the Counselor, the Holy Spirit, whom the Father will send in my name, will teach you all things and will remind you of everything I have said to you* (John 14:26). So, we see that the Holy Spirit spoke through the prophets (one of which was Moses, the human author of the first five books of the Bible), David, and the apostles. Peter also ascribed Paul's letters as part of sacred Scripture. He affirmed that *Paul also wrote you with the wisdom that God gave him" (2 Peter 3:15)* and gives credence to Paul by referring to his letters as Scripture (2 Peter 3:16). Finally, we can rest assured that the entire Bible we have today was written through men by the Holy Spirit. Paul encouraged Timothy by saying: *All Scripture is God-breathed and is useful for teaching, rebuking, correcting and training in righteousness, so that the man of God may be thoroughly equipped for every good work* (2 Timothy 3:16–17). Of special note is the fact that Paul told Timothy in the prior verse that he was made wise about salvation from the Scriptures, which must refer to the Old Testament Scriptures. Clearly, the Old

Testament was enough to point anyone seeking God to the Promised One, the Messiah!

2. **The Holy Spirit convicts.** He convicts the world of sin, righteousness, and judgment. In His discourse with His disciples the night before His crucifixion, Jesus explained the work of the Holy Spirit: *When he [the Holy Spirit] comes, he will convict the world of guilt in regard to sin and righteousness and judgment: in regard to sin, because men do not believe in me; in regard to righteousness, because I am going to the Father, where you can see me no longer; and in regard to judgment, because the prince of this world now stands condemned.* **(John 16:8–11)** Sin is the pervasive problem of man; it separates man from God, who is holy. Righteousness is not found in man's work, but only in the finished work of Christ on the cross. God *has entrusted all judgment to the Son* and the prince of this world (Satan) is condemned, as well as all those who do not trust Jesus Christ to save them from their sin (John 5:22).

3. **The Holy Spirit regenerates.** At the moment of regeneration, the Holy Spirit baptizes the new believer into the Body of Christ: *The body is a unit, though it is made up of many parts; and though all its parts are many, they form one body. So it is with Christ. For we were all baptized by one Spirit into one body* (1 Corinthians 12:12–13a). Jesus said: *The Spirit gives life; the flesh counts for nothing. The words I have spoken to you are spirit and they are life* (John 6:63). The Holy Spirit gives the Christian new life. Paul explained the key difference between the Old Covenant and the New Covenant: *He has made us competent as ministers of a new covenant—not of the letter but of the Spirit; for the letter kills, but the Spirit gives life* (2 Corinthians 3:6).

4. **The Holy Spirit indwells.** At the moment of conversion, the Holy Spirit takes up residence in the new believer. The Bible commands us to *be filled with the Spirit, walk by the Spirit,*

156

and *keep in step with the Spirit* (Ephesians 5:18; Galatians 5:16; 5:25). Because the Spirit lives inside of us, He assures our salvation, reminding us of this promise: *The Spirit himself testifies with our spirit that we are God's children* (Romans 8:16).

5. **The Holy Spirit gifts.** The Holy Spirit endows every believer with one or more spiritual gifts: *Now to each one the manifestation of the Spirit is given for the common good* (1 Corinthians 12:9). The rest of chapter twelve of Corinthians lists these various gifts, including wisdom, knowledge, faith, healing, miraculous powers, prophecy, discernment, tongues, and the interpretation of tongues. You can find more examples of spiritual gifts in Romans 12:6–8; 1 Corinthians 12:27–30; and Ephesians 4:11.

6. **The Holy Spirit guides.** He reveals truth as He guides and directs God's people. Jesus told His disciples: *But when he, the Spirit of truth, comes, he will guide you into all truth. He will not speak on his own; he will speak only what he hears, and he will tell you what is yet to come* (John 16:13).

7. **The Holy Spirit empowers.** The Holy Spirit emboldens and empowers us in our work of evangelism. When Jesus sent His apostles out, He explained that their witnessing would be led by the Holy Spirit: *do not worry about what to say or how to say it. At that time you will be given what to say, for it will not be you speaking, but the Spirit of your Father speaking through you* (Matthew 10:19–20).

8. **The Holy Spirit sanctifies.** The Holy Spirit makes us holy at conversion and progressively more holy as we grow in Christ. This is called sanctification, which is "the state or process of being set apart; that is, made holy."[10] Paul reminded the church at Thessalonica that *God chose you to be saved through*

10   *Theopedia: An Encyclopedia of Christianity*, s.v. "sanctification," November 2, 2012, www. theopedia.com/sanctification.

the sanctifying work of the Spirit and through belief in the truth (2 Thessalonians 2:13).

9. **The Holy Spirit seals.** At the moment of conversion, the Holy Spirit seals every born-again believer until the day of final redemption: *Having believed, you were marked in him with a seal, the promised Holy Spirit, who is a deposit guaranteeing our inheritance until the redemption of those who are God's possession—to the praise of his glory* (Ephesians 1:13b–14).

10. **The Holy Spirit unifies.** The Holy Spirit unifies by leading the church in worship. This is why many churches begin their services with an invocation, a prayer designed to invoke the presence and power of the Holy Spirit. If you have ever felt as if the preacher were speaking right to you on any given Sunday, now you know that the Spirit that inspired the Word of God is the same Spirit that indwells every believer and knows our lives intimately. Therefore, as God's truth is proclaimed, the Spirit penetrates our hearts to speak to us right where we are. That is why Paul encouraged the church at Ephesus to *keep the unity of the Spirit through the bond of peace. There is one body and one Spirit—just as you were called to one hope when you were called—one Lord, one faith, one baptism; one God and Father of all, who is over all and through all and in all* (Ephesians 4:3–6). The Holy Spirit also bestows both grace and discipline within the church body. In fact, when the body of Christ submits to the unifying Holy Spirit, then the body matures and attains to the *full measure of Christ* and ultimately manifests the fruit of the Spirit: *But the fruit of the Spirit is love, joy, peace, patience, kindness, goodness, faithfulness, gentleness and self-control* (Ephesians 4:13; Galatians 5:22). Notice that fruit is singular, indicating that the Spirit produces all of these behaviors in every Christian—to the extent that the Christian surrenders to the Holy Spirit's leadership in his or her life.

As you can see, we have covered a lot of ground digging into the first three doctrines: God the Father (theology); God the Son (Christology); and God the Spirit (pneumatology). We have truly entered the deepest stretch in our race of faith. God's teachings (doctrines) are the critical foundation upon which we build our faith. Knowing why we believe what we believe cements our faith, our confidence in Christ, and our capacity to persevere and even triumph during the storms of life. God is faithful, and when we earnestly seek Him, He rewards us. Let's keep up the pace as we dig into the next doctrine, the study of mankind (anthropology). But first, here is our next memory verse:

I have been crucified with Christ and I no longer live, but Christ lives in me. The life I live in the body, I live by faith in the Son of God, who loved me and gave himself for me.

(Galatians 2:20)

The Doctrine of Mankind

I once met a guy who was adamant in his stance that people are basically good. This is a common misperception in our culture. Most people would say they never murdered anyone, they don't make a living by robbing banks, and they try to do good for others. This may be true, but the premise is flawed. This mind-set compares humans to other humans. As a pastor friend of mine used to say, "In God's eyes, our very best is like our very worst." Adam and Eve disobeyed one command, and they were expelled from the Garden of Eden. This is a hard truth that causes a certain amount of discomfort. This mile tells the truth about God's highest order of creation, why we have fallen, and how God saves us from destruction.

How and Why Did God Create Human Beings?

We must begin the answer to this question by saying that God did not have to create humans. God was not lonely and in need of fellowship, because He has always been in perfect fellowship with Himself as Father, Son, and Spirit. So, the Trinitarian God created man for His glory: *Let us make man in our image, in our likeness...* (Genesis 1:26).

Man's purpose in this life is to glorify God. In fact, the inhabitants of heaven declare: *You are worthy, our Lord and God, to receive glory and honor and power, for you created all things, and by your will they were created and have their being* (Revelation 4:11). From a holistic perspective, God created the world and everything in it to reflect His glory through worship. Earlier, we learned that God seeks worshipers who worship Him in spirit and in truth. How can we bring the most glory to God? Solomon spent a lifetime looking for the meaning of life, gathering to himself wisdom and women and wine and work and wealth, but at every point, he determined that it was meaningless—chasing after the wind. Then he came to this conclusion: *Now all has been heard; here is the conclusion of the matter: Fear God and keep his commandments, for this is the whole duty of man* (Ecclesiastes 12:13). When we fear God and keep His commandments, we bring glory to Him.

God created mankind in His own image. God's image is what sets humans apart from the rest of creation. This means that humans have both a body and a spirit, that we are creative and cognitive creatures who possess an innate sense of the eternal. Furthermore, God gave us the power to choose to obey Him. As a result of Adam and Eve's disobedience, known as the Fall, mankind's image was marred but not lost.

God created Adam (the Hebrew term for man) from the dust of the ground. The body is physical matter. Then God breathed the breath of life into Adam's body, making him a living being, a man

(Genesis 2:7). God placed Adam in the Garden of Eden and commanded him not to eat of the tree of knowledge of good and evil. An interesting sequence occurs next. First, God says: *It is not good for the man to be alone. I will make a helper suitable for him* (Genesis 2:18). Then, God brought the animals, in pairs, to Adam and told him to name them. Then, the Scripture says: *for Adam, no suitable helper was found* (Genesis 2:20b). God showed Adam that he was different from all the animals and that he needed a partner, too. So, God formed Eve from Adam's rib. The word "woman" means "from man."

Why Did God Create Two Genders and Sexes?

God created humans for personal relationship. God created two genders, man and woman, both of whom are equal with respect to their standing before God and their contribution to the worship of God. The primary reason there are two sexes is procreation. God's first command to Adam and Eve was: *Be fruitful and increase in number; fill the earth and subdue it* (Genesis 1:28). As we said before, God created man and woman to bring Him glory and to increase the number of people who would glorify Him. From this same verse, mankind's second purpose is to subdue the earth, to tend and to keep it; in other words, God has given mankind the additional responsibility to serve as stewards of the earth, which He created.

God created male and female for different but complementary roles. The institution of marriage is introduced at the joining of Adam and Eve: *For this reason a man will leave his father and mother and be united to his wife, and they will become one flesh* (Genesis 2:24). When we consider how God is the One who joins a man and his wife so that they become "one flesh," we see that the marriage relationship should be made up of three persons, with the man and the woman both submitting to Jesus Christ. We also see that the marriage relationship is reflected in the church. Paul called Christ the "Head of the church," and the body of Christ is His bride. In fact, Jesus is the bridegroom and the church is the bride of Christ (Revelation 21:9). John the Baptist announced this relationship between Jesus and the church at Jesus's baptism, calling himself the *friend who attends the bridegroom.* In a sense, John the Baptist announced the arrival of the bridegroom, Jesus Christ (John 3:27–30).

What Is the Nature of Human Beings?

While we have learned that Jesus has both a human nature and a divine nature, humans only have one nature. Humans have a physical body, and since we are created in God's image, at the moment we are conceived, God gives us a spirit. There are some who believe that man consists of three parts—body, soul, and spirit. There are only two Bible verses that support this view (1 Thessalonians 5:23; Hebrews 4:12). However, greater biblical evidence supports the argument that man consists of body and spirit, where the words for "soul" (Hebrew *nephesh*; Greek *psuche*) and "spirit" (Hebrew *ruach*; Greek *pneuma*) are used interchangeably. For example, in her prayer, Mary said: *My soul magnifies the Lord, and my spirit rejoices within me* (Luke 1:46–47). From this verse, it is clear that she is using these terms in parallel.

Also, we see over and over in Scripture that each person consists of two parts—body and spirit. Jesus said: *The spirit is willing, but the body is weak* (Matthew 26:41). In addition, Paul expressed salvation this way, *But if Christ is in you, your body is dead because of sin, yet your spirit is alive because of righteousness* (Romans 8:10). Furthermore, Paul affirmed that the unmarried woman can be *devoted to the Lord in both body and spirit* (1 Corinthians 7:34). There are numerous other passages that describe the two parts of the human, but the idea that the body comes from below and the spirit comes from above is also borne out in Scripture, especially related to death.

What Is Sin?

Sin is disobedience to God's commands. There are numerous words in both testaments that are translated as sin. The most common Greek term for sin used in the New Testament is *hamartia*, which connotes the idea of missing the mark. Another term, *parabasis*, means to trespass or cross over the line. A third term, *anomia* and its close relative *paranomia*, connote lawlessness or lawbreaking. All three of these terms point to the pervasiveness of sin among all men. In fact, the Bible says that *all have sinned and fall short of the glory of God* (Romans 3:23).

When did sin begin? Sin began in the angelic realm with Satan's rebellion. While the creation of angels is not recorded specifically in Scripture, we can surmise that sin began somewhere between the creation of man, when God declared that His creation was *very good,* and the temptation in the Garden of Eden (Genesis 1:31; 3:1). Many scholars agree that there are two passages that address Satan's fall. In Isaiah 14:12–15, Isaiah denounces Babylon, but the description in these verses is not completely applicable to Babylon's ruler, but rather the evil influence of Satan himself. This passage references the *morning star* and *son of dawn,* and explains the reason he fell, for he said in his heart, *I will make myself like the Most High* (Isaiah 14:14). This *morning star,* translated as Lucifer in the King James Version of the Bible, allowed his pride to make him believe that he could be like God.

Second, Ezekiel 28:12–17 describes in even more detail this *guardian cherub* who was *in Eden, the garden of God.* While the prophet addresses the King of Tyre, surely we can conclude that the King of Tyre was not in Eden, but that he too had been influenced by the evil spirit of Satan, who, in the form of a serpent, deceived Eve. Similar to Satan, the King of Tyre allowed his pride to control him instead of submitting himself to God who created him.

While sin began with Satan's rebellion, it began in the human realm with the disobedience of Adam. A close study of the creation account shows that God gave the prohibition to eat from the tree of knowledge to Adam, prior to God's creation of Eve. We can glean from the text that Adam must have told Eve about the prohibition, but we cannot be sure exactly what he told her and what she made up. For example, in Genesis 3:3 Eve added the rule that they were to not even touch the tree. So, we are left to wonder if Adam said that or if she came up with that one all by herself!

As we read the dialogue between the serpent (Satan) and Eve, we see that Satan used doubt, deception, and desire to bring Eve to the point of choosing to disobey God. The narrative also tells us that Eve gave some of the fruit to Adam, and he ate. As a result of their disobedience, all humans are born with the sin of Adam: *Therefore, just as sin entered the world through one man, and death through sin, and in this way death came to all men, because all sinned* (Romans 5:12). This is why the Bible clearly states that *all have sinned and fall short of the glory of God* (Romans 3:23).

The penalty of sin, then, is death: *For the wages of sin is death, but the gift of God is eternal life in Christ Jesus our Lord* (Romans 6:23). The term "wages" refers to the payment that must be made. When Adam and Eve first sinned, two things happened to them. First, they began to die physically. Second, they immediately died spiritually, as they were separated from holy God. The good news about our sin condition can be found in the second part of that verse, which informs us of God's gift—eternal life offered because Christ paid that price! Therefore, for the Christian, sin's penalty has been paid, sin's power has been broken, but sin's presence still remains until we reach heaven. So, the Christian life is characterized by an ongoing battle whose outcome is assuredly victorious.

There are two key truths about sin that we must understand. First, every sin makes us legally guilty before God; however, the consequences of each sin can be different. That is to say that all sin is equally bad in the eyes of God, because all sin is an abomination to Him. So, a person who cheats on his test at school is just as much a sinner as a person who murders another person. This may not seem right until we see that the consequences for each sin are different. In either case, relationships are affected and repercussions are felt, but the consequences are more severe for the murderer.

The second truth about sin is this: when the Christian sins, her legal standing before God is unchanged, but her fellowship with God is disrupted. In other words, since our salvation is a gift from God, He does not take it away from us when we sin. Our relationship with Him cannot be broken because all of our sin—past, present, and future—was atoned for at Calvary once and for all. However, our fellowship with God is adversely affected. Sin causes us to push away from God. This is easy to see in our everyday life. When we are involved in sin, we tend to disengage ourselves from prayer, Bible study, and even church attendance. Sin also adversely affects our witnessing. Sin separates us both from God and God's message of hope to the world.

What about the "unpardonable sin"? This term is taken from Jesus's statement: *And so I tell you, every sin and blasphemy will be forgiven men, but the blasphemy against the Spirit will not be forgiven. Anyone who speaks a word against the Son of Man will be forgiven, but anyone who speaks against the Holy Spirit will not be forgiven, either in this age or in the age to come* (Matthew 12:31–32). We know from our study of the Seven Cs of Bible Study that context gives us great insight into verses like these. Therefore, the context of this statement is that the Pharisees had attributed Christ's miracle of casting out a demon to Satan himself. Jesus explained that a *household divided against itself will not stand* (Matthew 12:25). Finally, Jesus explained the reason for His coming, which was to bind the *strong man* (Matthew 12:29) (a reference to Satan) and to rob him, in order to rescue those who had been held captive by the forces of evil in this world, including those possessed by demons.

In summary, since the Holy Spirit convicts people of their sin and separation from God, and since He leads sinners to saving faith in Christ, Jesus concluded that those who reject the convicting and regenerating work of the Holy Spirit in their hearts will never be forgiven of their sins. Admission of one's sin and acceptance of Christ as Savior and Lord comprise the only remedy for man's sin condition.

What Happens when Humans Die?

The topic of the afterlife draws substantial interest among all people and it is also one of the most misunderstood topics in religion. Some of the most popular books and movies are the ones that describe or depict life after death experiences. The Bible teaches that the body dies but the spirit given by God lives on: *…the dust returns to the ground it came from, and the spirit returns to God who gave it* (Ecclesiastes 12:9).

Most people believe that they will go to heaven, but their sense of moral acceptance by God is based on their relative "goodness" compared to other people. As we just learned, everyone is sinful and therefore not acceptable to our holy God. In other words, no amount of good can get us into heaven. Instead, where our spirit goes depends on our relationship with God. For those who have believed and accepted Jesus Christ as Savior and Lord, God's judgment of our sin was satisfied by Christ's sacrifice on the cross. The spirits of Christians, then, will go immediately into the presence of God. Paul describes this truth: *Therefore we are always confident and know that as long as we are at home in the body we are away from the Lord. We live by faith, not by sight. We are confident, I say, and would prefer to be away from the body and at home with the Lord.* (2 Corinthians 5:6-8)

The spirits of those who die without Christ are judged based only on their works, which are never good enough to satisfy God's holy standard. They go to a place Jesus calls *Gehenna*, translated as the Valley of Hinnom. Jesus used this term because that valley was just outside the Dung Gate of the wall of the city of Jerusalem, and it was the place where trash and dead bodies of criminals were burned. He declares: *Do not be afraid of those who kill the body but cannot kill the soul. Rather, be afraid of the One who can destroy both soul and body in hell.* (Matthew 10:28) Hell is a real place and it is the destiny for all who have refused to accept God's free offer of salvation found only in Jesus Christ.

On Judgment Day, the body is raised to reunite with the spirit. Jesus is known as the "first fruits" of the resurrection, meaning that His body and spirit were rejoined immediately upon His resurrection from the grave (1 Corinthians 15:20). He was the first person whose body was raised from the dead. (Acts 26:23; 1 Corinthians 15:21–23). The promise of Scripture is that *the dead will be raised imperishable, and we will be changed* (1 Corinthians 15:52). When the end of this age comes, and after the Second Coming of Christ and His earthly reign of a thousand years, the final resurrection will take place and every person's body will be raised to reunite with its spirit. Those who are Christians will experience everlasting life in heaven, and those who are not Christians will experience everlasting life in hell.

What are the Biblical Covenants between God and Mankind?

The Bible clearly depicts the relationship between God and man as covenantal. The biblical term "covenant" (Hebrew *berith*; Greek *diatheke*) is often misunderstood, because it is often taught to be a binding agreement or contract whereby both parties are equally engaged in keeping the promise. However, that is not the nature of the covenants God made in the Old Testament. While God's covenants do involve two parties, only God is able to ensure He keeps His promise. There are six key covenants in the Old Testament. They are:

1. **God's covenant with Adam (Genesis 2:15–17; 3:15–21)**: God promised to provide Adam with future offspring who would destroy the devil's work. This promise was fulfilled in the First Coming of Jesus Christ.

2. **God's covenant with Noah (Genesis 9:12–17)**: God promised never to destroy the world with a flood again. This promise continues to be fulfilled, and every time we see a rainbow, we agree that God is long-suffering, compassionate, and faithful in withholding His judgment on humanity.

3. **God's covenant with Abraham (Genesis 15:1–21; 17:1–27; Galatians 3:15–16)**: God promised Abraham that he would be the father of many nations and that those nations would be blessed through him. This has come true, as the ultimate seed (Jesus Christ) is the promise of God's provision of the remedy for man's sin.

4. **God's covenant with Moses (Exodus 20:1–17; Matthew 5:17)**: God promised Moses and the Israelites that He would fulfill His Law. This was accomplished by Jesus Christ, who proclaimed Himself as the *fulfillment of the law* (Matthew 5:17).

5. **God's covenant with David (2 Samuel 7:5–16)**: God promised David that there would be a king in his ancestry who would never depart the throne and whose throne would be established forever. This was fulfilled in Jesus's First Coming and will be forever realized at His Second Coming.

6. **God's new covenant with his people (Jeremiah 31:31–34; Hebrews 8:6–13)**: God promised that the law would no longer be written on tablets of stone but instead on the hearts of men as they place their faith in the Promised One, fulfilled in the First Coming of Jesus Christ. The

essence of this New Covenant is the subject matter of the New Testament.

The doctrine of mankind encompasses God's creation of human beings and His condemnation of sin, whereby His Old Testament covenants paved the way for Christ to atone for our sins. Hallelujah! What a Savior!

Now that we have delved deeply into the doctrine of mankind, we press on to learn the unfathomable riches of God's deliverance. God is the great rescuer, and we are the rescued. The doctrine of salvation is critical for every person who places his or her faith in Christ, and so now we go even deeper. But first, here is our next memory verse:

Yet to all who received him, to those who believed in his name, he gave the right to become children of God—children born not of natural descent, nor of human decision or a husband's will, but born of God.

(John 1:12–13)

The Doctrine of Salvation

Someone once asked me if she was still saved if she couldn't recall the day she first trusted Jesus. Most people think of salvation as a one-time event. However, salvation is more than an event—it's a process. While I was saved at the age of seventeen, I have been working out my salvation ever since. The Race of Faith is truly a journey, and it begins when we decide to run it, but it lasts a lifetime. Most Christians would not be able to articulate the various aspects or phases of their salvation. In fact, most have heard the terms but never put them all together. This mile maps out the various phases of our salvation, which is the process of being saved from our sin.

Why Do We Need to be Saved?

The very first question we must answer is whether or not people need to be saved in the first place. This is perhaps one of the great barriers to choosing Jesus Christ; many people are not convinced they need Him. This is a legitimate question, and so we must lay the groundwork to answer it as completely as possible. We have three very compelling reasons why we need a Savior.

1. **Humans are sinful.** We established in the last chapter that man is fallen and sinful. While this is a hard truth, it is nevertheless true. Too many people have been told they need Jesus without first being told they are sinful. The Bible repeats over and over that *there is no one righteous, not even one* (Romans 3:10). This is a solemn truth and demands our attention. Today, many see themselves as basically good, but when we begin with a holy God, then even our best is filthy: *All of us have become like one who is unclean, and all our righteous acts are like filthy rags* (Isaiah 64:6).

2. **Humans are therefore separated from God.** The Bible further declares that no one is good enough to meet the holy standard of God's law: *Now we know that whatever the law says, it says to those who are under the law, so that every mouth may be silenced and the whole world held accountable to God. Therefore no one will be declared righteous in his sight by observing the law; rather, through the law we become conscious of sin* (Romans 3:19–20). These verses transition the reader from that bad news *(no one is righteous)* to the Good News in verse 21: *But now a righteousness from God, apart from law, has been made known, to which the Law and the Prophets testify.* That righteousness is Jesus. The point of these verses is twofold: to show that all men are accountable to God's law, and that no man will be declared

righteous by observing the law. The point of the law is to show us our sin.

3. **Humans are powerless to save ourselves.** Again, we turn to the book of Romans to gain insight: *at the right time, when we were still powerless, Christ died for the ungodly... But God demonstrates his own love for us in this: While we were still sinners, Christ died for us* (Romans 5:6, 8). This passage emphasizes that Christ died on our behalf. Because we are powerless to save ourselves and because we are still in our sin, God had to do for us what we could not do for ourselves—to pay the penalty for our sin. What a blessed Redeemer!

What Is the Process of Salvation?

Salvation can be defined as deliverance from the power and penalty of sin. Redemption is a closely linked term that emphasizes the act of deliverance and a buying back from sin's consequences. Many mistakenly believe that salvation is a one-time event. However, the Bible paints a much broader portrait of salvation. The Bible teaches that salvation is both an event *and* a process. We will now follow the process of salvation step-by-step.

1. Election

The doctrine of election has been debated since the days of the early church, and it can be very confusing even for the most mature believer. However, it is a biblical doctrine, and it must be understood. Volumes have been written on this topic alone, so please understand that this book is designed to give you only the basics. The doctrine of election begins with the fact that God has chosen us *in Christ*. Paul unveils this marvelous truth to us in his letter to the Ephesians: *For he chose us in him before the creation of the world to be holy and blameless in his sight. In love, he predestined us to be adopted as his sons through Jesus Christ, in accordance with his pleasure and will* (Ephesians 1:4–5).

The three biblical terms that speak to this doctrine are "election," "chosen," and "predestination." Jesus refers to the "elect" when describing the end-time events leading up to His Second Coming. (Matthew 24:22–31; Mark 13:20–27). Peter addresses all believers as the "elect" (1 Peter 1:1). Paul describes the "elect" as that remnant who would obtain salvation (Romans 11:7). And Peter calls all believers to make their calling and election sure (2 Peter 1:10). Paul refers to the Colossian believers as God's chosen people, and Peter calls the church *a chosen people, a royal priesthood* (Colossians 3:12; 1 Peter 2:9). Paul instructs the church at Rome that God has "predestined" them to be conformed to the likeness of Christ, and he tells the church at Ephesus that they have been "predestined" according to the plan of God (Romans 9:5; Ephesians 1:11). All of these passages build the doctrine that God has chosen us to accomplish His divine purposes. When someone becomes a Christian, he joins an army of believers who are tasked and empowered to work out God's plan in this world. What an awesome responsibility and privilege!

While we agree that we have been predestined for this purpose, we must be careful not to conclude that men are robots and have no choice in the matter of salvation. There are plenty of Scriptures that teach man's free will—Mark 16:16; John 1:12, 3:16, 6:28–29; Acts 16:31; Romans 10:9–13; 1 Timothy 4:10; 2 Peter 3:9; and Revelation 3:20; 22:17 to name a few—so we must hold election in proper tension with free will. If we take all of the Bible references above together, we could conclude that the doctrine of election is directed toward a group, a remnant, a people—not toward individuals. Therefore, the first step in the salvation process is that God has chosen us to be a part of His Kingdom.

2. Calling

And those he predestined, He also called (Romans 8:29). God's calling upon the hearts of humans is a critical component of faith. John described the dual actions of God calling and man responding: *No one can come to me unless the Father who sent me draws him, and I will raise him up at the last day. It is written in the Prophets: "They will all be taught by God." Everyone who listens to the Father and learns from him comes to me* (John 6:44–45). Notice that God draws and the person comes. The Bible also teaches that Jesus stands at the door of our heart and knocks (Revelation 3:20). He does not force Himself on us; rather, He gently knocks and allows us to open our hearts to Him. Some refuse to hear Him, and even more refuse to open their hearts.

Paul expounded on the process of the calling of God, whereby God uses His faithfully preached Word to draw men toward Him: *How, then, can they call on the one they have not believed in? And how can they believe in the one of whom they have not heard? And how can they hear without someone preaching to them? And how can they preach unless they are sent?* (Romans 10:14–15). He concluded with this statement: *Consequently, faith comes from hearing the message, and the message is heard through the word of Christ* (Romans 10:17). When we hear the Good News, the Holy Spirit convicts our hearts of our sin condition, our need of a Savior, and our compulsion to repent and believe. This is God's calling.

3. Conversion

Conversion is the act of accepting God's calling. This process consists of two steps. The first step of conversion is repentance, which is "the heartfelt sorrow for sin and renouncing of it."[11] The second step of conversion is faith, which is placing our trust in Jesus Christ

---

11 Wayne Grudem, *Systematic Theology* (Nashville: Zondervan, 1994), 713.

for the forgiveness of sin.[12] A way to picture this process is to see the world and the cross diametrically opposed to each other: *For the message of the cross is foolishness to those who are perishing, but to us who are being saved, it is the power of God* (1 Corinthians 1:18). Repentance is the act of turning away from the world and its values, and faith is the act of running to God and His offer of salvation.

Jesus began His public ministry by declaring: *The kingdom of God is near. Repent and believe the good news!* (Mark 1:15). When asked what they should do after hearing Peter's sermon on Pentecost, Peter replied, *Repent and be baptized, every one of you, in the name of Jesus Christ for the forgiveness of your sins* (Acts 2:38). John articulated the power of our faith as placing our trust in Christ: *This is the victory that has overcome the world, even our faith. Who is it that overcomes the world? Only he who believes that Jesus is the Son of God* (1 John 5:4–5). We convert and are born-again in Christ when we repent and believe.

4. Regeneration

"Regeneration" (Greek *palingenesia*) can be defined as that moment in which the convert is born again, or reborn spiritually. Let's repeat and continue Peter's reply to the crowd gathered on Pentecost: *Repent and be baptized, every one of you, in the name of Jesus Christ for the forgiveness of your sins. And you will receive the gift of the Holy Spirit. The promise is for you and your children and for all who are far off—for all whom the Lord our God will call* (Acts 2:38–39). These two verses highlight steps two through four of the salvation process. First, God calls. Then, we repent and believe (conversion). Then, we are regenerated (receive the gift of the Holy Spirit).

To repeat, the definition of "regeneration" is to be born-again. Jesus told Nicodemus, a Pharisee, that *no one can see the kingdom of God unless he is born again* (John 3:3). The phrase literally means to

---

12   Grudem, *Systematic Theology*, 710.

be born from above. This truth illustrates one of the more prevalent themes in Scripture – the physical versus the spiritual. Nicodemus was confused, because he was thinking of physical birth, while Jesus was talking about spiritual birth. Every person who places his or her faith in Jesus Christ is given the gift of the Holy Spirit at that very moment. This is a supernatural event that brings about the transforming work of God in our lives.

While the vast majority of Christians will say that they didn't feel any different when they trusted Christ, the Bible teaches that genuine regeneration bears fruit in our life. In fact, James boldly pointed out that the Holy Spirit living in us causes us to bear fruit: *As the body without the spirit is dead, so faith without deeds is dead* (James 2:26). We must keep in mind, however, that salvation is a process, and we will bear the fruit of the Holy Spirit only to the extent that we allow the Holy Spirit to control our thinking and our actions. The fruit of the Holy Spirit consists of *love, joy, peace, patience, kindness, goodness, faithfulness, gentleness, and self-control* (Galatians 5:22). If we truly desire to manifest this fruit in our lives, then we know that we have the Holy Spirit living in us.

5. Justification

To sum up salvation thus far, we have been chosen from the foundation of the world, called by the Word of God, converted through our response to the message of the Gospel, and regenerated by the power of the Holy Spirit. At the moment of regeneration, God justifies us. Simply stated, justification means "legal right-standing before God."[13] While we were once enemies of God, we are now declared "not guilty." Justification is a legal term and can best be understood in the setting of a court. God is the Judge and our plea is "guilty." Jesus Christ then steps in as our advocate, our lawyer, our attorney. He tells the Judge that He has already borne the sentence

---

13   Grudem, *Systematic Theology*, 722.

of our sin. God then declares the penalty justly paid, and we are set free.

Paul expressed this chain of events, which happens in the heavenly realm, as a result of our regeneration. He stated: *[We] are justified freely by his grace through the redemption that came by Christ Jesus. God presented him as a sacrifice of atonement, through faith in his blood. He did this to demonstrate his justice, because in his forbearance he had left the sins committed beforehand unpunished—he did it to demonstrate his justice at the present time, so as to be just and the one who justifies those who have faith in Jesus.* (Romans 3:24–26) Jesus paid the sacrifice for our sin, and since He was the perfect sacrifice, He satisfied God's wrath. His act of redemption demonstrated God's grace, which justified us in His sight and allowed us to be released from the shackles of sin and set free to live for Him.

Along with this declaration of "not guilty," God furthermore imputes Christ's righteousness to us. A good way to differentiate between justification and righteousness is to think of these two terms as such: justification is God's act of declaring us "not guilty," and righteousness is our consequential right-standing before God. While we must acknowledge that we are all sinful and deserving of eternal separation from God, we also can and should accept God's amazing love, which endows those who trust in Christ with His righteousness.

6. Adoption

Once we have been justified, we are immediately adopted into God's family. Over and over in Scripture we are taught that believers in Jesus Christ are members of God's family. John the apostle affirmed: *Yet to all who received him, to those who believed in his name, he gave the right to become children of God* (John 1:12). Paul encouraged the believers in Rome by telling them that *those who are led by the Spirit of God are sons of God...The Spirit himself testifies with our spirit that we are God's children* (Romans 8:14, 16). This is one of the main reasons we refer to God as "Our Father" when we pray.

Not only are we children of God, but even more amazingly, we are coheirs with Christ. If we think about the fact that God is the owner and ruler of the universe and everything in it, and if we understand that those of us who have chosen to follow Christ are heirs of God our Father, we can only fall down in worship of our heavenly Father for adopting us into His family! To continue that passage from Romans, Paul said, *Now if we are children, then we are heirs—heirs of God and co-heirs with Christ, if indeed we share in his sufferings in that we may also share in his glory* (Romans 8:17).

Paul also compared our life before Christ to our life after Christ. Before Christ, we were slaves to sin, but after Christ, we are heirs of God: *When we were children, we were in slavery under the basic principles of the world. But when the time had fully come, God sent his Son, born of a woman, born under law, to redeem those under law, that we might receive the full rights of sons. Because you are sons, God sent the Spirit of his Son into our hearts, the Spirit who calls out, "Abba, Father." So you are no longer a slave, but a son; and since you are a son, God has made you also an heir.* (Galatians 4:3–7)

We have full rights as sons and daughters of God, and the guarantee of our inheritance is marked by receiving the Holy Spirit at regeneration, which seals us until the day we will be glorified and welcomed into the Kingdom of God! (Ephesians 1:13–14).

7. Sanctification

The previous four steps of the salvation process (conversion, regeneration, justification, and adoption) happen in an instant. These next two steps, beginning with sanctification, take the rest of our lives on earth. Sanctification can best be described as the progressive work of God and man that makes us freer from sin and more and more like Christ. Paul encourages us with this promise of God: *he who began a good work in you will carry it on to completion until the day of Christ Jesus* (Philippians 1:6). God's gift of eternal life begins the moment we choose to follow Christ.

This book is built on this idea of progressive sanctification—the process of becoming a mature disciple of Christ. Earlier, we defined "sanctification" (Greek *hagiosmo*) as "the state or process of being set apart; that is, made holy."[14] This is the essence of the Christian life—to discover and achieve our God-given purpose in Christ. Paul encouraged the Thessalonians with these words: *from the beginning, God chose you to be saved through the sanctifying work of the Spirit and through belief in the truth. He called you to this through our gospel, that you might share in the glory of our Lord Jesus Christ* (2 Thessalonians 2:13–14). These verses capture multiple steps in the salvation process: election, calling, conversion, sanctification, and glorification.

How are we sanctified? Our growth and development in Christ occurs through training, trials, and temptations. As we learn to obey Jesus Christ and place our trust in Him in every area of our life, we are further sanctified. As we face trials in life—illness, death, disability, job loss, financial crisis, marital stress, wayward children, persecution, or suffering—we rely upon Jesus to walk us through them and are further sanctified. When we face temptations to sin, God will show us a way to resist that temptation; the result is increased sanctification (1 Corinthians 10:13). The Holy Spirit living in us is our guide, our comforter, and our protector. We are called upon to *continue to work out your salvation with fear and trembling, for it is God who works in you to will and to act according to his good purpose* (Philippians 2:12–13). This is what the process of sanctification is all about.

---

14   *Theopedia: An Encyclopedia of Christianity*, s.v. "sanctification," November 2, 2012, www.theopedia.com/sanctification.

8. Perseverance

This next step in the process of salvation also lasts a lifetime. The Bible teaches that all who are truly born-again will "endure" (Greek *hypomone*) to the end. The author of Hebrews, having just recounted all the faithful ones who had finished the race and are now in heaven with Jesus, encourages all of us who are still alive and actively running the race of faith today: *Therefore, since we are surrounded by such a great cloud of witnesses, let us throw off everything that hinders and the sin that so easily entangles, and let us run with perseverance the race marked out for us* (Hebrews 12:1). We are to run with perseverance the race marked out for us. This is the essence of the Christian's life. The powerful allegory, *Pilgrim's Progress*, portrays the ups and downs, the strides and setbacks, and the highs and lows of the Christian journey.

Perseverance is characterized by a long-term pattern of spiritual growth. Trials and tribulations produce a steadfast endurance, a holding on, a keep-on-keeping-on attitude. God promises that He will not let go of those of us who have genuinely placed their faith in Jesus Christ. John the apostle quoted Jesus as saying: *My sheep listen to my voice; I know them, and they follow me. I give them eternal life, and they shall never perish; no one can snatch them out of my hand. My Father, who has given them to me, is greater than all; no one can snatch them out of my Father's hand. I and the Father are one* (John 10:27–30). Those who are in Christ will persevere to the end.

Peter also confirmed that it is the power of God to guard us until our salvation is culminated in our glorification: *According to his great mercy, he has caused us to be born again to a living hope through the resurrection of Jesus Christ from the dead, to an inheritance that is imperishable, undefiled, and unfading, kept in heaven for you, who by God's power are being guarded through faith for a salvation ready to be revealed in the last time* (1 Peter 1:3–5). These verses highlight several of the steps of salvation, including regeneration, adoption, perseverance, and glorification. We now turn to the final step in the process of salvation.

9. Glorification

"Glorification" (Greek *doxazo*) occurs when our dead bodies are raised and reunited with our spirits in heaven. This is the culmination of our existence and occurs when Christ returns. Paul affirmed this as the final abiding state of the redeemed: *And those he predestined, he also called; those he called, he also justified; those he justified, he also glorified* (Romans 8:30). Here again, we see several of the steps of salvation in their proper sequence.

When we as Christians die, our spirits return to God, and our bodies are committed to the ground. The spirit returns to heaven, and the body returns to earth. Paul explains the supernatural reunion of the body and spirit at the Second Coming of Christ: *So will it be with the resurrection of the dead. The body that is sown is perishable, it is raised imperishable; it is sown in dishonor, it is raised in glory; it is sown in weakness, it is raised in power; it is sown a natural body, it is raised a spiritual body* (1 Corinthians 15:42–44). Paul goes on to explain that the natural comes first and the spiritual comes second. The same order is seen in the first Adam, who comes from the earth and the second Adam (that is, Jesus Christ), who comes from heaven.

The final abiding state of the redeemed is with Christ forever in heaven. Paul helps us to understand that the Christian's home is not here on earth, but instead in heaven: *But our citizenship is in heaven. And we eagerly await a Savior from there, the Lord Jesus Christ, who, by the power that enables him to bring everything under his control, will transform our lowly bodies so that they will be like his glorious body* (Philippians 3:20–21). All Christians profess the hope that one day we will be with Jesus in heaven, where the final dwelling of God is with men (Revelation 21:1–7). What a blessed inheritance!

Now we have a better understanding of the foundational basis for our salvation. We learned a lot about the need for and the process of salvation. We should be encouraged by the path that we are on and our ultimate destination. We have Jesus as the One who paved the way for us to be reconciled to our Father, and we have all those who have gone before us, who have faithfully run and completed the race marked out for every Christian. Paul, in his final letter, encouraged Timothy with these words: *I have fought the good fight, I have finished the race, I have kept the faith. Now there is in store for me the crown of righteousness, which the Lord, the righteous Judge, will award to me on that day—and not only to me, but also to all who have longed for his appearing* (2 Timothy 4:7–8). Those of us who are in Christ do in fact long for His appearing.

Having completed a very difficult and steep leg of our marathon, it may be a good idea to rest just for a bit and drink in the awesome truth we have just learned. Allow these truths to refresh you and renew your strength. The next leg of our journey takes a sharp turn and evens out. There is a gradual transition over the next few miles from learning to living; from doctrine to duty; from believing to being. This is the part of the race where we really learn to exercise our faith outwardly. The core has been trained and nurtured, and our foundation is firm. Now, we are equipped for the work of the saints! As we rest for just a few more minutes, let's take a look at our next memory verse:

For it is by grace you have been saved, through faith—and this is not from yourselves, it is the gift of God—not by works, so that no one can boast. For we are God's handiwork, created in Christ Jesus to do good works, which God prepared in advance for us to do.

(Ephesians 2:8–10)

The Race of Faith

The Fifth Leg: Equip

None of us begins a task or a mission without first equipping ourselves. When a person first becomes a follower of Jesus Christ, the Holy Spirit endows her with certain spiritual gifts that she is to use in the ministry of God's Kingdom. The church cannot function well unless every believer does his or her part. God has gifted each of us so that we might do great things for His glory.

Mile 17: The Doctrine of the Church

Mile 18: Spiritual Gifts Overview

Mile 19: Discovering and Using Our Spiritual Gifts

The Doctrine of the Church

A friend of mine and his family moved to a new city and began visiting churches. After a couple of months of viewing websites and attending worship services at various churches, they concluded that churches come in every shape and size. Some are very traditional, some very contemporary. Some use a pipe organ to accompany the singing of songs while others have a band with drums and guitars. In some churches, the pastor wears a robe and in others he wears a t-shirt and jeans. Some churches have committees and other churches have a leadership team that makes all the decisions. Some are active in their community and some are not. When Jesus told Peter He would build His church, what did He have in mind? This mile presents Jesus's purpose for His church.

What Is the Church?

Back at the four-mile marker, we discussed the church at length. Here in mile seventeen, we will build on that foundation to truly understand why God ordained the church (His "called-out" ones) to accomplish His purpose in redemption. While there are a lot of opinions about what the church is, why it exists, and what it is supposed to do, and while most of us have certain preconceptions of church based on our own experience, we have learned during the first sixteen miles that our beliefs and behaviors must be based on the Bible.

The church can be defined as "the community of all true believers for all time."[15] Jesus said, *I will build my church and the gates of Hades will not overcome it* (Matthew 16:18). Hades is the place of the dead. The word "overcome" comes from the Greek word, *katischusousin*, which connotes an inability to stand against or to resist some force. That said, Jesus meant that the church's mission is to be on the offensive in reclaiming the souls of man for God. Jesus used this same imagery in Matthew 12: *How can anyone enter a strong man's house and carry off his possessions unless he first ties up the strong man? Then he can rob his house* (Matthew 12:29). In order to interpret this passage, let us understand that Satan is the strong man, and his house is this world; Jesus referred to Satan as the prince of this world (John 16:11). His binding represents Jesus's resistance against Satan in the wilderness. With these truths in mind, we can conclude that Jesus was commissioning the army of God (the church) to reclaim God's people from captivity. The mission of the church is to join God in His rescue mission.

Taking this mission one step further, we now see that the church is like an army, with each and every soldier equipped for battle. We are part of God's Special Forces, sent out to seek those who are held captive and to rescue them. So, with this biblical description of the

---

15   Grudem, *Systematic Theology*, 853.

church, we can now conclude that "church" is not some building people go to on Sunday mornings. Instead, the church is both a local and universal army, commissioned with a grand battle plan to make disciples of all nations. No wonder the Bible's authors repeated Jesus's Great Commission five times! We are left to wonder how many times Jesus said it throughout His ministry.

Now, the Bible does not describe the church as some hostile force, for Jesus never coerces people to join Him. Instead, our only weapon is the Word of God, to be used to withstand the devil's schemes. Paul explained to the Ephesians: *Put on the full armor of God so that you can take your stand against the devil's schemes. For our struggle is not against flesh and blood, but against the rulers, against the authorities, against the powers of this dark world and against the spiritual forces of evil in the heavenly realms* (Ephesians 6:11–12). So, the enemy is Satan and his forces of evil. We fight against those evil forces. God has given us armor—the belt of truth; the breastplate of righteousness; feet fitted with the readiness of the Gospel of peace; the shield of faith; and the helmet of salvation. Our only weapon is the *sword of the Spirit, which is the word of God* (Ephesians 6:17). Jesus resisted all three of Satan's temptations by using the sword, the Word of God. Each time, he quoted from the book of Deuteronomy.

War brings victory, but it also brings casualties. How many people have died for the Christian faith? Paul encouraged Timothy with these words, *Endure hardship with us like a good soldier of Christ Jesus* (2 Timothy 2:3). The Christian's mission is not easy. It is hard. It is uncomfortable. It is dangerous. This is perhaps why Jesus emphasized the cost of following Him throughout His ministry. We are in a war, and too many sit back at base camp in complacency, never venturing out into the battle zone. Can we even imagine what might happen if every born-again believer became a fully devoted follower of our Commander, Jesus Christ? We should thank God every day for the missionaries spread all across the globe penetrating the darkness and bringing the captives into the light!

This leads us to the next truth about church. The church is invisible, yet visible. This means that none of us can know for certain who is really part of the Kingdom of God and who is not. Church attendance cannot and must not be the measure of our salvation. Sadly, there are a lot of people who attend worship every Sunday thinking they are good enough and are therefore a part of the family of God. The truth is that we can only be saved by genuine faith in Christ: *Salvation is found in no one else, for there is no other name under heaven given to men by which we must be saved* (Acts 4:12). Since Jesus is the only way, then our obedience to Him is our only appropriate response, which, if practiced, will bear "much fruit." He said, in effect: *As you go, make disciples of all nations.* (Matthew 28:19) The phrase "as you go" implies that at every moment of every day, we are to be on mission for Christ. This book was written to help you become a disciple who makes other disciples.

The local church, then, is a body of believers, associated by covenant in the faith and practice of the Gospel. This is the geographic element of church. Unfortunately, there are so many denominations and so many different shapes and sizes of church that the world gets confused. What distinguishes one church from another? Simply put, the answer is that every denomination has some nuance of difference in either church dogma or tradition. That is why the Bible must be the final authority on all matters of faith and practice. Hopefully, this book clarifies certain biblical teachings and at the same time challenges our traditional training and thinking.

What Does the Church Represent?

We have already touched on how the church is represented in Scripture back in the fourth mile, so we will expound on the five representations of the church and add some explanation here:

1. **The church is the bride of Christ (2 Corinthians 11:2; Ephesians 5:21–33; Revelation 19:1–10).** Jesus is the bridegroom, and all Christians of all ages are His bride. Paul compared the relationship of husband and wife to that between Christ and the church: *Wives, submit to your husbands as to the Lord. For the husband is the head of the wife as Christ is the head of the church, his body, of which he is the Savior. Now as the church submits to Christ, so also wives should submit to their husbands in everything. Husbands, love your wives, just as Christ loved the church and gave himself up for her.* **(Ephesians 5:22–25)** This passage is often misunderstood. The Greek word for "submit" is *hupotasso*, which implies a voluntary yielding to the authority of another. In this case, wives are called to follow the lead of their husbands, since God has made the husband accountable for his family. The key is the next verse, where husbands are commanded to love their wives as Christ loved the church. Christ loved the church so much that He laid down His life for her. That is the ultimate expression of love. What woman would not want to respect a man who loves her like that?

2. **The church is the body of Christ (1 Corinthians 12; Ephesians 4:7–16).** The body has many parts, all of which are vital, and all of which play a different role. This image of the church highlights the diversity of the church, with each person bringing something of unique value to the whole: *There are different kinds of gifts, but the same Spirit. There are different kinds of service, but the same Lord. There are different kinds of working, but the same God works all of them in all men* (1 Corinthians 12:4–6). Notice that the Trinity is represented in these verses—the same Spirit, same Lord (Jesus), and same God. Spiritual gifts are given for the common good, so that the body can be effective in carrying out God's ordained mission.

3. **The church is the family of God (Galatians 6:10; Ephesians 3:14–15; 1 Peter 4:17).** When we become Christians, we are immediately adopted into the family of God. We are no longer aliens or strangers, but we are sons and heirs. A famous saying is applicable here: "Blood runs thicker than water." In the same way, the church of Jesus Christ is unified by His blood. Therefore, unconditional love should be our guiding principle as we relate to our faith family. Paul instructed the church in Galatia to *carry each other's burdens*, for this is an act of goodness: *Therefore, as we have opportunity, let us do good to all people, especially to those who belong to the family of believers* (Galatians 6:2, 10).

4. **The church is the building of God (1 Corinthians 3:9–11; Ephesians 2:19–22; 1 Peter 2:4–12).** Salvation for the Christian includes adoption into God's family and membership into His household, so that *we are no longer foreigners and aliens, but fellow citizens with God's people and members of God's household, built on the foundation of the apostles and prophets, with Christ Jesus himself as the chief cornerstone* (Ephesians 2:19–20). The foundation is formed by the words of the prophets and the proclamations of the apostles that Jesus Christ is the Messiah. Every Christian is part of this beautiful building of God.

5. **The church is the army of God (Philippians 2:25; 2 Timothy 2:1–5; Revelation 19:19).** The Bible calls Christians soldiers, and soldiers have both a commander and an enemy. The Commander is Jesus Christ (see Joshua 5:13–15 for a preincarnate appearance of Christ), and the enemy is Satan and his forces of evil who hold humankind captive. Paul encouraged Timothy to *endure hardship with us like a good soldier of Christ Jesus. No one serving as a soldier gets involved in civilian affairs—he wants to please his commanding officer* (2 Timothy 2:3–4). Jesus is our Commander and

we are His soldiers, commissioned to "make disciples of all nations."

What Is the Threefold Purpose of the Church?

During the warm-up session, we explored the threefold mission of the church, which includes worshiping, working and witnessing. These three activities bring glory to God, which is the chief end of mankind. A good way to think about our mission is to see it as three-pronged, reaching out in three directions. Remember the triangle in our Spiritual FITNESS diagram? We reach up to God in worship. We reach out to our fellow believers in our Kingdom work. We reach out to the world as witnesses. This is an apt description of our mission, as it addresses each of the three entities to which we must relate—God, the church, and the world.

Worship is our awe-filled response to who God is and what He does. Work involves training up and tasking God's army to do the work God has called us to do; we become mature believers and achieve Spiritual FITNESS through the process of working out our salvation and working within God's Kingdom. Witnessing consists of serving others with the love of Jesus Christ and sharing the Good News with the world, so that they too can become a part of God's family.

What Are the Marks of an Effective Church?

There is one letter in the New Testament that fully develops the doctrine of the church. Paul wrote to the church at Ephesus, and after he established the truth that we have been chosen by God, made alive by God, and adopted as children of God, he then explained God's intentions for the church: *His intent was that now, through the church, the manifold wisdom of God should be made known to the rulers and the authorities in the heavenly realms, according to his eternal purpose which he accomplished in Christ Jesus our Lord* (Ephesians 3:10–11). God commissioned His church to be a herald of His wisdom and purpose. Paul prayed that the saints *grasp how wide and long and high and deep is the love of Christ* (Ephesians 3:18). With the immeasurable love of Christ as our foundation, Paul unveils the three marks of an effective church:

1. **Unity (Ephesians 4:1–10)** - *There is one body and one Spirit— just as you were called to one hope, when you were called—one Lord, one faith, one baptism, one God and Father of all, who is over all and through all and in all.* (Ephesians 4:4–6) The Church of Jesus Christ must be unified if it is to be effective in its mission. Unity can only come when every Christian submits to the leadership of the Holy Spirit.

2. **Maturity (Ephesians 4:11–16)** - *... So that the body of Christ might be built up until we all reach unity in the faith and in the knowledge of the Son of God and become mature, attaining to the whole measure of the fullness of Christ. Then we will no longer be infants, tossed back and forth by the waves, and blown here and there by every wind of teaching and by the cunning and craftiness of men in their deceitful scheming.* (Ephesians 4:13–14) Maturity is an imperative to effectiveness in the church. The church today must get back to teaching the body the deeper truths of the faith. This is the premise of this book—maturity!

3. **Purity (Ephesians 4:17–32)** - *You were taught, with regard to your former way of life, to put off your old self, which is being corrupted by its deceitful desires; to be made new in the attitude of your minds; and to put on the new self, created to be like God in true righteousness and holiness.* (Ephesians 4:22–24) Purity begins with our decision to obey Jesus, to feed our mind and our heart with the things of God, and to demonstrate genuine

kindness, compassion, and forgiveness for each other—first, within the church, and second, outside the church.

How Is the Church Governed?

According to the Bible, God has ordained two church offices: pastors and deacons.

1. **Pastors (1 Timothy 3:1–7; 1 Peter 5:1–4)** *If anyone sets his heart on being an overseer, he desires a noble task.* **(1 Timothy 3:1)** The office of pastor is identified by three separate terms in the Bible. These three terms are not titles per se, but are instead functional descriptors. As "overseer" (Greek *episcopos*), also traditionally called "bishop," the pastor oversees the affairs of the church and provides leadership for the congregation in carrying out its God-given mission. As "elder" (Greek *presbuteros*), the pastor provides the teaching and training of the congregation. As "shepherd" (Greek *poimen*), the pastor provides for the protection and care of the congregation. The qualifications for pastor are listed in verses 2–7 of this passage.

2. **Deacons (1 Timothy 3:8–13)** *Deacons, likewise, are to be men worthy of respect, sincere, not indulging in much wine, and not pursuing dishonest gain. They must keep hold of the deep truths of the faith with a clear conscience. They must first be tested; and then if there is nothing against them, let them serve as deacons.* (1 Timothy 3:8–10) The deacons' function is highlighted in Acts 6:1–7. Deacons (Greek *diakonos*) take on the service-oriented needs within the church, thereby freeing up the pastors for preaching and prayer. Some churches have only male deacons, and some have both male and female deacons. 1 Timothy 3:11 reads this way: *In the same way, their wives are to be women worthy of respect, not malicious talkers but temperate and trustworthy in everything.* The word for

"wives" can also be translated as "women" (Greek *gunaikas*), and that is how some churches interpret that verse. They also point out that Phoebe was a deaconess: *I commend to you our sister Phoebe, a servant of the church in Cenchrea* (Romans 16:1). The word "servant" in this verse is the same word for "deacon," the Greek word *diakonos*.

In addition to these two offices, the local church needs the entire body to support the overall goal of making disciples. Therefore, many non-ordained members, known as laypersons, are gifted and equipped to lead specific ministries. These lay leaders are a critical component to church functionality. Depending on the church, there can be endless opportunities to serve God meaningfully using the spiritual gifts with which He has endowed us.

What Are the Ordinances of the Local Church?

Another key component of a church involves Scriptural ordinances. There are two church ordinances specifically called out in Scripture – baptism and communion. We have addressed these ordinances already, but we will add a few more points for each here:

1. Baptism:

In the New Testament, baptism always follows conversion. First of all, Jesus was baptized as an adult, to set an example for us. Second, Luke explained that after Peter's sermon on Pentecost, *those who accepted his message were baptized* (Acts 2:38). Third, the Samaritans who heard the word from Philip believed and then were baptized (Acts 8:12–13). Furthermore, the Ethiopian eunuch believed and then was baptized (Acts 8:34–38). In addition, those to whom Peter preached in Cornelius's home were baptized after they received the Holy Spirit (Acts 10:44–48). Finally the Philippian jailer and his family all believed and were then baptized (Acts 16:30–34).

Perhaps the most compelling reason to baptize people after they have converted is found in the meaning of baptism. According to Romans 6, the symbolic meaning of baptism is our identification with Christ in His death, burial, and resurrection. That is, we die to our old life, we are buried (under the surface of the water, thus immersion is the best symbol of burial), and we are raised out of the water as a symbol of our resurrection to walk in the new life we now have with Christ as our Lord. Paul affirmed this by saying: *We were therefore buried with him through baptism into death in order that, just as Christ was raised from the dead through the glory of the Father, we too may live a new life* (Romans 6:4).

2. Communion:

Communion is also known as the Eucharist (which is the Greek word for "thanksgiving") and the Lord's Supper. Jesus instituted this ordinance at His Last Supper the night before He was crucified:

> *While they were eating, Jesus took bread, gave thanks and broke it, and gave it to his disciples, saying, Take and eat; this is my body. Then he took the cup, gave thanks and offered it to them, saying, Drink from it, all of you. This is my blood of the covenant, which is poured out for many for the forgiveness of sins. I tell you, I will not drink of this fruit of the vine from now on until that day when I drink it anew with you in my Father's kingdom.*

(Matthew 26:26–29)

The bread symbolizes Jesus's body, which was offered the next morning at His crucifixion. The bread was unleavened bread in keeping with the Passover feast. Leaven represents sin or corrupting influence, and God instructed the Israelites to get rid of all leaven to allow for a hasty departure from their bondage (1 Corinthians 5:6–8). Since Jesus was without sin, the unleavened bread He offered at His Last Supper best represented His sinless body.

The "fruit of the vine" symbolizes Jesus's blood, which fulfills the New Covenant promise God gave to His people through Jeremiah (Jeremiah 31:31–34; Hebrews 8:8–13). There is life in the blood. The Bible declares, *without the shedding of blood, there is no forgiveness* (Hebrews 9:22). The blood symbolizes the death of Christ, the unity of all believers in Him, and the anticipation of His coming again.

Paul said that whenever the church observes communion, we *proclaim the Lord's death until he comes* (1 Corinthians 11:26). There is nothing in Scripture that dictates the frequency of communion; Scripture simply states that as often as we take it, we proclaim the sacrifice of Christ as the atonement (covering) for our sin. This ordinance is a fitting participatory element of worship, as it unifies the body of Christ under a single blood type, identifying us all as the children of God.

Paul also issued a warning to us: *So then, whoever eats the bread or drinks the cup of the Lord in an unworthy manner will be guilty of sinning against the body and blood of the Lord. Everyone ought to examine themselves before they eat of the bread and drink from the cup* (1 Corinthians 11:27–28). We are to examine ourselves and be reverent when we take communion. Paul alludes earlier in this passage to the fact that some came to the Lord's Supper drunk with the wine they had at their regular meal. Whatever the issue, we must not partake of communion in an "unworthy manner."

We should now be a little more comfortable with the meaning of the church, its purpose, and what it represents. We have also identified the three marks of an effective church—unity, maturity, and purity. In addition, we have reviewed the biblical offices and ordinances of the church. Now, as we prepare to head into our next mile, let's review our next memory verse:

Now to him who is able to do immeasurably more than all we ask or imagine, according to his power that is at work within us, to him be glory in the church and in Christ Jesus throughout all generations, for ever and ever! Amen.

(Ephesians 3:20–21)

Spiritual Gifts Overview

When I think about someone knowing and using his spiritual gifts to build up the church, I think of a man with whom I attended church many years ago. I had torn my ACL playing basketball (not very much fun at all!). As I lay on my back in my upstairs bedroom letting the Continuous Passive Movement (CPM) machine do its work, I suddenly heard a lawnmower starting up outside my window. Unsolicited, my friend had determined that I would be unable to do my yard work, and so, as an act of service and an expression of his gift of helping others, he did my yard work for me. Many times, we use our gifts without even knowing it. This mile lists and explains the spiritual gifts administered by the Holy Spirit to His church.

What Is a Spiritual Gift?

A spiritual gift is any ability that is empowered by the Holy Spirit and used in the ministry of the church. Paul gave a thorough explanation of spiritual gifts in his letters to the churches in Rome, Corinth, and Ephesus. In his letter to Corinth, he addressed a host of issues that had arisen within the church, including questions about leadership, immorality, lawsuits, marriage, acceptable foods, worship, spiritual gifts, and the resurrection. He turned to the topic of spiritual gifts by saying: *Now about spiritual gifts, brothers, I do not want you to be ignorant* (1 Corinthians 12:1). As with the other issues Paul addressed, there must have been quite a bit of confusion about spiritual gifts within the church. Sadly, there remains a good deal of confusion even today, especially regarding some gifts in particular, such as healings and tongues.

In his letters to Rome, Corinth, and Ephesus, Paul laid out several principles about spiritual gifts that are instructive for us to gain agreement:

1. All spiritual gifts are given by God for the common good (1 Corinthians 12:3–6; Ephesians 4:3–6:1; Corinthians 12:7).
2. There are different kinds of gifts (Romans 12:4–6; 1 Corinthians 12:4, 8–10).
3. All spiritual gifts serve to unify and equip the church to carry out its mission until Christ returns (1 Corinthians 12:12; Ephesians 4:12–13).
4. All spiritual gifts are equally important (1 Corinthians 12:2–26).
5. Every born-again believer possesses one or more spiritual gifts (1 Corinthians 12:11, 27; Ephesians 4:7).
6. No spiritual gift is required for salvation or endows the believer with a greater spiritual experience or level (1 Corinthians 12:28–30).

7. Spiritual gifts should not be confused with human talents, because spiritual gifts are given only to those who have been saved.

How Are Spiritual Gifts Categorized?

There are four specific passages in Scripture that list or describe the different spiritual gifts—Romans 12:3–8; 1 Corinthians 12:27–31; Ephesians 4:11; and 1 Peter 4:11. Not every list is the same, and, frankly, one could conclude that there may be other spiritual gifts that simply were not included in the letters to the early church. In other words, there does not seem to be a definitive list of gifts.

Upon a closer review of these lists, we learn that the spiritual gifts can be categorized in a couple of different ways. First, the lists include specific gifts as well as the names and titles of people who possess them. For example, Paul said, *And in the church God has appointed first of all apostles, second prophets, third teachers, then workers of miracles, also those having gifts of healing, those able to help others, those with gifts of administration, and those speaking in different kinds of tongues* (1 Corinthians 12:28). Notice that this list begins with official titles, such as apostles, prophets, and teachers, but ends with actual gifts as they are used, such as healings and administration.

Another way to categorize the spiritual gifts is to group them as speaking gifts versus serving gifts. For example, teaching and prophecy both use speech to convey God's truth, whereas gifts like helping or serving require physical action. Peter summarized the purpose of spiritual gifts related to these two categories: *If anyone speaks, he should do it as one speaking the very words of God. If anyone serves, he should do it with the strength God provides, so that in all things God may be praised through Jesus Christ. To him be the glory and the power for ever and ever. Amen* (1 Peter 4:11). This one verse captures the essence of how our spiritual gifts should bring glory to God. When every member of the local church discovers and uses his or her spiritual gifts, that church becomes a beacon for the community in which God planted it.

What Are the Spiritual Gifts?

Based on the four passages we have already identified, we will list the spiritual gifts and say a brief word about them. The names/titles of those possessing these gifts—apostles, prophets, evangelists, pastors, and teachers—are not listed. We will list the spiritual gifts in the order in which they are first mentioned in Scripture, followed by their references. Only two of the gifts are mentioned in all lists: prophecy and teaching.

1. Prophecy (Romans 12:6; 1 Corinthians 12:10; Ephesians 4:11)

Prophecy is the bold proclamation of God's truth. Many think of the Old Testament prophets in reference to this gift. Prophecy is oftentimes mistaken as involving only the prediction of future events because the word, "prophesy" (Greek *propheteis*) is a combination of two words, *pro,* which means "before," and the verb *phemi,* which means "to speak." However, the fullest expression of the gift of prophecy is speaking God's revealed word to others, whether it regards the present or predictions for the future.

2. Teaching (Romans 12:7; 1 Corinthians 12:28; Ephesians 4:11)

Teaching is conveying biblical truth in a way that others can understand. "Teaching" comes from the Greek word *didasko* and connotes a special ability to understand complex biblical principles and terms and the ability to break them down in such a way as to impart understanding to others. Teaching is oftentimes borne out of a passion for personal Bible study.

3. Serving (Romans 12:7)

"Serving" (Greek *diakonon*) comes from the same word that is rendered "deacon." A person with this spiritual gift is great at identifying what needs to get done and then is instrumental in getting it done. This same word is used in Acts 6, which recounts the church's need of spiritual servants to assist the gentile widows with getting food.

4. Encouraging (Romans 12:8)

"Encouragement" (Greek *parakalon*) is formed from two words: *kaleo*, meaning "call" and *para*, meaning "alongside." Therefore, someone with this gift calls to another to come alongside him or her. Some Bibles translate this word as "exhortation," which implies some form of pressure or warning, while the translation of "encouragement" is a positive urging to keep a spiritual perspective when a person is going through a difficult time.

5. Giving (Romans 12:8)

All Christians are commanded to give, but those who have the spiritual gift of giving (Greek *metadidous*) are passionate about providing material or non-material resources for a given need. The word, *metadidous* is another combination of two words: *meta*, translated as "with" and *didomi*, translated as "give." The context of this gift is also emphasized by the generosity or liberality of the giver.

6. Leading (Romans 12:8)

Leaders motivate and inspire others to get involved in achieving God's purposes in the church. The word, "leading" (Greek *proistamenos*), connotes one person who stands before others and exerts a profound influence. In this context, leadership in the church is characterized by diligence.

7. Mercy (Romans 12:8)

Persons with the spiritual gift of mercy display a special sensitivity and kindness toward those who are suffering. Mercy (Greek *eleos*) is extended by God and involves not giving someone what he or she deserves. Those who possess the spiritual gift of mercy do not judge others for their sins or shortcomings.

8. Wisdom (1 Corinthians 12:8)

Wisdom can be defined as perfectly applying one's biblical knowledge in daily life and ministry. The Greek word for "wisdom" is *sophia*, which connotes an inner intuition or understanding. This appropriately describes the leadership of the Holy Spirit as the one imparting such a gift.

9. Knowledge (1 Corinthians 12:8)

Knowledge is simply the ability to understand biblical truth. While all who are born-again, and thus have the Holy Spirit to guide them into all truth, will increase their knowledge through Bible study, those with the spiritual gift of knowledge (Greek *gnosis*) possess an expanded insight into a passage or principle of Scripture, which helps to strengthen the ministry and mission of the church.

10. Faith (1 Corinthians 12:9)

Faith is certainly a part of salvation, but it is also a spiritual gift. Faith is the active conviction within a person to trust in the supernatural power and promises of God. The Greek word for "faith," *pistis*, means to be persuaded and convicted about relying on and petitioning God, no matter the circumstances or seeming hopelessness of any given situation.

11. Healing (1 Corinthians 12:9, 28)

The phrase from 1 Corinthians 12:9 is "gifts of healing" (Greek *charismata iamaton*), which confirms that there are many kinds of ailments (physical, emotional, or spiritual) and many ways to heal. This gift, like that of faith, is evidenced by a person's assurance that God can and wants to demonstrate His power and authority over the natural world. People with the gifts of healing acknowledge that they themselves do not possess any power to heal, but they have an unshakeable confidence to ask and plead to God for healing.

12. Miracles (1 Corinthians 12:10, 28)

The spiritual gift of "miracles" (Greek *dunamis*) connotes an intense burden of calling on the power of God to be displayed in order to bring Him glory. Similar to the gifts of healing, miracles are supernatural and are therefore only performed by God. People with this gift have an acute sensitivity to God's will in a given situation and the boldness to appeal to Him for divine intervention.

13. Discernment (1 Corinthians 12:10)

"Discerning of spirits," or, in Greek, *diakriseis pneumaton*, is the ability to distinguish and judge between what is true and what is false. While the Holy Spirit guides all Christians to discern good from evil, people with this gift also possess an inner awareness of truth and falseness as well as the drive to alert others.

14. Tongues (1 Corinthians 12:10, 28)

The Greek word for "tongues" is *glosson* (the singular form is *glossa*), from which we get our English word "glossary." The two uses of this word in the New Testament either describe a literal tongue or a language spoken by a certain group of people. This spiritual gift is a God-given ability to know and speak another language in order to communicate God's Word effectively and powerfully to others.

15. Interpretation of Tongues (1 Corinthians 12:10)

Interpretation goes hand-in-hand with the gift of tongues. The Greek word for "interpretation" is *hermeneuo*, which connotes the translation of a language unknown by others. Essentially, the gift of interpretation involves the supernaturally inspired translation of a message spoken by someone speaking in tongues.

16. Helps (1 Corinthians 12:28)

The spiritual gift of "helps" (Greek *antilepsis*) involves offering assistance, aid, or support to others, especially those who are in great need. While the gifts of serving and helping may seem similar, the server does something for someone else while the helper joins that person in an activity or project in which he or she is already engaged.

17. Administration (1 Corinthians 12:28)

The gift of administration involves planning, organizing, and accomplishing a task. The Greek word for "administration" is *kubernesis*, and connotes one who steers a ship. People who possess this gift are able to take a leaders' vision and direct resources effectively and efficiently to accomplish what needs to be done.

Are All Spiritual Gifts Still Active Today?

We have just listed and briefly explained the seventeen gifts that are given in the Bible. Some biblical scholars conclude that the gifts of healings, miracles, tongues, and the interpretation of tongues ceased after the apostles all died. They make the point that the apostles used these gifts to authenticate the message of Jesus and His apostles in the early church. In those days, the New Testament had not yet been written and circulated, so God wrought miracles and healings through His chosen messengers to confirm the truth of Christ and His resurrection before God's Word was written. These scholars argue that once the Word of God was written, these manifestational gifts were no longer necessary.

This group of scholars point to several verses to support their position. Mark concluded his Gospel with these words: *Then the disciples went out and preached everywhere, and the Lord worked with them and confirmed his word by the signs that accompanied it* (Mark 16:20). Furthermore, the author of Hebrews attested: *This salvation, which was first announced by the Lord, was confirmed to us by those who heard him. God also testified to it by signs, wonders and various miracles, and gifts of the Holy Spirit distributed according to his will* (Hebrews 2:3b–4). Finally, Paul asserted that the mark of a true apostle of Christ was through the miraculous: *The things that mark an apostle—signs, wonders and miracles—were done among you with great perseverance* (2 Corinthians 12:12). Based on these verses, one could conclude that God used miracles, signs, and wonders in the first century to authenticate and corroborate Jesus's message of salvation until that message was written down by His apostles.

An alternative perspective may be offered based on the following four points. First, we must acknowledge that miracles and healings are always in concert with God's will. Second, we must agree that God is sovereign and always has the power to manifest the miraculous in every generation. Third, we must also acknowledge that miracles do still happen today. Fourth, the Bible is fully applicable to every generation. Therefore, one could conclude that God still gifts certain believers with the spiritual gifts of healings and miracles. However, as described above, these gifts are Spirit-led assurances of God's ability to perform a miracle in specific situations. People with these two gifts are always first to acknowledge that they don't do anything to bring about the miracle but simply point others to trust God in accomplishing His will.

Regarding the spiritual gifts of speaking in tongues and interpreting tongues, the church in Corinth placed a lot of emphasis on speaking in tongues, and Paul dedicated three chapters in his first letter to address the issue. In 1 Corinthians 12, Paul explained the purpose of spiritual gifts and then listed them; he then used the analogy of the human body being made up of many parts, and then gave a second but slightly different list of the spiritual gifts. He concluded the chapter by asking a series of questions: *Are all apostles? Are all prophets? Are all teachers? Do all work miracles? Do all have gifts of healing? Do all speak in tongues? Do all interpret? But eagerly desire the greater gifts* (1 Corinthians 12:29–31a). The answer Paul obviously sought was "No." We must conclude from these verses that not all gifts are given to every believer.

It may at first seem odd that Paul then launched into the "Love Chapter" (1 Corinthians 13). He had ended the previous discussion on gifts with these words: *And now I will show you the most excellent way* (1 Corinthians 12:31b). Why does he make this transition? The reason is quite simple. Paul was teaching the Corinthians that the superior demonstration of the Holy Spirit's power in the life of the believer is through the fruit of the Spirit, of which love is the first and most important attribute. As Paul taught the Galatians, *the fruit of the Spirit is love, joy, peace, patience, kindness, goodness, faithfulness, gentleness, and self-control. Against such things there is no law* (Galatians 5:22). His transition from the manifestational gifts to love is a powerful lesson that without love, our spiritual gifts are powerless in their testimony: *If I speak in the tongues of men and of angels and have not love, I am only a resounding gong or a clanging symbol* (1 Corinthians 13:1). Paul issued quite a stinging indictment to those in the church at Corinth who touted their gifts as greater than all the others; by doing so, they were not displaying love.

The first mention of tongues in the Bible is found in Mark 16, where Jesus predicted that His disciples would speak in tongues. This would be fulfilled in Acts 2, during the Pentecost, fifty days after Jesus's resurrection. The disciples were gathered in one room and *all of them were filled with the Holy Spirit and began to speak in other tongues as the Spirit enabled them* (Acts 2:4). The narrative goes on to say that *each one heard them speaking in his own language* (Acts 2:6). The Greek term that is translated as "language" is *dialecto*, from which we get the word "dialect."

This significant event marked the indwelling of the Holy Spirit into God's people for the specific purpose of sending them back to their nation to proclaim the Gospel in their own tongue. Jesus had told them that they were to wait for the Holy Spirit to come, and then the Spirit came. This description of these early disciples speaking in other tongues also verifies that these were actual languages and not gibberish, for those gathered heard their own language. The narrative continues by naming as many as fifteen ethnicities that were represented in that one room. Jesus's Great Commission began in Jerusalem and was then taken to the ends of the earth, beginning with that miraculous outpouring of the Holy Spirit to all people.

Paul confirmed the purpose of the spiritual gifts of tongues to the church in Corinth: *Undoubtedly there are all sorts of languages in the world, yet none of them is without meaning. If then I do not grasp the meaning of what someone is saying, I am a foreigner to the speaker, and he is a foreigner to me. So it is with you. Since you are eager to have spiritual gifts, try to excel in the gifts that build up the church* (1 Corinthians 14:10–12). Clearly, Paul was explaining that the languages (tongues) being spoken in the church at Corinth were foreign languages, whereby the speakers desired to be important by demonstrating this gift to the rest of the church. He then encouraged those persons to interpret (translate) the message or prayer being offered in that foreign tongue in order to edify the church.

Paul concluded his instruction with this fact about speaking in tongues: *Tongues, then, are a sign, not for believers but for unbelievers; prophecy, however, is for believers* (1 Corinthians 14:22). The point he made was that the Gospel of Jesus Christ needs to be spoken in every language in order to accomplish Jesus's Great Commission – that is, to make disciples of all nations. The spiritual gift of prophecy is to speak the Word of God to the body of Christ. This is why Paul emphasized prophecy over that of speaking in tongues in church.

So, we see that all spiritual gifts are to be used to bring glory to God and to spread the Gospel. As with the gifts of healings and miracles, we ask, "Are speaking in tongues and interpreting tongues still viable gifts today?" Both of these gifts are still viable today but have been misused by many. When both of these gifts, truly given by the Holy Spirit to people He chooses, are used in accordance with God's will, then God is glorified, and the world witnesses the power of God in the mission of His church.

Now that we understand the purpose of spiritual gifts, and we know what they are, it's now time for you to discover the gifts the Holy Spirit has given to you. In the next mile, there will be a series of questions that will help you discover your spiritual gifts, but first, let's take a moment to memorize our next memory verse:

If anyone speaks, he should do it as one speaking the very words of God. If anyone serves, he should do it with the strength God provides, so that in all things God may be praised through Jesus Christ. To him be the glory and the power for ever and ever. Amen.

(1 Peter 4:11)

Discovering and Using Our Spiritual Gifts

I love to teach God's Word. I know that it is one of my spiritual gifts, but I also know that it is God who gave it to me. I consider it a privilege and a responsibility to faithfully use my gifts for His glory. I will never forget all the people God used in my life to help me realize that I had the gift of teaching. They encouraged me by sharing with me how my teaching had helped them better understand a Bible passage or a principle of truth. Very often, God uses other people to help us identify our spiritual gifts. Perhaps you have never really thought about what your spiritual gifts are, so this mile polls those who know you best to help you identify your spiritual gifts and how to put them to use for God's glory.

What Is the Purpose of a Spiritual Gifts Inventory?

There are at least three purposes for a spiritual gifts inventory. The first purpose is to help you discover your spiritual gifts. This is most often accomplished by the person completing the inventory, but I propose a different approach in this mile, as you will soon see. The second purpose is to affirm your passion for certain areas of ministry. We all have God-given desires to make an impact on specific areas of the kingdom's work. The third purpose is to develop a plan to get involved. God does not endow His children with spiritual gifts so that they can suppress or ignore them. God's church is an organism, whereby every member of the body needs each other. Every believer must discover, develop, and use his or her spiritual gifts.

What Are Your Spiritual Gifts?

Now we come to the actual inventory. So, your task is to find two people who are Christians and who know you well. There are two inventories included. They are to read the following descriptions and circle the score that best characterizes your actions and passions. You can also complete the inventories online at www.theraceoffaith.com.

After both inventories are completed, you can score yourself. Remember, this is not a test; there are no right or wrong answers. It is an inventory designed to show you how God has gifted you for His work. So, think about who you want to ask to conduct this inventory, and then ask them to complete the inventory and give you their scores.

Inventory # 1:

1. Loves to plan, organize, and manage projects; takes a leaders' vision and directs resources effectively and efficiently to accomplish what needs to be done.

0 Seldom/Never   **3** Sometimes   **5** Regularly   **7** Often/Always

2. Demonstrates an ability to distinguish and judge between what is true and what is false; possesses an inner awareness of and prompting to read people and their true motives.

   0 Seldom/Never   **3** Sometimes   **5** Regularly   **7** Often/Always

3. Encourages others; seeks to draw close to those who are hurting or discouraged; helps others keep a spiritual perspective when they are going through a difficult time.

   0 Seldom/Never   **3** Sometimes   **5** Regularly   **7** Often/Always

4. Trusts in the supernatural power and promises of God; relies fully on God and petitions Him without fail, no matter the circumstances or seeming hopelessness in any given situation.

   0 Seldom/Never   **3** Sometimes   **5** Regularly   **7** Often/Always

5. Provides material or non-material resources for a given need; takes great joy in being generous because God owns everything and has made us stewards of His resources.

   0 Seldom/Never   **3** Sometimes   **5** Regularly   **7** Often/Always

6. Evidences an assurance that God can and wants to demonstrate His power and authority over the natural world; exudes an unshakeable boldness to ask and plead to God for healing.

   0 Seldom/Never   **3** Sometimes   **5** Regularly   **7** Often/Always

7. Offers assistance, aid, or support to others, especially those who are in great need; joins others in an activity/project in which they are already engaged in order to help them get it done.

   0 Seldom/Never   **3** Sometimes   **5** Regularly   **7** Often/Always

8. Demonstrates an ability to translate a language unknown by others in attendance; able to interpret a message spoken by someone speaking in another language.

   0 Seldom/Never   **3** Sometimes   **5** Regularly   **7** Often/Always

9. Has the distinct ability to understand biblical truth; possesses great insight into passages and principles presented in Scripture; able to see how the entire Bible message is woven together.

   0 Seldom/Never   **3** Sometimes   **5** Regularly   **7** Often/Always

10. Motivates and inspires others to get involved in achieving God's purposes in the church; possesses a profound influence on others to see and buy into the larger vision.

    0 Seldom/Never   **3** Sometimes   **5** Regularly   **7** Often/Always

11. Displays a special sensitivity and kindness toward those who are suffering; does not judge others for what they have done but instead shows compassion and empathy.

    0 Seldom/Never   **3** Sometimes   **5** Regularly   **7** Often/Always

12. Carries an intense burden to call on the power of God to be displayed over the natural world in order to bring Him glory; has an acute sensitivity to God's will in a given situation and the boldness to appeal to Him for divine intervention.

    0 Seldom/Never   **3** Sometimes   **5** Regularly   **7** Often/Always

13. Boldly proclaims the truth of God's Word, regardless of whether that truth is popular with others or not; able to connect the Bible's message with current events.

    0 Seldom/Never   **3** Sometimes   **5** Regularly   **7** Often/Always

14. Identifies what needs to get done and then is instrumental in getting it done; has an awareness of others' resource limitations and takes joy in meeting those needs.

    0 Seldom/Never   **3** Sometimes   **5** Regularly   **7** Often/Always

15. Conveys biblical truth in a way that others can understand; known for passionate study of the Bible; able to take complex biblical principles/terms and explain them in such a way as to impart understanding to others.

    0 Seldom/Never   **3** Sometimes   **5** Regularly   **7** Often/Always

16. Has been given the supernatural ability to know and speak another language in order to communicate God's Word effectively and powerfully to others.

    0 Seldom/Never   **3** Sometimes   **5** Regularly   **7** Often/Always

17. Appropriately applies biblical teaching in daily life and ministry; garners an inner intuition or understanding that guides him or her in seeing and responding to difficult life circumstances.

    0 Seldom/Never   **3** Sometimes   **5** Regularly   **7** Often/Always

Inventory # 2:

1. Loves to plan, organize, and manage projects; takes a leaders' vision and directs resources effectively and efficiently to accomplish what needs to be done.

    0 Seldom/Never   **3** Sometimes   **5** Regularly   **7** Often/Always

2. Demonstrates an ability to distinguish and judge between what is true and what is false; possesses an inner awareness of and prompting to read people and their true motives.

0 Seldom/Never   3 Sometimes   5 Regularly   7 Often/Always

3. Encourages others; seeks to draw close to those who are hurting or discouraged; helps others keep a spiritual perspective when they are going through a difficult time.

0 Seldom/Never   3 Sometimes   5 Regularly   7 Often/Always

4. Trusts in the supernatural power and promises of God; relies fully on God and petitions Him without fail, no matter the circumstances or seeming hopelessness in any given situation.

0 Seldom/Never   3 Sometimes   5 Regularly   7 Often/Always

5. Provides material or non-material resources for a given need; takes great joy in being generous because God owns everything and has made us stewards of His resources.

0 Seldom/Never   3 Sometimes   5 Regularly   7 Often/Always

6. Evidences an assurance that God can and wants to demonstrate His power and authority over the natural world; exudes an unshakeable boldness to ask and plead to God for healing.

0 Seldom/Never   3 Sometimes   5 Regularly   7 Often/Always

7. Offers assistance, aid, or support to others, especially those who are in great need; joins others in an activity/project in which they are already engaged in order to help them get it done.

0 Seldom/Never   3 Sometimes   5 Regularly   7 Often/Always

8. Demonstrates an ability to translate a language unknown by others in attendance; able to interpret a message spoken by someone speaking in another language.

0 Seldom/Never   3 Sometimes   5 Regularly   7 Often/Always

9. Has the distinct ability to understand biblical truth; possesses great insight into passages and principles presented in Scripture; able to see how the entire Bible message is woven together.

   0 Seldom/Never   **3** Sometimes   **5** Regularly   **7** Often/Always

10. Motivates and inspires others to get involved in achieving God's purposes in the church; possesses a profound influence on others to see and buy into the larger vision.

    0 Seldom/Never   **3** Sometimes   **5** Regularly   **7** Often/Always

11. Displays a special sensitivity and kindness toward those who are suffering; does not judge others for what they have done but instead shows compassion and empathy.

    0 Seldom/Never   **3** Sometimes   **5** Regularly   **7** Often/Always

12. Carries an intense burden to call on the power of God to be displayed over the natural world in order to bring Him glory; has an acute sensitivity to God's will in a given situation and the boldness to appeal to Him for divine intervention.

    0 Seldom/Never   **3** Sometimes   **5** Regularly   **7** Often/Always

13. Boldly proclaims the truth of God's Word, regardless of whether that truth is popular with others or not; able to connect the Bible's message with current events.

    0 Seldom/Never   **3** Sometimes   **5** Regularly   **7** Often/Always

14. Identifies what needs to get done and then is instrumental in getting it done; has an awareness of others' resource limitations and takes joy in meeting those needs.

    0 Seldom/Never   **3** Sometimes   **5** Regularly   **7** Often/Always

15. Conveys biblical truth in a way that others can understand; known for passionate study of the Bible; able to take complex

biblical principles/terms and explain them in such a way as to impart understanding to others.

0 Seldom/Never   **3** Sometimes   **5** Regularly   **7** Often/Always

16. Has been given the supernatural ability to know and speak another language in order to communicate God's Word effectively and powerfully to others.

0 Seldom/Never   **3** Sometimes   **5** Regularly   **7** Often/Always

17. Appropriately applies biblical teaching in daily life and ministry; garners an inner intuition or understanding that guides him or her in seeing and responding to difficult life circumstances.

0 Seldom/Never   **3** Sometimes   **5** Regularly   **7** Often/Always

Once both people have completed their inventories, calculate the scores below. The numbered descriptions above correlate to the gifts listed below. Add the score for each gift for each of the inventories and enter them in the "Total Score" space provided.

SPIRITUAL GIFT	INVENTORY 1 SCORE	INVENTORY 2 SCORE	TOTAL SCORE
1. Administration			
2. Discernment			
3. Encouragement			
4. Faith			
5. Giving			
6. Healings			
7. Helps			
8. Interpretation			
9. Knowledge			
10. Leadership			
11. Mercy			
12. Miracles			
13. Prophecy			
14. Service			
15. Teaching			
16. Tongues			
17. Wisdom			

What Are Your Top Three Gifts?

Based on the highest scores in the table above, what are your top three spiritual gifts?

1. _____

2. _____

3. _____

Do the scores surprise you? As you read through the spiritual gift explanations before asking others to complete the inventory, did you identify with one or more of the gifts? Are they the same gifts in which you scored highest?

Remember, the purpose of knowing your spiritual gifts is not for your benefit but for the benefit of others. In other words, when you discover and develop your spiritual gifts within the context of your local church, you help to produce maturity and unity within the body. This is a powerful teaching that should not be overlooked. When there is a deficit in the number of church members using their God-given gifts, then the church cannot fully carry out its God-given mission.

Understand also that as we run our race of faith, our gifts may change somewhat. If you have taken several spiritual gift inventories before, you may have noticed that your top three gifts today are different from what they were before. This does not mean that you have lost a gift. It could mean that your life circumstance and experience have helped you to develop other gifts, especially in the context of your local church situation. It could also mean that with every inventory there is a chance for varying results. No inventory is an exact science. The key is to get a sense of your spiritual gifts, then develop them and use them for God's glory.

What Are the Results of Using Our Gifts?

As we develop and find ways to use our spiritual gifts, the Holy Spirit works within us to mold and shape us into the image of Christ. Through our obedience, we see that God faithfully carries out His promises. Peter encouraged the church with these words: *Each one should use whatever gift he has received to serve others, faithfully administering God's grace in its various forms* (1 Peter 4:10). From this verse, we learn that we participate in the administration of God's grace within the church when we faithfully use our gifts.

224

There are also two benefits to using our spiritual gifts—fulfillment and fruitfulness. When we use our gifts, we are fulfilled in the ministry for which God has gifted us. Our purpose, whether it is behind the scenes or in front of the church, is realized as we boldly follow the leadership of the Holy Spirit. We will also bear fruit that has a positive and powerful impact on the Kingdom, because the church will be more unified and mature in carrying out its mission as a result of our using the gifts God has given to us.

Which Church Ministries Need Your Spiritual Gifts?

Once you discover your spiritual gifts, then you have to find ways to use them. Now is the time to brainstorm how you can use your spiritual gifts within your local church. Take a moment and think of the ministries that need your help:

1. _____ 2. _____
3. _____ 4. _____

Now that you know your gifts and have taken a few moments to brainstorm how to employ them in the ministry of your church, we can look forward to the next leg of our marathon. As we round the bend and look ahead to the next mile marker, take a moment to memorize our next memory verse:

There is one body and one Spirit—just as you were called to one hope when you were called—one Lord, one faith, one baptism; one God and Father of all, who is over all and through all and in all.

(Ephesians 4:4–6)

The Race of Faith

The Sixth Leg: Serve

Jesus said that the greatest in the kingdom of heaven will be those who serve. True spiritual leadership is earned from a life of service to others. We are called by Christ to serve others—our family, our community, and the world. Service is the natural by-product of the grace-filled life of the Christian, and it is the chief means by which we accomplish God's mission.

Mile 20: God's Mission

Mile 21: Our Mission Field

Mile 22: Other Mission Opportunities

God's Mission

I remember the first time I learned about missionaries. I was quite impressed that these super-Christian people would leave the comfort and coziness of American culture to dedicate their lives to sharing the Good News with people they had never met. Then, I heard one of these missionaries tell our church that every Christian is called to be a missionary. That was a new concept to me. I furthermore came to understand that the term "missions" is not an accurate depiction of what the Bible teaches about God's plan. The Bible clearly teaches that God has one mission only—redeeming the world to Himself. This mile explains God's mission, which He has given to the church to accomplish.

What Is God's Mission?

The Bible declares, *faith by itself, if it is not accompanied by action, is dead* (James 2:17). This is an often misunderstood concept, as it may appear at first to contradict Paul's clear teaching that *it is by grace you have been saved, through faith—and this not from yourselves, it is the gift of God—not by works, so that no one can boast* (Ephesians 2:8–9). Instead of seeing these two truths in conflict with each other, it is best to think of these two statements as addressed to two different audiences.

Paul was addressing a group called the "Judaizers," who were a religious sect that taught that salvation included both faith in Jesus *and* keeping the rituals and ceremonies of the Jewish tradition. James, on the other hand, was addressing a group who had accepted Christ in faith but did not put their newfound faith into action. Therefore, it was as if the two men were standing back-to-back and fighting two different misapplications of the Good News. To clear the matter, Paul continued his statement that we are saved by grace alone with these words: *For we are God's workmanship, created in Christ Jesus to do good works, which God prepared in advance for us to do* (Ephesians 2:10). So, in summary, our works do not save us; rather, our salvation impels us to do good works.

The work of every Christian is the same. We have received Jesus's Christ Great Commission recorded in various ways in each of the four Gospels and also in Acts. The text most often quoted is the Great Commission statement in Matthew: *Therefore, go and make disciples of all nations, baptizing them in the name of the Father and of the Son and of the Holy Spirit, and teaching them to obey everything I have commanded you* (Matthew 28:19–20). Notice that it is a "commission," whereby we join God in His mission.

There is only one imperative in this commission: to make disciples! This commission is our mission. We are to make disciples. The picture that Jesus painted when He said, "Therefore, go...," is best rendered, "As you go..." That is, as we go about our daily life, we are to "make disciples." When you are at school, at work, at a sporting event, at the grocery store or coffee shop, on vacation or on a mission trip halfway around the globe—wherever you are—make disciples!

There are two components of making disciples. The first component of making disciples is baptizing new believers *in the name of the Father and of the Son and of the Holy Spirit*. Baptism is our identification with Christ in His death, burial, and resurrection. The new disciple is transformed from his or her old life of wandering in darkness to a new life of running in the light. Baptism is the outward symbol of the inward change that takes place when one first chooses Jesus Christ as Savior and Lord.

The second component of making disciples is *teaching them to obey everything I have commanded you*. Teaching occurs through expounding the Word of God and exampling the life of Jesus Christ. Jesus taught by word and by deed. We are called to emulate Jesus in word and deed. At mile 1, we explained this concept with these two components of being a disciple of Christ:

- Knowing, adhering to, and proclaiming His commands
- Knowing, adhering to, and portraying His actions

We can't know Jesus's commands and actions unless we devote ourselves to daily Bible study. We can't adhere to His commands and actions unless we align our will with His will. We can't proclaim His commands or portray His actions unless we take up our cross daily and follow Him. Teaching occurs when we consistently employ these components of discipleship.

Our mission, therefore, is the ongoing act of making disciples "of all nations." God's mission is the duty and privilege of every believer and every church to make disciples of every nation. The word, "evangelism," is an important term for new Christians. The word is derived from the Greek *euangelizo*, which literally means good message, alternatively called "Good News." Therefore, our mission is to serve others and to share the Good News: *God demonstrates his own love for us in this: While we were still sinners, Christ died for us* (Romans 5:8). That is the Good News!

Is God's Mission Found in the Old Testament?

The simple answer to this question is "Yes!" In fact, the Fall of Adam and Eve in the Garden of Eden formed the foundational need for God's mission. God did not have to give Adam and Eve the freedom to choose to obey God's commands but He did. Just imagine if God had created robots instead. As a parent, I much prefer that my children choose to obey me as a demonstration of their love for me than obey me simply because I have coerced them. This is the wisdom of God as Creator.

When Adam and Eve sinned, they immediately died spiritually and were separated from their holy Creator. Their one sin brought them spiritual and eventual physical death, but even more devastatingly, it separated them from God. However, God already knew humans would sin, and therefore He provided a solution. To Satan (appearing in the form of the serpent), God declared: *And I will put enmity between you and the woman, and between your offspring and hers; he will crush your head, and you will strike his heel* (Genesis 3:15).

The ultimate offspring of Eve referred to here is Jesus Christ, who did in fact crush Satan's head when He died on the cross, paying for our sin once and for all. This is known as the gospel before the Gospel. God had already set His redemption plan in motion!

Also, even before God called people to Himself, He wanted all people, everywhere, to know God's blessing. The calling of Abram (later renamed Abraham) expressed God's global plan to bless all nations through Abram's seed: *I will make you into a great nation and I will bless you; I will make your name great, and you will be a blessing. I will bless those who bless you, and whoever curses you I will curse; and all peoples on earth will be blessed through you* (Genesis 12:2–3).

Furthermore, the prophet Isaiah prophesied that God would send the Promised One to be a light for the gentiles: *I, the LORD, have called you in righteousness; I will take hold of your hand. I will keep you and will make you to be a covenant for the people and a light for the Gentiles, to open eyes that are blind, to free captives from prison and to release from the dungeon those who sit in darkness* (Isaiah 42:6–7).

In fact, Jesus quoted Isaiah 61, which contains a similar description of His mission, and declared that He is the fulfillment of this promise by God: *The Spirit of the Lord is on me, because he has anointed me to preach good news to the poor. He has sent me to proclaim freedom for the prisoners and recovery of sight for the blind, to release the oppressed, to proclaim the year of the Lord's favor* (Isaiah 61:1–2a; Luke 4:18–19). Jesus then rolled up the scroll of Isaiah and declared: *Today this scripture is fulfilled in your hearing* (Luke 4:21).

Yet another foreshadowing of God's mission in the Old Testament is in the book of Jonah, which details the story of a reluctant missionary. God called Jonah to go to Nineveh and preach, but Jonah, convinced that the people of Nineveh were too evil to receive God's forgiveness, refused to go. God disciplined Jonah by causing him to be swallowed by a great fish, and Jonah prayed to God and repented. God then caused the fish to vomit him upon dry ground. Jonah then went and preached to the people of Nineveh, and they repented and called upon the Lord. As a result of Jonah's work, God spared Nineveh.

We can peruse the Old Testament and repeatedly find the same message throughout: God desires that all men, from every nation, know about His great love for them and His great plan to save them. The scarlet thread that runs throughout the Old Testament is the promise of the coming Messiah to reconcile the world back to God. In fact, the Bible describes this act of reconciliation: *All this is from God, who reconciled us to himself through Christ and gave us the ministry of reconciliation: that God was reconciling the world to himself in Christ, not counting men's sins against them. And he has committed to us the message of reconciliation* (2 Corinthians 5:18–19). The message of reconciliation is the Good News!

Is God's Mission in the New Testament?

As we saw God's mission in our examination of the Old Testament, we also see God's mission expounded in the New Testament. The Gospel of John begins with the universal God sending His Son, Jesus, the universal Word, as the universal Savior for all humanity: *In the beginning was the Word, and the Word was with God, and the Word was God...Yet to all who received him, to those who believed in his name, he gave the right to become children of God* (John 1:1, 14). The beauty of this passage is that Jesus Christ is offered to all and that all who receive Him are adopted into God's family.

In all four Gospels, Jesus's primary purpose was to preach the Good News: *Jesus went through all the towns and villages, teaching in their synagogues, preaching the good news of the kingdom...* (Matthew 9:35). He consistently preached that *the harvest is plentiful but the workers are few* (Matthew 9:37; John 4:35). Also, Jesus repeated His Great Commission five times (Matthew 28:19–20; Mark 16:15; Luke 22:46–48; John 20:21; Acts 1:8). Obviously, since Jesus repeated this command so many times, it must have been extremely important. His Great Commission laid out the outward mission of the church—to be a witness to the world and to tell them the Good News that God loves the world and wants to save them from His wrath and judgment. His mission is our mission; therefore, every Christian is a missionary.

Let's be clear. Every born-again Christian is a minister *and* a missionary. Many Christians think of ministers as those few who lead the local church and missionaries as those few who go to some foreign country to share the Gospel. The Bible teaches that we are all to be ministers and missionaries. Ministry is the means by which we accomplish God's mission. We can look at the apostle Paul and the three elements of his calling from God.

1. **He was selected.** God called Paul while he was on the road to Damascus. God said of Paul, *This man is my chosen instrument to carry my name before the Gentiles and their kings and before the people of Israel* (Acts 9:15). God chose Paul to carry the name of Christ to the world.

2. **He was sent.** In his testimony before King Agrippa, Paul explained his commission from the risen Lord: *I will rescue you from your own people and from the Gentiles. I am sending you to them to open their eyes and turn them from darkness to light, and from the power of Satan to God, so that they may receive forgiveness of sins and a place among those who are sanctified by faith in me* (Acts 26:17–18). Jesus sent Paul to be a light for the gentiles and to show them His truth.

3. **He was sustained.** Throughout his four missionary journeys, Paul faced opposition, persecution, starvation, and isolation: *I have worked much harder, been in prison more frequently, been flogged more severely, and been exposed to death again and again. Five times I received from the Jews the forty lashes minus one. Three times I was beaten with rods, once I was stoned, three times I was shipwrecked, I spent a night and a day in the open sea, I have been constantly on the move. I have been in danger from rivers, in danger from bandits, in danger from my own countrymen, in danger from Gentiles; in danger in the city, in danger in the country, in danger at sea; and in danger from false brothers. I have labored and toiled and have often gone without sleep; I have known hunger and thirst and have often gone without food; I have been cold and naked. Besides everything else, I face daily the pressure of my concern for all the churches.* **(2 Corinthians 11:23–28)** Throughout his ministry, God sustained Paul.

When Paul pleaded with God three times to remove his thorn in the flesh, God's reply was simple: *My grace is sufficient for you, for my power is made perfect in weakness* (2 Corinthians 12:9). While there has been much speculation as to the identity of Paul's thorn, truthfully we cannot know. Perhaps that is the greatest teaching from this narrative. We all have thorns, and so we all can claim God's sufficient grace for our mission in life.

All of us who profess to be Christians are called to be missionaries; God selects, sends, and sustains us in that calling. Whether we are called by God to go across the street or across the globe, we are all called. This is the mystery of God's wisdom—to use His church, filled with His Holy Spirit, to testify to the world of His unconditional love and forgiveness, which is offered only through His Son Jesus Christ!

Where Is God's Mission Accomplished?

We will discuss the different ways to accomplish God's mission in great detail over the course of the next two miles, but it is important at this point to establish that God's mission must take place at every geographic level: local, regional, national, and global. We find this pattern in Jesus's Great Commission statement in Acts: *You will be my witnesses in Jerusalem, and in all Judea and Samaria, and to the ends of the earth* (Acts 1:8).

The apostles' local city was Jerusalem. Jerusalem was located in the region of Judea. Samaria was an adjacent region within the nation of Israel. The ends of the earth included the rest of the word outside the nation of Israel. What is your Jerusalem? What is your Judea? What is your Samaria? What is your world?

Notice also that the commission's focus begins close and spreads outward like ripples in a pond. There is a strategic element to Christ's order. Our spheres of influence begin where we are and branch outward. This is why our missionary work begins at home—with our family, friends, neighbors, classmates, and coworkers.

Our missionary work then extends to those we don't know but who need to hear the Good News. Christian efforts in disaster relief, education, church planting, Bible translation and distribution, and counseling are all designed to establish a platform of service in order to introduce the Gospel message to the world. When missionary projects adhere to the biblical model and mandate, they result in the creation of disciples—the addition of worshipers to God's Kingdom from *every nation, tribe, people and language* (Revelation 7:9).

How Can We Accomplish God's Mission?

Being an everyday missionary requires intentionality. We must determine in our mind, heart, and will to be obedient to Jesus Christ. Obedience to Christ is to carry out His Great Commission – making disciples of all nations. Therefore, if we desire to please our Savior and Lord, then we must make a habit of being His witness wherever we are. To help us do this, just remember the acrostic PLANT.

> ⇨ **P**ray for opportunities to share your faith. The apostle Paul constantly prayed for a door to be opened to the Gospel: *And pray for us, too, that God may open a door for our message, so that we may proclaim the mystery of Christ…* (Colossians 4:3).

> ⇨ **L**ook where God is working. A common misunderstanding in the Christian life is that we choose a ministry or mission and expect God to join us in that effort. By contrast, the Bible teaches that we are to look for where God is working and join Him in that work: *it is God who works in you to will and to act according to his good purpose* (Philippians 2:13).

> ⇨ **A**sk people questions. The only way to truly know another person's understanding of God, sin, and salvation is to

ask. Paul expressed the need to ask questions in order to gain a hearing. Asking questions tells others we care about and are interested in them: *Be wise in the way you act toward outsiders; make the most of every opportunity* (Colossians 4:5).

⇨ Nurture your relationships with others. The Gospel is offensive enough, so we do not need to be offensive or pushy with others. We are to let His Word be our only word to them: *Let your conversation be always full of grace, seasoned with salt, so that you may know how to answer everyone* (Colossians 4:6).

⇨ Tell them about your relationship with Christ. Peter emphasized the importance of sharing the reason for the faith we profess: *Always be prepared to give an answer to everyone who asks you to give the reason for the hope that you have. But do this with gentleness and respect* (1 Peter 3:15).

Our faith drives our ministry, and our ministry drives our mission, which is to proclaim the Good News to all nations. This is the Great Commission of Jesus Christ. Now that we have a basic understanding of what God's mission is all about, we can make this aspect of serving more practical by looking at our mission field. But first, let's take a moment to memorize our next memory verse:

Then Jesus came to them and said, "All authority in heaven and on earth has been given to me. Therefore go and make disciples of all nations, baptizing them in the name of the Father and of the Son and of the Holy Spirit, and teaching them to obey everything I have commanded you. And surely I am with you always, to the very end of the age."

(Matthew 28:18–20)

Our Mission Field

I used to teach a Bible study class a long time ago. I noticed that a woman would attend but her husband stayed at home. When I inquired, she explained that he did not feel comfortable coming because his family owned a local liquor store. I asked if I could meet him for lunch. He agreed, and we had a great lunch and conversation. He expressed that he felt conflicted between his work and going to church. I told him flatly, "That's nonsense." I told him that Jesus welcomes every person, regardless of occupation or past. Then I said that maybe God will use him to witness to his customers, a group of people who would probably never darken the doors of the church. He then took the step of faith and he has been a devoted follower of Jesus Christ ever since. He still works at the liquor store, sowing seeds of the Gospel! This mile describes our mission field and how we can impact it for Christ.

What Is Our Mission Field?

I introduced the concept of geographic missions in the previous mile. Now we will delve a little more deeply into how we develop and execute strategies to impact our communities for Christ. It is no accident that you live where you do. This is God's providence at work. When I graduated from college, I found myself relocating to Charleston, South Carolina. I knew virtually nothing about the city, and yet, twenty-five years later, I call it my home. I sometimes wonder why God brought me here, but I quickly embrace the fact that I am here and that God wants me to get busy doing His work.

Wherever you are right now is your mission field! God wants us to get busy. Jesus took notice of the woman at the well and changed her life. He not only changed her life, but she then became a powerful witness that changed other people's lives as well. It was like a domino effect. The woman met Jesus and received Him as the Messiah; then she ran into town and told everyone she met about Him. John describes the result of her witnessing: *Many of the Samaritans from that town believed in him because of the woman's testimony...* (John 4:39). Jesus told His disciples to *open your eyes and look at the fields! They are ripe for harvest* (John 4:35). In the same way, we are to open our eyes and look at our mission field.

Think about your family, friends, neighbors, coworkers, classmates, and community. If you were to make a list of all the people you know, how many people would that be? How many contacts do you have in your address book? Where are they spiritually in relationship to God? When you boil it all down, the Gospel is meant to be shared personally and boldly. It is a deeply personal message and one that many never hear from those closest to them.

Have you ever wondered why God has brought certain people into your life? Think back to the circumstances that brought you into a relationship with each of your closest friends. When is the last time you had a spiritual conversation with them? Are all your friends

Christians? If so, have you thought about ways to connect with others who are not yet members of God's Kingdom?

It is easy to conclude that we are too busy or that we are too uncomfortable to devote time to the seemingly long and awkward process of introducing Jesus to other people. We have many fears to justify our lack of engagement in the Great Commission. First, some of us are afraid of being rejected or even ridiculed by our friends and acquaintances. Second, others of us are not confident about our biblical knowledge and are afraid of handling questions or objections. Third, still others of us believe our lives do not measure up enough to tell others about Jesus.

The truth is that our testimony is as simple as telling our story and His story. We discussed this topic at length back at mile 10. The goal of God's mission is to combine our service to others with the message of Jesus. Our service may be targeted to meet temporal, physical, and emotional needs, but our witnessing is targeted to meet people's eternal, spiritual needs. Missionary endeavors combine both service and witnessing to profoundly impact the world.

What Does Our Mission Field Look Like?

Every city or town can be divided into three major sectors: public, private, and social. The public sector includes services such as governmental departments, police and fire departments, public schools, military, roads and transportation, parks and recreation, and some healthcare and postal services. The private sector includes retail and private businesses, banking, healthcare, legal firms, construction, and real estate. The social sector includes religion, arts and entertainment, athletics, politics, nonprofits, and volunteer organizations. In which of these three sectors do you work? How can your church make a positive impact on these three sectors?

The church is called by Christ to make an impact on every segment of its community. When even one believer enters one of these sectors, the church can have an influence on that sector. The influence could be negative, nonexistent, or positive. This is why our witnessing is so significant.

Jesus said: *You are the light of the world. A city on a hill cannot be hidden. Neither do people light a lamp and put it under a bowl. Instead they put it on its stand, and it gives light to everyone in the house. In the same way, let your light shine before men, that they may see your good deeds and praise your Father in heaven* (Matthew 5:14–16). Jesus boldly declared us as the "light of the world." This statement establishes the following truths: the world is in darkness; Satan is evil; and man's sinful nature is prone to do evil rather than good. As Paul attested: *The god of this age has blinded the minds of unbelievers, so that they cannot see the light of the gospel of the glory of Christ, who is the image of God* (2 Corinthians 4:4). Every Christian and every church must make it our mission to dispel the darkness by being the light that Christ made us through His salvation.

How Can We Reach Our Community?

In addition to thinking strategically about how to make an impact on the three sectors of society, we can also build relational networks within our social circles. Just think about all the ways in which you come into contact with other people. For example, you could have an eternal impact on your workplace by hosting a prayer group or Bible study during lunch hour or after work. You could also go with your coworkers to happy hour and form stronger bonds in that venue; perhaps you could even offer to be the designated driver for others. This may seem like a forbidden practice for the Christian, but based on the life of Jesus portrayed in the Gospels, we can safely assume that Jesus would be right there with you.

Students could have a profound influence on their peers in school. Teenagers are a very difficult demographic to reach, primarily because of all the opposing influences that pervade their lives.

With all the social media deluging this demographic, it seems like it would be impossible to have any positive impact. One study estimated that teenagers spend more than fifty-three hours per week using media such as television, music, phones, computers, and movies.[16] Furthermore, Christians are often stigmatized in popular culture, which can cause young Christians to stay quiet, all the while being subtly estranged from their weekend church activities.

While there have been a plethora of books written about the declining influence of Christianity on our teenagers and the resulting dropout rate when they get their driver's licenses and/or go to college, the answer to this dilemma is truly quite simple and biblical:

> *Love the LORD your God with all your heart and with all your soul and with all your strength. These commandments that I give you today are to be upon your hearts. Impress them on your children. Talk about them when you sit at home and when you walk along the road, when you lie down and when you get up. Tie them as symbols on your hands and bind them on your foreheads. Write them on the doorframes of your houses and on your gates.*
>
> **(Deuteronomy 6:5–9)**

Faith begins with the parents. If we truly love God with every fiber of our being, then we will know God's commandments and teach them to our children. Our teaching must be all-encompassing—we must model godly living and mold our children into the purpose for which God created them. Notice that this text includes the four extreme points in a child's life: at home, away from home, asleep, and awake. The point is that God commands us to teach our children all the time and to take whatever steps necessary, even tying symbols to our hands, to remind ourselves of the high calling of producing godly offspring.

---

16   *Generation M2: Media in the Lives of 8- to 18-Year-Olds*, given at a forum in Washington, DC, January 20, 2010, http://www.kff.org/entmedia/mh012010pkg.cfm

Sadly, most parents (myself included) too often expose ourselves, and therefore our families, to the negative influences of this world. We can sit back and blame the culture, but we must own the fact that we play our part in feeding the culture. The truth is that if everyone made the decision to not watch a particular channel or show on television, that show or channel would cease to exist. Interestingly, our greatest influence on the world begins in our own homes. Regardless of what everyone else does, the best way to make a difference is to raise the next generation to revere God and delight in His law. This is certainly easier said than done, but it begins with a decision. Our mission field begins at home!

Another relational network consists of athletic teams or the arts. Whether you are an adult involved in club sports within your school or city or you are part of an art class or hobby group, you can have a positive impact for the Kingdom of God, even more so if you choose to participate in a secular sport/activity as opposed to a church league. Maybe your children are involved in sports or other activities. In every case, the group of people (fellow teammates, students, parents, etc.) with whom you interact are all created in God's image, and God has placed us in an excellent position to share God's love in tangible ways. How many conversations can you have during the course of a season? How many of those conversations can result in a spiritual discussion that literally transforms a life? Our mission field can be an art class or a soccer field, a basketball court or the stands. The key is that if we take Christ's Great Commission seriously, we will be intentional about introducing Jesus to those in our world.

Still another relational network is your neighborhood. How many of your neighbors do you actually know? We live in such a hustle-bustle world that we miss opportunities to develop meaningful relationships with the people who live in our immediate vicinity. If every Christian made it her goal to meet a new neighbor every week, consider the impact. Is there some kind of act of service that would show the kindness of Jesus to our community? What if the church worked together with a local community or neighborhood to host a cookout? Again, our intentionality is the key ingredient to our mission's impact.

There are so many more relational networks within our reach. How often do we visit fitness clubs, coffee shops, parks, stores, banks, hairdressers/barber shops, nail salons, etc? The list could go on, but the point remains the same. God created us for relationships. Our relationship with Him has been broken by our sin nature, but for those of us who have accepted the salvation offered by Jesus Christ, we are no longer enemies of God but His children. Our mission from our Savior is simply to see our earthly relationships as God-given opportunities to offer others that same restored relationship with God that we now enjoy. To follow that mission on a daily basis requires us to be intentional in our actions. We are called to invest and invite!

You may be asking how you can engage people in your relational networks. Our mission is to engage others in conversation in order to establish a relationship. Sadly, some people have been confronted too many times by well-meaning Christians who appear to have only one agenda—to save sinners from hell.

In order to be successful, we must act with the right motive as well as the right method. The first imperative to our witnessing is authenticity. The second imperative is compassion. Without authenticity and compassion, we will never truly show Christ to the world. Jesus's conversations with people always began by establishing common ground before transitioning from the physical world to the spiritual. Jesus always ended his conversations by sharing spiritual truth.

How can we establish common ground? Most of us have heard the acrostic FORM:

> Family
> Occupation
> Recreation
> Message

Nonthreatening conversations can begin with family and move to occupation and recreation. The message part of this acrostic directs us to move our conversation to the Good News about Jesus Christ. The key to engaging others in conversation is to be truly interested in learning about them—their experiences, worldview, and motivations. In other words, what makes that person tick? Where is that person in relationship to God? Over time, we should be able to learn enough about the other person to be able to pray for them specifically.

In the first few centuries of the church, people used the Greek word *icthus* ("fish") to identify themselves and others as Christians. One person would form one half of the fish in the sand, and if the other person was a fellow believer, he or she would complete the sign. This greeting ensured a measure of protection against the brutal persecution Christians faced. We do not have this threat today, but the point is still valid. We should make it known to others early on in our conversations that we are Christians. This helps to establish authenticity and opens up the opportunity to build strong relationships with others to whom God has called us to bear witness.

What Are the Three Phases of Being a Missionary?

As we contemplate what it means to be a missionary we can use the metaphor of spreading good to our world: good deeds, goodwill, and the Good News. Paul's missionary trip to Athens provides us with a great example to follow. The Greeks were always eager to learn of new ideas and philosophies. Paul took the opportunity to establish common ground and then transition to the Gospel during a meeting of the Areopagus: *Men of Athens! I see that in every way you are very religious. For as I walked around and looked carefully at your objects of worship, I even found an altar with this inscription: TO AN UNKNOWN GOD. Now what you worship as something unknown I am going to proclaim to you* (Acts 17:22b–23).

Notice Paul's good deeds. First, he actually went to the people. We cannot overlook or minimize the importance of this first step in establishing a connection. Can you imagine a Jew from Tarsus engaging a throng of intelligent and religious men in the heart of the Greek culture? Such an act required a great deal of humility and courage. Paul could have come up with any number of excuses to not take this step in being missional, but He considered obedience to Christ to be of prime importance. He once said to the Corinthian church: *Woe to me if I do not preach the gospel!* (1 Corinthians 9:16). His going to Athens was a good deed.

Second, Paul shared goodwill. That is, he complimented the gathering on their religiosity, thus establishing common ground based on religion. This is a critical step in building a relationship with others. We must find out what excites them. Paul could tell that they considered religion to be a very important aspect of their society. Paul used his own observations to build the transition to the Gospel. He noticed the altar erected to the unknown god. In just one sentence, Paul turned the conversation from many gods to the one, true God.

Third, Paul presented the Good News. He gained a hearing with the group in Athens because He performed a good deed and offered goodwill. He now had the platform to present the Good News: *What you worship as something unknown I am going to proclaim to you.* He was knowledgeable and intentional. In the verses that follow, Paul laid out the Gospel, ending with the fact of the resurrection of Jesus Christ (Acts 17:31). When we are convinced of the truth of the Gospel message, then we are convincing to others.

Are you persuaded? Paul declared to his protégé Timothy: *Yet I am not ashamed, because I know whom I have believed, and am convinced that he is able to guard what I have entrusted to him for that day* (2 Timothy 1:12). We should never be ashamed of the Gospel. We must continually keep in mind that it is the Spirit's work to convict and convince others of their need for a Savior. He simply uses us as His instruments to bear testimony to His goodness.

It is important to note that when Paul presented the Gospel to the men of Athens, he encountered three types of responses: *When they heard about the resurrection of the dead, some of them sneered, but others said, "We want to hear you again on this subject." At that, Paul left the Council. A few men became followers of Paul and believed* (Acts 17:32–34a). So it is with every missionary as we share the Gospel. Some will sneer at us, some will ask for more information, and some will believe. We must always remember that our efforts to serve others with the love of Jesus Christ should not be based on immediate results but instead on the principle that we are planting seeds for the future.

We will delve into this topic even more over the next several miles, but I hope that you now have a better understanding of your mission field and how God will use you intentionally to make a positive, eternal impact upon your world. As we approach the next mile marker, let us take a moment and commit to memory our next memory verse:

But the Counselor, the Holy Spirit, whom the Father will send in my name, will teach you all things and will remind you of everything I have said to you.

(John 14:26)

Other Mission Opportunities

Gas prices affect nearly everyone. One summer not too long ago, the prices had spiked so high that they had fundamentally changed the way people used their cars. A member of our church came up with a way for our church to make an immediate, positive impact on our community. He suggested that we do a "gas buy-down." So, for an hour on three consecutive Saturday afternoons, a group of volunteers from our church stood out by the pumps of the local gas station and informed customers that their per gallon price was now 25 cents less than what was on the sign. Most people were skeptical and confused, but a few of them showed up to church the following Sunday! They were touched by the creative generosity of their local church. This mile offers practical ways to get involved in God's worldwide mission.

What Other Mission Opportunities Are There?

At mile 20, we quoted Jesus's Great Commission statement from Acts. We will repeat it here: *But you will receive power when the Holy Spirit comes on you; and you will be my witnesses in Jerusalem, and in all Judea and Samaria, and to the ends of the earth* (Acts 1:8). Jesus not only wanted His disciples to be witnesses in Jerusalem but also Judea, Samaria, and the ends of the earth. This text is the basis for spreading the Gospel message throughout the world in order to give every people group the opportunity to receive salvation.

Therefore, in addition to our everyday mission fields of home, work, school, neighborhood, coffee shops, and a number of other relational networks, God commanded the church to spread His message worldwide. So, our "Judea" is our region, and our "Samaria" is our nation, and "the ends of the earth" is the world. Many Christians are called by God to become full-time missionaries in some region of the world. Many more Christians take the step of faith in becoming part of a mission team serving for a definitive period of time in any of those three regions.

This mile will help you to take that step of faith. This mile is more of a practicum to drive you to obey the Great Commission. Maybe you can get involved in a community impact event your church is planning. Maybe there is an opportunity for you to participate in a mission trip to some other region in the United States. Maybe there is an opportunity for you to leave our nation and serve on a mission team in some other continent. All of these endeavors must be bathed in prayer and preparation, but for now, let's begin the process of thinking beyond our world and taking on a more global perspective.

In the book of Acts, we read a story about how Philip, an early deacon of the church and later a pastor in Samaria, was called by God to head south and meet up with an Ethiopian eunuch on his way home to Africa (Acts 6:5; 8:4–8). By all accounts, Philip's ministry in Samaria was tremendously successful. So why did God pull him away and send him down to Gaza to meet with this one man? The story gives us our answer. The Ethiopian eunuch was reading Isaiah 53, and when Philip joined him, the eunuch asked him about the passage.

What happens next is the quintessential purpose of missions: *Then Philip began with that very passage of Scripture and told him the good news about Jesus* (Acts 8:35). The fact that Philip began with that very passage was in a sense the common ground we look to establish. It was also important for Philip to know the passage well enough to be able to explain it and ultimately to show the eunuch the truth about Jesus Christ. The outcome of this meeting was that the eunuch believed and was baptized. And because Philip obediently left Samaria to share the Good News with this one man, the entire Gospel spread to the African continent.

Whether we are called to go across the street or to Africa is up to God. Our obedience to that call is up to us. Where would you be willing to go if God called you? What is holding you back from taking that leap of faith to share the Good News with people who may not speak your language or understand your culture? When God told Abraham that all nations would be blessed through him (Genesis 12:3), perhaps not even Abraham had any idea how far God's love would reach beyond the desert of Iraq.

How Can We Become More Active in Our Community?

The very first phrase of Jesus's Great Commission is "Go..." As we have already discussed, the rendering of that word implies "As you go..." Many churches today are much more about enticing people to *come*. But that is not the commission of the Christian church. Jesus continually taught that the church is to be on the offensive, on the move, out in the community, heralding the message of salvation.

What can the church do to impact its community? There are a number of regular service projects that can have a very positive impact. Some examples might include serving food to the homeless and hungry; providing clothes and supplies to the needy; offering after-school tutoring; visiting nursing homes, assisted living centers, or prisons; planning neighborhood cookouts; handing out free bottled water or ice cream in parks; and hosting community movie nights. All of these activities are designed to establish common ground with a certain sector of society.

The best way for churches to have a sustained impact on their communities is to become known as the church that meets needs—physical, emotional, and, ultimately, spiritual. When people sense that the church cares enough to take care of their physical or emotional needs, and when they discover over time that there are no strings attached, then they will, over time, open up to the church's message. It may not even be your church that ultimately delivers the saving message of Christ to those you serve, and that is perfectly okay.

How often do we see this dynamic play out in Scripture? Whether it was the paralytic, the blind man, the demon-possessed man, the sick woman, the man with leprosy, the crippled woman, the woman at the well, the four thousand, or the five thousand, Jesus established His platform by meeting people's most basic needs. Jesus's sermons and parables served to deliver the message of hope to those who were physically or mentally sick, but who had never considered how sick they were spiritually. The life of Christ provides the church with guidelines for transitioning conversation from the physical to the spiritual, from the temporal to the eternal.

Our challenge is to invest and invite. We must invest into the lives of others—those in our home, neighborhood, community, and city. Most of us would say we don't have the time to make that kind of commitment. If that is you, then answer these hard questions. What could you give up doing today to free up one hour? That extra hour of sleep in the morning? That television show you just watched because it happened to be on? That idle hour of browsing social media? That video game, which lures you to the next level? In that extra hour a day, you could:

- Take a walk around your community and pray for the people in each house as you pass by.
- Strike up a conversation with your neighbor using FORM (Family, Occupation, Recreation, and Message).
- Take your son or daughter to get an ice cream and just talk about what God is doing in your life and theirs.
- Stop by on your way home from work to visit the elderly at a local nursing home.
- Stop at a drive-through and get a burger for the man with the cardboard sign.
- Ask your server how you can pray for her.
- Buy five paperback Bibles and hand them out on a local college campus.
- Take your dog to the dog park and make a new friend.

The different ways you can use that one hour are limitless. It takes only creativity and intentionality. The good news for Christians is that our God is never short on creativity. He is the author of creativity, and so all we have to do is ask Him to guide us.

Why Should We Become Involved in National and International Missions?

Much of the Christian race is about stepping outside our comfort zone. Taking a national and/or an international mission trip stretches us so we can see the bigger picture of the Christian movement. Most people report that these mission trips have changed their lives. What about you? Have you ever served on a mission team? If so, did the experience change your life? If not, do you think you would be open to taking that next step in your faith journey?

There are at least five reasons we should take mission trips.

1. We get to participate in what God is doing in other parts of the world. Paul and Barnabas were able to share with the apostles in Jerusalem how God was working in other areas: *The church sent them on their way, and as they traveled through Phoenicia and Samaria, they told how the Gentiles had been converted. This news made all the brothers very glad* (Acts 15:3). Local churches can be so encouraged when they hear how God is working in other parts of the world.

2. We gain a greater appreciation for how big our God is. Traveling halfway around the globe and finding a group of people from a vastly different culture worshiping the same God is an awesome experience. We recognize that the God of the universe has revealed Himself to the world, and that His offer of salvation is available to all people, no matter their race, gender, education, cultural background, financial status, or social class. Paul declared this truth when he said, *There is neither Jew nor Greek, slave nor free, male nor female, for you are all one in Christ Jesus* (Galatians 3:28).

3. Our conventions and traditions are challenged, which can result in increased maturity. I once attended a traditional church that showed an International Missions video of a worship service in Africa. Those African worshipers were smiling, singing, and dancing to handmade drums. When the video was over, the congregation applauded. The irony was that this congregation would not allow drums in their worship service! Mission trips help us to evaluate and differentiate God's ways of telling His story from man's ways. Paul said, *I have become all things to all men so that by all possible means I might save some* (1

Corinthians 9:22b). It is important to note that Paul was not changing or diluting the message of the cross, but instead taking whatever steps necessary to gain a hearing with those to whom God called him to bear witness.

4. We experience great joy in seeing other lives impacted by our efforts to share the love of Christ. One of the most powerful responses from others, especially those in third world nations, is to be blown away by the fact that some group of people who does not know them would take the time and spend the money to come and minister to them! I will never forget the sense of joy I felt as I went from hospital room to hospital room in a very poor country, seeing literal tears well up in the eyes of those who had been ill for months and even years. Despite their physical infirmities, they were grateful to hear about the hope of eternal healing found in Jesus Christ.

5. Our mission activities build the capacity to reach even deeper into the unreached areas of our world. In other words, as more and more believers devote time, money, and ministry resources to making a mission trip or trips, the penetration of the Gospel allows for greater efforts beyond those regions. Paul attested this truth to the Corinthian church: *Our hope is that, as your faith continues to grow, our area of activity among you will greatly expand, so that we can preach the gospel in the regions beyond you* (2 Corinthians 10:15–16). When we are obedient to the call of God to *go into all the world and preach the good news to all creation,* then the return of Jesus Christ draws ever closer (Mark 16:15).

How Can We Prepare for a Mission Trip?

If you have never been on a mission trip before, there are some very specific ways to prepare yourself. As you can imagine, a trip like this can be life-changing, but it can also be very stressful. After all, you are not only going to a new place but you are perhaps going with a group of people you may or may not know all that well. Moreover, you are about to be thrust into unchartered waters that may cause you discomfort. Finally, mission trips require spiritual, emotional, physical, and financial preparations. How can you approach this life-changing endeavor in a way that best honors God?

First, you must pray. Prayer is critical to God's work. You are to pray for clarity in your call to go in the first place. If your motives are not pure, you most probably will experience a lot of fatigue and frustration. Once you know that God has called you to join a mission team, you can then pray boldly for His protection, provision, and purpose.

Second, you must study. This includes studying God's Word as well as the culture of the new place. Study God's Word to know the plan of salvation. You must be prepared to give an answer for the hope you have in Christ. This is not only the mission team leader's responsibility, but it is the responsibility of every member. Also, study God's Word to become bolstered by the awesome power of God displayed throughout Scripture as His children obeyed His call to go out into the world. In addition to studying God's Word, you can mentally and spiritually prepare yourself by studying the culture. A mission team can be so much more effective if it understands beforehand the customs, culture, and the language of the people to whom they are going to serve and bear witness. This acclimation is critical to getting the most accomplished in a relatively short period of time.

Third, you usually need to raise financial and prayer support. This is oftentimes one of the hardest things to do, for obvious reasons. It bears mentioning that this aspect of the trip can be and usually is a tremendous blessing for those who are a part of the process. You may know people who cannot physically go themselves but who want to be a tangible support to you as you go. Do not underestimate the generosity of God's people. In fact, God's resources are limitless. Therefore, if you are called to go, the money will be taken care of supernaturally in ways that only God could accomplish. Just be careful not to let the fundraising aspect of the mission trip overtake its real purpose. This can dampen the team's spirit, and that is never a good thing. Trust God and He will provide.

Fourth, you must plan. Most of the time, this element of preparation is done in the context of the larger mission team, but you should also have personal goals as well. The key to planning is to understand that you are part of a larger group, that your group is part of a mission project in the region to which you are going, and that that mission project is probably a part of a larger mission strategy. Therefore, every defined mission trip should have specific goals to support the local contacts in the mission field. Without proper planning, mission teams can become more of a burden than a help to the local community. Planning establishes specific objectives and ways the team can drive its mission forward.

Serving others with the love of Jesus Christ begins in the church when we use our spiritual gifts to edify and unify the body of Christ. Serving others then moves to our local mission field—where we live, work, and play. Our impact on our local community increases as we intentionally and compassionately meet people's needs. Serving others then moves beyond our local mission field to other regions and nations. This work is far-reaching and obedient to the clarion call of Christ—to make disciples of all nations.

We have now completed the sixth leg in our marathon. We gain a kick in our step as we begin the final leg; a mere 4.2 miles remain in our race of faith. As we pass mile marker 22, let's take a moment to reflect on our next memory verse:

Then I heard the voice of the Lord saying, Whom shall I send? And who will go for us? And I said, Here am I. Send me!

(Isaiah 6:8)

The Race of Faith

The Seventh Leg: Share

Jesus came to *seek and to save that which is lost.* (Luke 19:10) His mission is our mission. Not only are we to demonstrate a life of sharing the Gospel, but we are also to lead others to proclaim the Good News as well. The Kingdom of God cannot advance without our sowing the seeds of Christ's love to a world that is so desperately searching for hope!

Mile 23: Sharing Our Faith

Mile 24: Spiritual Mentorship

Mile 25: Bible Study Leadership

Mile 26: Influencing Our World

Sharing Our Faith

While working in her yard one Saturday afternoon, Stacy had observed her next-door neighbor—a harried Mom of three children between the ages of three and eight—come to the brink of losing it. Prompted by the Holy Spirit, Stacy (never one to interfere) cautiously approached the young mother. "It seems like you need a break! I will be glad to watch your kids while you go upstairs and take a nice long nap or bath." The mother immediately broke down in tears, explaining all the stress and strain she was under. After she unloaded, she accepted the offer and came back outside an hour later, refreshed and rejuvenated. Knowing that Stacy was a Christian, the mother asked her if she would come over sometime to talk about her faith. Uneasy about sharing her faith, Stacy reluctantly agreed to meet with her the next afternoon. The next morning, Stacy prayed for guidance and then there was a knock on her door. It was her neighbor, asking if it was okay to invite eight of her friends over to hear about Jesus as well. Though overwhelmed, Stacy put it in God's hands and witnessed a miracle—three women entered eternal life that afternoon, all because one woman saw a need and met it! This mile offers practical steps to sharing your faith.

Why Do We Need to Share Our Faith?

We have covered the first six legs of our marathon: follow, invest, train, nurture, equip, and serve. The final leg is *Share*. We share the Good News with others who then make the decision to become followers and begin their own race of faith. Therefore, the process is never-ending, and this is why the FITNESS path is a circle in the triangle above. Once we become followers, we are called to introduce others to Jesus Christ so that they, too, can become followers. Our goal should be to get to heaven and to take as many others with us as possible.

This discipline is very difficult for many Christians, whether they have been Christians for a short period or for most of their lives. A few miles back, we discussed the reasons why many do not actively share their faith. In review, we are sometimes afraid of rejection or ridicule; we lack confidence in our ability to convey biblical truth; or we feel that our lives don't measure up to the expected behavior of a Christian. In this mile, we will discuss the reasons we must share our faith.

1. **Obedience.** We are to share our faith in order to be obedient to Jesus Christ. Jesus said, *Go into all the world and preach the good news to all creation* (Mark 16:15). Jesus did not suggest or encourage this practice; He commanded it. This has been God's plan from the beginning. In fact, our obedience to His Great Commission appears to have some bearing on when Christ returns. In His answer to His disciples' question about His Second Coming, Jesus said, *And this gospel of the kingdom will be preached in the whole world as a testimony to all nations, and then the end will come* (Matthew 24:14). We do not know when and exactly how this preaching to all nations happens, but Jesus certainly emphasized the significance of preaching the Gospel to all nations.

2. **Love for Christ.** We share our faith because our witnessing testifies to our love for Christ. Countless nonbelievers have been disappointed by those of us who say we believe in an actual hell and yet refuse to demonstrate our love for Christ by sharing the Good News with them. Jesus said: *Whoever acknowledges me before men, I will also acknowledge him before my Father in heaven. But whoever disowns me before men, I will disown him before my Father in heaven* (Matthew 10:32–33). When we share our faith, we actively acknowledge Jesus as the world's Savior.

3. **Love for Others.** We share our faith because God desires that everyone be saved. Peter declared God's heart this way: *The Lord is not slow in keeping his promise, as some understand slowness. He is patient with you, not wanting anyone to perish, but everyone to come to repentance* (2 Peter 3:9). Paul shared the same truth about God: *This is good, and pleases God our Savior, who wants all men to be saved and to come to a knowledge of the truth* (2 Timothy 4:3–4). Since we are God's children, then we will certainly share God's desire. He wanted all men to become saved, and He gave us the privilege and the responsibility to carry out that task.

What Are the Steps to Sharing Our Faith?

Since sharing our faith demonstrates our obedience to Christ, our love of Christ, and our love for other people, then we should plan how to do it. If we each take this process seriously, then we can make a profound impact upon the lives of so many other people all over the world. Many people know of the informal theory of six degrees of separation, meaning that each of us is approximately six steps away, by way of introduction, from any other person on earth. Therefore, through a series of introductions, any person can know any other person on earth. So, with that in mind, let's correlate that theory with these six steps of sharing our faith:

1. **Prepare:** Pray, study, and look for opportunities to share.
2. **Prompt:** Use prompting questions or comments to direct the conversation to spiritual topics.
3. **Present:** Clearly present the Gospel.
4. **Persuade:** Answer any questions or objections.
5. **Pray:** Pray that the Holy Spirit will convict and convince the person of the Gospel truth.
6. **Promise:** Promise to follow up with the person.

This process may take one hour or it may take years. The key to witnessing is to be authentic and compassionate. Be faithful to the process, but trust the Holy Spirit for the results. Someone else may reap the crop from which your seed is sewn, and you may reap the crop from someone else's witnessing. As Jesus pointed out to His disciples, we are always on the lookout for the harvest:

> *Do you not say, Four months more and then the harvest? I tell you, open your eyes and look at the fields! They are ripe for harvest. Even now the reaper draws his wages, even now he harvests the crop for eternal life, so that the sower and the reaper may be glad together. Thus the saying 'One sows and another reaps' is true. I sent you to reap what you have not worked for. Others have done the hard work, and you have reaped the benefits of their labor.*
>
> **(John 4:35–38)**

It may be helpful to think of faith as a spectrum; everyone in the world is at some place along this spectrum. For example, Jim may be anywhere from -10 to +10. Let's assume the person who first trusts in Christ has moved from 0 to +1. Then every step of growth toward Christian maturity increases from +1 to +10. Now, imagine Jim meeting Steve who is at -10. Steve is essentially an atheist, someone who does not believe God exists. Once Jim exposes Steve to the love of Christ either in word or deed, Steve may move to -9. However, he is still far from ever making the decision to follow Jesus. And Jim was not unsuccessful in his witnessing. Instead, even though Steve was not immediately born-again, Jim nevertheless made a positive impact on him. This is what happens when Christians sow seeds of the Gospel.

Imagine what would happen if all Christians in your city shared their faith consistently. It would be an amazing movement toward God. The key is to remember that while we are instruments of God's grace to others, God is the One who regenerates the people to whom we witness: *What, after all, is Apollos? And what is Paul? Only servants, through whom you came to believe—as the Lord has assigned to each his task. I planted the seed, Apollos watered it, but God made it grow. So neither he who plants nor he who waters is anything, but only God, who makes things grow* (1 Corinthians 3:5–7).

In summary, we actively fulfill God's commandment to share our faith when we prepare our hearts and minds; look for ways to prompt spiritual discussions with others; present the Gospel; persuade others of the Gospel's truth; pray with or for others; and promise to follow up. Once we have prepared to share our faith, we must then take steps to prompt spiritual conversations.

How Do We Prompt Spiritual Conversations?

We should begin every day by asking God to give us opportunities to share our faith that day. One of my favorite sayings is, "You get good at what you do." Whether it is riding a bike, learning to play the piano, shooting foul shots, or sharing your faith—it all takes practice. The more we do any of these activities, the better we become. Therefore, we must determine to look for opportunities to prompt spiritual discussions.

Let's assume Sharon sees you on Monday morning and asks, "How was your weekend?" You could say, "It was fine." Or, you could say, "Our pastor spoke yesterday about the power of forgiveness." This simple transition may amount to no further discussion about your worship experience, but it does establish that you are a Christian and that one important topic within the Christian faith is forgiveness. In an answer to a pretty generic question, you have formed the basis of a spiritual relationship.

Now, imagine several weeks later that Sharon experiences a crisis in her life. Who do you think she might go to for a little perspective or guidance? That's right. You! And the truth is that either everyone is going into a crisis, or is in the middle of a crisis, or is just coming out of a crisis. So, our opportunities to have a positive influence on others increase when we acknowledge who we follow. In all my years as a Christian, I have met countless people who did not have nice things to say about Christians and Christianity, but I have never met anyone who had anything bad to say about Jesus. If we keep our focus on Jesus when talking with nonbelievers, then the conversation will stay positive.

So, what are some other transitional questions that we can ask? We could ask our server at a restaurant, "While we are thanking God for our meal, can we also pray for you?" You may find this to be a little hokey, but let me share a story. My good friend David and I were in seminary and our Evangelism professor encouraged us to ask this question whenever we went out to eat. Well, David and I found ourselves at an Outback Steakhouse. The young lady came to our table, took our drink orders, and then left. When she came back to get our meal order, David said, right on cue, "We are about to pray for our meal. Can we pray for you?" In an instant, her eyes grew wet with tears, and she ran away from the table. Jokingly, I said, "Way to go, David! You sure know how to make a person feel good!" A few minutes later, another server came to the table and announced that he was going to be our server. David and I looked at each other and plotted to discourage our Evangelism professor from giving students that assignment in the future. Well, we prayed for our waitress nonetheless and ate our meal. Just as we were paying the bill, our first server came to our table and explained. She said that just before she'd left for work, she and her dad had gotten into a horrible argument, and by the time she arrived at work, she felt really bad about it. David's simple question brought all her bottled emotion to the surface, and she then went and asked her boss for a fifteen-minute break, during which she called her dad and reconciled over the phone. She then thanked us for caring that much to ask her if we could pray for her. She said obviously God knew exactly what she needed when He sat us down at her table. I never ribbed David again for being such a faithful witness for His Savior.

I remember that story fondly because David taught me many other lessons through His walk with Christ, in particular that we are to make the most of *every* opportunity to share a good word on behalf of Christ. David never missed an opportunity to witness for his Savior. At the age of forty-two, cancer took his life from those of us who knew and loved him, but his funeral service was perhaps the most powerful celebration of a man who had so faithfully devoted himself to Jesus's Great Commission.

There are a number of other transitional statements that we can use to turn a conversation toward the spiritual realm. For example:

- When talking about sports, ask, "I wonder if there will be sports in heaven."
- When talking about the weather, inquire, "Do you believe that God causes natural disasters or just allows them to happen?"
- When talking about relationships, state, "I am so glad that I can take any concern or worry to Jesus. For me, that is the most important relationship I have."
- When talking about politics, ask, "Do you think God cares for one candidate over another?"

- When talking about a recent book, movie, or television show, share, "I learned something really cool about the life of Christ this week, when I was reading the Bible. Do you want to know what I learned?"

You get the idea. If we have a devotional life with Jesus Christ—if we read the Scriptures daily, if we memorize verses, if we are in continual prayer asking God to provide opportunities—we will be more tuned in to seeing those opportunities that come across our path. We shouldn't be nervous because the Holy Spirit gives us confidence. Remember, you get good at what you do. Trust God for the words as you take the next step of presenting the Gospel.

How Do We Present the Gospel?

The Gospel of Jesus Christ is simple and can be presented in any number of ways. There are a plethora of resources available that cover virtually every possible way to present it. This book offers a simple four-step process. At mile 10, we introduced this method of presenting the Gospel. We repeat this method here as a review:

1. **God**
   a. He is love (1 John 4:16).
   b. He is holy (1 Peter 1:16).
   c. He is just (2 Thessalonians 1:6).

2. **Man**
   a. We are sinful from birth (Romans 3:23).
   b. We deserve death (Romans 6:23).
   c. We are spiritually helpless (Isaiah 64:6).

3. **Jesus**
   a. He is God, who also became man (John 1:1, 14).
   b. He died as our substitute (1 Peter 2:24).

    c. He offers forgiveness as a free gift (Ephesians 2:8–9; Romans 6:23).

4. **You**
    a. You must respond to His offer (John 1:12; Romans 10:13).
    b. You must trust Christ for salvation and make Him Lord of your life (Romans 10:9–10; 1 Peter 3:15).
    c. You will be transformed and gifted by the Holy Spirit (2 Corinthians 5:17; 1 Corinthians 12).

This process begins with God and ends with the person, an appropriate reflection of the sequence of becoming a Christian. Jesus said, *No one can come to me unless the Father who sent me draws him* (John 6:44). Notice the order: God draws and man comes. Notice also that both God and man take action; God initiates the action, but man must choose. God does not compel man, but instead extends the invitation for man to come. God offers salvation to all, but relatively few accept it. Jesus said, *Enter through the narrow gate. For wide is the gate and broad is the road that leads to destruction, and many enter through it. But small is the gate and narrow the road that leads to life, and only a few find it* (Matthew 7:13–14).

Another common method of presenting the Gospel is known as the Roman Road. This method uses specific verses from the book of Romans. They are:

1. *All have sinned and fall short of the glory of God.* (Romans 3:23)
2. *But God demonstrates his own love for us in this: While we were still sinners, Christ died for us.* (Romans 5:8)
3. *For the wages of sin is death, but the gift of God is eternal life in Christ Jesus our Lord.* (Romans 6:23)
4. *Therefore, there is now no condemnation for those who are in Christ Jesus.* (Romans 8:1)

5. *If you confess with your mouth, "Jesus is Lord," and believe in your heart that God raised him from the dead, you will be saved. For it is with your heart that you believe and are justified, and it is with your mouth that you confess and are saved...for "Everyone who calls on the name of the Lord will be saved." (Romans 10:9–10, 13)*

These five statements summarize the essence of the Good News. They emphasize God's love, humanity's sin, God's solution, humanity's responsibility, and the ultimate reward—eternal life and fellowship with God for everyone who believes.

A great way to remember either one of these two methods is to tape them to the inside cover of your Bible. Or, you can remember the first verse, and then at each verse in the sequence, write the next reference verse. This will guide you through each part of the process. Either way, commit your favorite Gospel presentation to memory and then you will always be ready to give an answer for the hope that you have. This leads us to the next step of persuasion.

How Do We Persuade Others of the Truth of the Gospel?

The word "persuade" can sometimes connote a negative emotion, as if we are twisting someone's arm to break down and become a Christian. According to Merriam-Webster, the word "persuade" means "to cause someone to believe something, especially after a sustained effort; to convince."[17] Paul spent every Sabbath in the synagogues of each city he visited, trying to *persuade Jews and Greeks* (Acts 18:4). From this verse and so many others in Scripture, we learn that the Gospel is not just some emotional response akin to blind faith, but it is a logical truth from which we can consciously agree to a reasonable argument.

---

17 *Merriam-Webster OnLine*, s.v. "persuade," November 15, 2012, http://www.merriam-webster.com/dictionary/persuade

A key passage in helping us to understand the importance of persuasion in the Gospel presentation is found in Paul's second letter to the Corinthians: *Since, then, we know what it is to fear the Lord, we try to persuade men* (2 Corinthians 5:10). Paul continued his appeal with these words:

> *All this is from God, who reconciled us to himself through Christ and gave us the ministry of reconciliation: that God was reconciling the world to himself in Christ, not counting men's sins against them. And he has committed to us the message of reconciliation. We are therefore Christ's ambassadors, as though God were making his appeal through us. We implore you on Christ's behalf: Be reconciled to God.*
> **(2 Corinthians 5:18–20)**

In this passage, Paul used two seemingly incongruent illustrations—that of an ambassador and that of a "beggar" (taken from the Greek word "deomai"). Ambassadors are very important people in society and begging is a very lowly act of society's least esteemed people. This is a beautiful picture of what it means to be a witness. We are beggars holding out the "bread of life" for others to be fulfilled! Jesus said, *I have come that they may have life, and have it to the full* (John 10:10).

So, now that we know that persuasion is a key ingredient to witnessing, how can we do it? The truth is that we will never be prepared in the human sense to answer every question or satisfy every objection. However, the Christian is empowered by the Holy Spirit. Therefore, we can review some of the more common objections here, but we can also claim Jesus's promise: *But the Counselor, the Holy Spirit, whom the Father will send in my name, will teach you all things and will remind you of everything I have said to you* (John 14:26). It is important to acknowledge that what Jesus said has been captured for us in the four Gospels (Matthew, Mark, Luke and John). So, we study the Bible so that its truth will come to the surface at the appropriate point in our conversations with others. Let's now review some of the more common objections and suggested responses:

1. "The Bible has errors." Gently ask, "Can you show me where they are, and I will be glad to try to reconcile them for you?"

2. "God wouldn't send people to hell." Soberly respond, "The Bible says that God does not want anyone to perish (2 Peter 3:9). The sad truth is that everyone, because of our sin, is going to hell. God doesn't send people to hell; they choose not to accept God's offer of salvation, which can only be found in Jesus Christ."

3. "I just can't believe that Jesus is the only way." Calmly explain, "Jesus said He is the only way. That makes sense, since He is the only person ever born who was without sin. Do you believe Jesus would lie and deceive the world about who He really is?"

4. "I think I am good enough to go to heaven." Respectfully ask, "How much good is good enough for God? The Bible clearly teaches that no one is righteous enough without Christ."

5. "God wouldn't accept me after all I have done." Assure him or her with these words, "God said that where sin abounds, grace abounds all the more. God's grace is bigger than any sin we can ever commit. The only unforgivable sin is not trusting Christ as God's answer for our sin condition."

Obviously, there are a number of other objections that people can raise, but remember to be compassionate and authentic. If we don't know the answer, we should just simply say that we don't know the answer, but we ought to make sure to follow up with the person who asks the question. Also, don't be confrontational. Chances are that if someone is having this kind of conversation with us, he or she is searching for the truth. Once again, we are not responsible for the salvation of others; we *are* responsible, however, for sowing the seed. God is responsible for the results, which leads us to our next step of praying for that other person.

How Do We Pray with and for the Other Person?

This step in the witnessing process serves one of two purposes. The first purpose is to encourage the new believer to approach God in prayer about his decision to follow Jesus. This is sometimes called the sinner's prayer. That label emphasizes the fact that we are all sinful and in need of the Savior. There are a number of ways to say it, but remember that this prayer is the moment at which a person repents of his sin, trusts Jesus as his Savior and commits to following Him as his Lord for the rest of his life. This prayer is an individual's response to God's call on his life. He may choose to pray to God alone or he may ask you to help him. Either approach is valid. A simple way to think about this prayer is ABC:

Admit that you are a sinner.
Believe in Jesus Christ as your Savior from sin.
Commit to following Jesus for the rest of your life.

This may seem like a very simplistic approach to the single most important decision in a person's life, but it speaks so clearly to the beauty of the Christian faith—there are no prerequisites to becoming a child of God. Faith is all that is required, but the outcome of our faith is a fruitful life. Paul emphasized this truth in this way: *For it is by grace you have been saved, through faith—and this not from yourselves, it is the gift of God—not by works, so that no one can boast. For we are God's workmanship, created in Christ Jesus to do good works, which God prepared in advance for us to do* (Ephesians 2:8–9). Once the Holy Spirit convicts us of our sin, humility brings us to our knees to repent of that sin, accept His offer of salvation, and then join Him in His redemptive mission.

Each aspect of the prayer above comes with its own set of hurdles for the searcher. For example, because most people think that they are basically good, it may be very difficult to persuade them that they are sinful before a holy God. Obviously, the hard truth is that the entire premise of this thinking is flawed. An honest study of God's holiness and humanity's sinfulness would produce a separation so great that we would never be able to approach God without accepting His salvation. As Isaiah pointed out, *all our righteous acts are like filthy rags; we all shrivel up like a leaf, and like the wind our sins sweep us away* (Isaiah 64:6). Even our best is an abomination to God; God is so holy that sin and God cannot coexist.

The next hurdle is accepting that Jesus Christ is not only our personal Savior but the Savior of the world. When John the Baptist saw Jesus coming toward him, he proclaimed, *Look, the Lamb of God, who takes away the sin of the world* (John 1:29). This is an important truth. While Jesus's death brings life to individuals, we must be careful not to make Christianity an option among many different faith traditions. I went door-to-door asking people how I could pray for them, and one woman remarked that she believed in many gods, and then quickly added, "But Jesus is my favorite!" I responded, "He's my favorite too!" The sad truth is that most people in the world have no issue with Jesus except that He claimed to be the only way to heaven. In this prayer, new converts must confess that Jesus is the Savior of the world and not just their personal Savior.

The final step is perhaps easy to say, but it takes a lifetime of discipline and effort to accomplish. I have often said it is oh-so-easy to take Jesus as our Savior, but it is oh-so-difficult to make Him our Lord! Why is this? Paul, a born-again follower of Jesus Christ, confessed, *"For what I do is not the good I want to do; no, the evil I do not want to do—this I keep on doing. Now if I do what I do not want to do, it is no longer I who do it, but it is sin living in me that does it* (Romans 7:19–20). The biblical truth is that when a person trusts Jesus as his Savior and Lord, sin's penalty has been paid, and sin's power has been broken, but sin's presence remains until we die and go to heaven. Paul would declare a few verses later: *What a wretched man*

I am! Who will rescue me from this body of death? Thanks be to God—through Jesus Christ our Lord! (Romans 7:24–25). Commitment to Jesus as Lord is what this book is all about! *The Race of Faith* begins with a decision to follow Jesus, no matter what!

How Do We Promise to Follow Up?

When we have had the chance to present the Gospel of Jesus Christ to another person, regardless of whether that person trusted Jesus by the end of that meeting or if that person left the meeting undecided, we must make sure to follow up. Before we part company, we should already have a follow-up meeting scheduled. The reason is simple. Time will tick away, and we will both sink back into our busy lives. Exchanging contact information and setting up the next meeting are imperative actions to take.

Before you part ways, promise the other person that you are available to answer any follow-up questions or to meet again to go over Scripture. Also, promise the other person to pray for him or her. Before your next meeting, pray that God will bring that person to a decision to follow Christ and involve others in your prayer process. Wouldn't it be awesome if church prayer meetings had more of these kinds of prayer requests? "I just had a great meeting with Joe, and he is really close to making a decision to follow Jesus. He still has some questions, but when I presented the Gospel to him the other day, he seemed to have a better understanding of the importance of this faith step. Please pray for Joe." I can only imagine what God would do if the entire Christian community were proactively, intentionally, compassionately, and consistently sharing the faith that we profess. The world would be changed forever!

We now know why we must share our faith. We also know the six steps involved: preparing, prompting, presenting, persuading, praying, and promising. We acknowledge that the process is often a journey over the course of time, but we also know that we are called to be diligent and patient. God is in control. We have learned a few strategies for turning a conversation to the spiritual, and we have learned at least two methods of presenting the Gospel. We also talked about how to handle some of the more common objections. Now, as we press on past mile marker 23, we set our eyes on the next mile. And here is our next memory verse:

I pray that you may be active in sharing your faith, so that you will have a full understanding of every good thing we have in Christ.

(Philemon 6)

Spiritual Mentorship

I remember when my former pastor began to mentor me. While we were still in seminary, he had scheduled David and me to preach on a couple of Sunday nights. We were each given our passage and then assigned to develop our sermon outline, highlighting the main theme and key points. Little did David and I know that our next meeting would involve going into the sanctuary and delivering our sermons out loud, while our pastor moved from pew to pew to get a read on our eye contact, voice inflection, and gesture proficiency. What a humbling experience, but one that truly helped both David and me to own the faith that we profess and to take preaching God's Word seriously. This mile explains the Scriptural basis for and the benefits of being a spiritual mentor.

What Is the Scriptural Basis for Spiritual Mentorship?

Spiritual mentorship is a very important part of the Christian faith. Jesus was the ultimate mentor to His apostles during His earthly ministry. Examining His life helps us to understand what it takes to be a spiritual mentor today. His earthly ministry was characterized by modeling and molding. Everything He did and said became lessons for His followers. Whether the principle involved how to pray, forgive, serve, or love, Jesus taught by example and instruction.

Jesus was a spiritual mentor to His apostles and the other disciples, but was spiritual mentorship a key activity of the early church? We find our answer throughout the New Testament, and the answer is yes! One clear passage is found in 2 Timothy, where Paul explains the process of passing on the faith from generation to generation: *You then, my son, be strong in the grace that is in Christ Jesus. And the things you have heard me say in the presence of many witnesses entrust to reliable men who will also be qualified to teach others* (2 Timothy 2:2).

From this one verse, we can surmise four attributes of the spiritual mentor. First, every spiritual mentor must display spiritual strength in God's grace. Notice that Paul commanded Timothy to *be strong in the grace that is in Christ Jesus.* Being strong in God's grace is gained through daily exercise and conditioning. The FITNESS model for discipleship expounded in this book teaches the process of strengthening during the race of faith. The Christian, who has been tested, tried, stretched, and strained, is more apt to better handle tougher life circumstances that come his or her way. While every Christian goes through trials, only those who are mature respond to those trials in a way that honors God, obeys Christ, builds the church, and serves as a powerful witness to the world.

Another attribute of a spiritual mentor is scriptural knowledge. Paul instructed Timothy through his teaching. In the same way, we cannot be obedient to our Lord if we do not know what He taught.

Maturity comes through consistent study of God's Word, the understanding of the deeper truths of our faith, and the application of those truths in our daily living. As the author of Hebrews states: *Therefore let us move beyond the elementary teachings about Christ and be taken forward to maturity, not laying again the foundation of repentance from acts that lead to death, and of faith in God, instruction about cleansing rites, the laying on of hands, the resurrection of the dead, and eternal judgment* (Hebrews 6:1–2). Our knowledge of the Scriptures enables us to comprehend the big picture of God's redemption plan, noting principles introduced in the Old Testament and fulfilled in the New Testament. This knowledge produces a holistic understanding of God and consequent maturity within the believer.

In addition, a spiritual mentor sows seeds for the next generation. Notice that Paul told Timothy to entrust his teaching to reliable men. This trust takes on the idea of sowing seeds to the next generation of believers. As we have discussed through this race, our mission is to share the Gospel with the world, beginning at home and moving outward into our various spheres of influence. Paul told the Corinthians: *Now he who supplies seed to the sower and bread for food will also supply and increase your store of seed and will enlarge the harvest of your righteousness* (2 Corinthians 9:10). The principle of this verse is that God rewards those who faithfully sow the seeds of the Gospel by granting them greater influence in the world.

Finally, a spiritual mentor models and teaches sanctification. Paul explained that those men to whom Timothy entrusted the Gospel message would be *qualified to teach others.* Qualification implies one who has grown up in the faith. Paul encouraged the Roman church with these words: *I myself am convinced, my brothers, that you yourselves are full of goodness, complete in knowledge and competent to instruct one another* (Romans 15:14). As spiritual mentors, our qualification comes not by our outward works, but by the inward working of the Holy Spirit in our lives, for it is the Holy Spirit who sanctifies us, as Paul continued in his address to the Roman church: *the grace*

God gave me to be a minister to the Gentiles with the priestly duty of proclaiming the gospel of God, so that the Gentiles might become an offering acceptable to God, sanctified by the Holy Spirit (Romans 15:16). While no Christian is perfect, we are called by Christ to become more and more submissive to the Holy Spirit as we progress on our journey. This is the essence of sanctification.

What Are the Requirements to Being a Spiritual Mentor?

1. **Be a fully devoted follower of Christ.** When we are distracted or disengaged in our walk with Christ, we cannot effectively mentor others into a deeper relationship with Jesus. When we are growing in Christ, then we can lead others to grow in Christ. This is what it means to model our faith.

2. **Bear fruit regularly.** Jesus told his disciples: *I am the vine; you are the branches. If a man remains in me and I in him, he will bear much fruit; apart from me you can do nothing* (John 15:5). Jesus emphasized that fruit-bearing cannot happen unless we are *in Him.* What fruit does he mean? We cannot be sure, but later Paul listed the fruit of the Spirit when he said: *But the fruit of the Spirit is love, joy, peace, patience, kindness, goodness, faithfulness, gentleness and self-control* (Galatians 5:22–23a). Christian men and women who consistently portray these attributes of the Spirit of God can serve as spiritual mentors.

3. **Have a consistent worship lifestyle.** Worship attendance is a given among most Christians, but the mature Christian understands that worship is not about getting but about giving. The mature Christian actively worships throughout each day and approaches the worship experience reverently and soberly, acknowledging one's sinfulness and God's holiness. Jesus said to the woman at the well: *A time is coming and has now come when the true worshipers will worship the Father in spirit and truth,*

for they are the kind of worshipers the Father seeks (John 4:23). As we have discussed in earlier miles, God seeks worshipers who worship in *spirit and truth*. The spiritual mentor must be a true worshiper who pursues God and leads others to a life of deeper worship.

4. **Practice the spiritual disciplines.** We reviewed the various spiritual disciplines back at mile 8. They include learning, praying, worshiping, witnessing, serving, giving, fasting, journaling, meditating, and mentoring. The Christian who knows how to feed herself by consistently practicing the spiritual disciplines of her faith is ready to model and teach others to feed themselves in order to work out their salvation.

5. **Use your spiritual gifts.** As we learned back in the fifth leg of our race, every Christian is called to discover and then use his or her spiritual gifts for the building up, maturing, and unification of the church. When a person is aware of one's God-given gifts and uses them for His glory, she can then serve as a mentor to others who are in the process of learning about, discovering, and utilizing their gifts.

6. **Demonstrate spiritual maturity in handling varied life circumstances.** In other words, a spiritual mentor needs to have enough life experience to have gone through some trials and temptations. This does not necessarily mean that young people cannot be mentors; rather, a mature response to different life circumstances builds credibility and leadership characteristics that best prepare us to share how God has sustained us through these trials.

7. **Be willing to devote the right amount of time and investment into the life of others.** In today's world, this is perhaps one of the greatest disqualifiers, as true mentoring takes a lot of time and is a big commitment. Weekly meetings and ongoing check-ups are critical to the success of the mentor-mentee relationship. Jesus's apostles were with Him virtually every day for three-and-a-half years!

What Are the Six P's of Spiritual Mentorship?

Once we determine that we have met the criteria to become a spiritual mentor, we need to partner with someone who is an infant in the faith. We need to be on the lookout for people within our church or within our sphere of influence, come alongside them, and begin this important relationship. Paul's relationship with Timothy is a great illustration of spiritual mentorship. As we learn from Paul's letters to Timothy, the mentor engages in six specific activities in the process of helping his protégé to become a fully devoted follower of Jesus.

1. **Pray:** Paul consistently prayed for his protégé. Paul opened his second letter to Timothy with these words: *I thank God, whom I serve, as my forefathers did, with a clear conscience, as night and day I constantly remember you in my prayers* (2 Timothy 1:3). When we act as spiritual mentors, we are to be in constant prayer for our mentees, asking God to use His Word and the person's relationships and life circumstances to draw that person into a deeper intimacy with Him.

2. **Prepare:** Paul prepared Timothy for greater ministry. He encouraged him to oppose false teaching (1 Timothy 1:12–17; 4, 6); taught him about proper worship and church leadership (1 Timothy 2–3); and instructed him about relationships both inside and outside the church (1 Timothy 5). A quick survey of this letter highlights the importance of laying out the reality of the journey to our mentee. Too many times, people enter the faith assuming that everything will go well, but they become easily disillusioned and discouraged when the trials, temptations, and tribulations come. Mentors must prepare their protégés for the hard road ahead.

3. **Praise:** Paul took the opportunity to praise Timothy for his faithfulness and his progress. In each letter, he

referred to Timothy as his *true son in the faith* and *his dear son* (1 Timothy 1:2; 2 Timothy 1:2). Further, Paul boldly declared Timothy to be a *man of God* and he praised Timothy for his *sincere faith* (1 Timothy 6:11; 2 Timothy 1:5). The mentor should always look for the positive in his mentee, pointing out areas for growth and progress. This will serve as great encouragement.

4. **Push:** Paul pushed and challenged Timothy not only to stand firm in his faith but also to develop it over time. We are to not stay idle in our race of faith. Paul challenged Timothy with these words: *Do not neglect your gift, which was given you through prophecy when the body of elders laid their hands on you. Be diligent in these matters; give yourself wholly to them, so that everyone may see your progress. Watch your life and doctrine closely. Persevere in them, because if you do, you will save both yourself and your hearers.* (1 Timothy 4:14–16) Paul saw God's gift in Timothy and challenged him to use it for God's glory. The result would be the saving of many lives.

5. **Protect:** Paul was very protective of Timothy as well. Even though Timothy was young, Paul instructed the churches to accept him as one approved by God: *But you know that Timothy has proved himself, because as a son with his father he has served with me in the work of the gospel* (Philippians 2:22). Paul also protected Timothy by warning him about the false teachers and those who would desert him in the journey. Like Paul, every mentor must put a hedge of protection around his protégé to keep him or her from stumbling.

6. **Promote:** Paul promoted Timothy. He established Timothy as a credible leader in the church: *For this reason I have sent to you Timothy, my son whom I love, who is faithful in the Lord. He will remind you of my way of life in Christ Jesus, which agrees*

with what I teach everywhere in every church (1 Corinthians 4:13). Eventually, every mentee must transition into the role of mentor. The mentor's job does not end until he has translated a disciple into a disciple-maker. Timothy became the pastor of the church in Ephesus.

What Are the Benefits of Spiritual Mentorship?

With the relational and emotional commitment required of the spiritual mentor, we have to ask ourselves, "Is it worth it?" We could very easily contend that the new believer has the Bible as his guide and that he has the church to offer whatever training is necessary to achieve spiritual growth; therefore, spiritual mentorship is unnecessary. However, as we have already discussed in this mile, spiritual mentorship has biblical origins, and it is an important component to the propagation of the Christian faith.

There are a number of benefits of spiritual mentorship. First, our faith increases when we pray, teach, and guide others in the race of faith. Teaching others is one of the best ways to learn afresh the doctrines of God's Word and to further build our faith. I have been studying and teaching the Bible for twenty-five years, and yet I am amazed more and more by how much I learn with each new reading. The fact is that we will never get to the bottom of the Word of God; its depths are so great that we will never be able to mine all the treasures contained there. Spiritual mentorship provides a great environment for our continued development as Bible students and disciples of Christ.

The second benefit of being a spiritual mentor is spiritual fulfillment. Jesus said: *It is more blessed to give than to receive* (Acts 20:35). Paul quotes Jesus as teaching this truth, which supports the larger principle that seems counterintuitive in today's secular worldview. In fact, a lot of Jesus's statements were paradoxical. For example:

- *For whoever wants to save their life will lose it, but whoever loses his life for me will find it.* (Matthew 16:25)
- *Instead, whoever wants to become great among you must be your servant, and whoever wants to be first must be slave of all.* (Mark 10:43–44)
- *So do not worry, saying, "What shall we eat?" or "What shall we drink?" or "What shall we wear?" For the pagans run after all these things, and your heavenly Father knows that you need them. But seek first his kingdom and his righteousness, and all these things will be given to you as well.* (Matthew 6:31–33)
- *So the last will be first, and the first will be the last.* (Matthew 20:16)
- *You have heard that it was said, "Eye for eye, and tooth for tooth." But I tell you, Do not resist an evil person. If someone strikes you on the right cheek, turn to him the other also.* (Matthew 5:38–39)
- *Love your enemies and pray for those who persecute you.* (Matthew 5:44)
- *Enter through the narrow gate.* (Matthew 7:13)

These principles are counterintuitive and paradoxical. Jesus truly came to establish a Kingdom that was not of this world. All of these commands direct us to do those things that our earthly mind would not allow. Therefore, when it comes to spiritual mentorship, we may feel like we will be drained and exhausted trying to help another believer along in his or her journey. In truth, according to Jesus's Kingdom principles, the more we give to the work of His Kingdom, the greater is the blessing and the greater is our sense of fulfillment in accomplishing His purposes.

This principle works in every facet of our faith journey. Those who tithe faithfully and with a cheerful heart will attest that they live better off the 90 percent than they ever lived off the 100 percent. Those who go and serve others, whether in a community impact project or on a mission trip halfway around the globe, will all attest that they went to be a blessing to others but that *they* received the blessing. Those who feel tired and lethargic but push themselves to go for a run or do the yard work they have been putting off will attest that they were more energized as they expended their energy in those activities. Those who carry the busiest schedules will attest that they have learned how to be efficient in their use of time. Busy people get things done. We could go on, but the point is that when we dedicate ourselves to the work of Christ's Kingdom, including the work of a spiritual mentor, we are fulfilled.

A third benefit of spiritual mentorship is stronger churches. One of the great challenges within the church has been how to grow our church members to maturity. The church has wrestled with how best to foster a lifestyle of teaching and training for new believers. The truth is that the vast majority of born-again Christians are not grounded in the deeper truths of the faith. This has resulted in a compartmentalized Christianity, which then lacks power in impacting the world for Christ. Most church members in America today go to worship services on Sunday to sing some songs, listen to some prayers, hear a message, sing another song, and then go home. Sadly, their Christian activity essentially ends at that moment and then picks back up the following Sunday.

Some churches offer new member classes and maybe even have a discipleship program for those who sign up for it. However, real, life-transforming discipleship is messy and is not a check-the-box program. It requires group training as well as one-on-one mentoring. When a church develops a comprehensive approach to discipleship, including spiritual mentorship, over time that body of Christ becomes stronger, healthier, more unified, and more mature!

A corollary benefit of spiritual mentorship is more effective ministries. When the various ministries of the local church are being led and developed by mature believers, then those ministries will be more effective in accomplishing God's purposes. More often than not, churches struggle to get enough workers to support its various ministries. And more often than not, this is because most of the members are not mature or confident enough to take on important roles in ministry. Spiritual mentorship fosters a gradual development of disciples to take on simple tasks or behind-the-scenes jobs and then move on to greater responsibilities, such as ministry leadership roles. Spiritual mentorship lays the groundwork for Christ's high expectations of His followers.

One final but critical benefit of spiritual mentorship is Kingdom realization. What this means is that as we pray for, prepare, praise, push, protect, and promote the next generation of spiritual leaders, we create greater capacity to tackle the larger Kingdom initiatives to which Christ called us. Jesus said: *The kingdom of God does not come with your careful observation, nor will people say, "Here it is," or "There it is," because the kingdom of God is within you* (Luke 17:21). This is why we never say that we are building the Kingdom or establishing the Kingdom, but say instead that the Kingdom is being "realized." As more and more followers of Jesus Christ come to a full realization of His Kingdom within them, then the church of Jesus Christ will have a more profound impact upon our world.

As we look around the bend, we see our next mile marker, and it is a sweet sight. We are closing in on the finish line of our race of faith. We are not only challenged to be mentored but to mentor others. As we press on past this mile marker, we can take a moment to reflect on our next memory verse:

Even youths grow tired and weary, and young men stumble and fall; but those who hope in the LORD will renew their strength. They will soar on wings like eagles; they will run and not grow weary, they will walk and not be faint.

(Isaiah 40:31)

Bible Study Leadership

I was twenty-three years old and fresh out of college. I had recently relocated to a new city and knew virtually no one. I attended a church and its Sunday school and joined the church within a month. Then I attended a new member class. That was October/November of 1988. In February 1989, I was asked if I would teach the college Sunday school class. I was mortified. I felt ill-prepared. I was overwhelmed at the thought. And frankly, I didn't understand the level of commitment. I am sure some of my first students had a laugh, but over time, I found that my fear forced me to prepare, which pushed me to study more, which helped me to solidify my faith foundation. I am grateful to that church for pushing me out of the nest. It changed my life. This mile explores the reasons why many Christians never lead Bible studies and also lists some of the keys to doing so.

What Is Bible Study Leadership?

Have you ever led a Bible study? Does the thought of leading a Bible study make you sick to your stomach? Most Christians would answer, "No" and "Yes!" to those two questions, respectively. Leading a Bible study is a daunting activity, and most people feel unqualified. But before we review the reasons why people do not want to lead a Bible study, let's define what Bible study means. It consists of at least three important components.

1. **Communicating biblical truth.** We know that communication can be one-way or two-way—sending and/or receiving. Biblical truth is a fact (or facts) concerning a command, principle, promise, prophecy, etc. declared in the Bible. Communication of biblical Truth occurs when a Bible book, passage or verse is read, recited, memorized, explained, argued, interpreted, cross-referenced, illustrated, and/or applied. When the Bible teacher or the student reads the Word of God, biblical truth is communicated without any human fallacy. The greatest part of any sermon or lesson occurs when the Bible is read. When the preacher or teacher opens his or her mouth to offer any words other than those contained in the Bible, he or she is immediately subject to fallibility. Sadly, many preachers today begin with a human topic, thought, or idea and then go to the Bible to find a suitable verse or passage to make their human point. This is called proof-texting. Expositional preaching, on the other hand, produces spiritual wisdom by beginning with the Word of God and then making its point, irrespective of the preacher's opinions, values, experiences, or thoughts.

2. **Conveying biblical knowledge.** Conveyance implies a transporting of knowledge from one person to another, whereby the receiver accepts and makes that knowledge his or her own. This is an extremely important truth. While communication

of biblical truth lays down the truth, conveyance of biblical knowledge picks up that truth. Knowledge is not only transferred but understood and ultimately applied in the student's life. The process of learning begins with listening, moves to understanding, follows with acceptance, and ends with application. There is no benefit to knowing the Scriptures only; we must also apply them. James declared: *Do not merely listen to the word, and so deceive yourselves. Do what it says* (James 2:17). Our application of biblical knowledge is the spiritual result of hearing, understanding, and accepting it.

3. **Cooperating with the Spirit.** Since the Holy Spirit is the writer of the Bible, then the Spirit is the ultimate communicator of its truth. Peter emphasized this truth to the churches by saying: *Above all, you must understand that no prophecy of Scripture came about by the prophet's own interpretation of things. For prophecy never had its origin in the human will, but prophets, though human, spoke from God as they were carried along by the Holy Spirit* (2 Peter 1:20–21). The supernatural "carrying" of the Holy Spirit explains how men from different generations, walks of life, occupations, and educational levels could write God's Word as it was given to them and deliver a consistent message of God's plan of redemption. In addition to the Bible being inspired by the Holy Spirit, we also know that since the Holy Spirit dwells within every believer, He is the One who bears testimony to the truth of God's Word when it is read and taught. This is why each person who hears a sermon or a lesson can be convicted, comforted, or challenged in a different way from other people. We can say that a passage has spoken to us in a unique way because the Holy Spirit, who lives within us, knows exactly where we are spiritually in relation to God and others. He knows the intimate details of our spiritual walk and uses God's Word to speak to us directly.

These three components help us to understand what Bible study is all about. When we communicate biblical truth, when we convey the knowledge of God and His redemptive mission, and when we cooperate with the Holy Spirit as He uses the Word to teach, guide, and direct us, then we experience transformation. Paul said: *Do not conform to the pattern of this world, but be transformed by the renewing of your mind. Then you will be able to test and approve what God's will is—his good, pleasing and perfect will* (Romans 12:2). Our knowledge of and desire to align with God's will begins with a sincere desire to study God's Word.

Why Don't More Christians Lead Bible Studies?

There are a number of reasons that Christians give for not wanting to lead a Bible study. We will mention a few of them here. Perhaps you can identify with one or more of these reasons.

1. **Confidence.** Public speaking is often considered to be people's number one fear, and teaching the Bible fits right into that category. In fact, many popular lists rank fear of public speaking higher than fear of death, meaning people would rather die than get up in front of a group of people and talk! Many lack confidence in leading a group, speaking before a group, and answering the tough questions that may be asked.

2. **Competence.** Most Christians feel unqualified to teach the Bible. They have the mind-set that only someone who is a seminary graduate can teach the Bible to others. They may have attended church their entire lives, and they may know a lot of the stories from the Bible. In fact, they may feel qualified to teach children but leading adults is a whole different story. They don't feel capable to articulate the deeper truths and principles presented in the Word of God. They don't

have a holistic understanding of the Bible's message, and so they feel inadequate at pulling it all together for others.

3. **Comparison.** They don't feel quite up to par with the Bible teachers from whom they have learned. When they compare themselves to other preachers and teachers, they say, "I could never do that!" They weren't there when that other seasoned teacher first tried to lead a Bible study and fumbled and stumbled through the lesson. So, instead of acknowledging that any new activity is going to come with its share of bumps and bruises, they compare themselves, a mere newbie, to that seasoned teacher who has been at it for quite some time, thus creating a barrier.

4. **Conscience.** Many of us are afraid to teach because our lives don't measure up to whatever standard we have established for a person in that esteemed role. Whether we are still wrestling with a certain sin in our lives, or we're afraid of others finding out about our sinful lives before we became Christians, we discount ourselves as being qualified to teach. Perhaps we don't take on the role because we know we struggle in our flesh, and we don't want to put ourselves into a position to fall. We live in a culture where we put our leaders on a pedestal, and then when they show that they are human, we respond with disappointment and disgust.

I have been there. I know the feeling of being put on a pedestal, and I know what it feels like to be knocked off the pedestal. One of the most beautiful motifs expressed throughout the Bible is that God chooses to use the sinful, the weak, the broken, the uneducated, the dirty, the poor, the wretched, and the outcasts to do His work. Do you believe Moses was a great teacher? He murdered a man, displayed a bad temper, deliberately disobeyed God, and had fierce disagreements with his own family. Do you believe David was a great leader? He committed adultery, lied about it, and then murdered another man to cover it up. Do you believe Peter was a great preacher? He was impetuous, impatient, and denied even knowing His Lord three times to three different people. Do you believe Paul was a great teacher? He led the persecution of the church, was very impatient and confrontational with some of his brothers in the faith, and admitted to his constant struggle with sin.

We could go on and on, but the point remains that God uses imperfect people to do His work. No one is perfect except Jesus. In fact, let's think about it another way. If God chose to use men who had it all together, there might be a temptation for those men to take the credit for their spirituality themselves. Paul acknowledged this truth:

Brothers and sisters, think of what you were when you were called. Not many of you were wise by human standards; not many were influential; not many were of noble birth. But God chose the foolish things of the world to shame the wise; God chose the weak things of the world to shame the strong. God chose the lowly things of this world and the despised things—and the things that are not—to nullify the things that are, so that no one may boast before him. It is because of him that you are in Christ Jesus, who has become for us wisdom from God—that is, our righteousness, holiness and redemption. Therefore, as it is written: Let the one who boasts boast in the Lord.

(1 Corinthians 1:26–31)

God will take our mess and transform it into His message! Christ's righteousness, holiness, and power make us useful to God. Once we understand that truth, we will boast in the Lord only!

What Are the Seven Keys to Being a Bible Study Leader?

There is perhaps no greater way to advance our understanding of God's plan of redemption from the first *In the beginning...* of

Genesis to the final *Amen* of Revelation than to be a Bible student and teacher. Before we actually lead a study alone, we should learn from an experienced teacher.

There is a common acrostic for the experienced teacher to use when training a new teacher; it's called MAWL, which stands for model, assist, watch, and leave. The teaching mentor models how to teach, and the student observes. Then the mentor assists the new student teacher in leading a study. Then the mentor watches the student teach. Finally, the mentor leaves, meaning that the new teacher is ready to lead his or her own study. This process can take weeks or months, depending on the readiness of the new teacher. We should be careful not to throw a new teacher into a leadership position until he or she is ready, but we also should not make it a virtual impossibility to take on that position either. In truth, none of us is ever completely ready. If we feel called to teach, God will orchestrate our learning curve if we commit to diligent prayer and preparation.

In order to help us get an idea of what it takes to lead a Bible study, let's explore the following seven keys:

1. **Passion for God's Word.** This may not seem as obvious to us at first, but remember that part of discovering our spiritual gifts includes our passion for a particular aspect of ministry. Our passion about the Bible will be evident to our students and will foster a transformational environment. Paul declared: *For when I preach the gospel, I cannot boast, since I am compelled to preach. Woe to me if I do not preach the gospel!* (1 Corinthians 9:16). When we have a compulsion to preach or teach, our hearers or students will be profoundly impacted by the truth of God's Word.

2. **Preparation through personal study.** Preparation is critical for all teachers, not just novice Bible study leaders. When we prepare to lead a study, we are plowing earth

and dirt in order to share a new nugget of wisdom with others. Being a student ourselves is the greatest preparation, as continual learning produces continual excitement and anticipation for the deeper truths of God's Word. Remember, too, that our students should be like the Bereans, who did not take Paul's word as gospel, but *received the message with great eagerness and examined the Scriptures every day to see if what Paul said was true* (Acts 17:11). As a Bible study leader, you are not the authority; God's Word is.

3. **Planning of the Bible study objective.** Every Bible study leader needs to answer the question, "So what?" The objective of every lesson must be clearly communicated and met, or else the study has the potential to fall far short of God's desire for transformation. Therefore, the teacher must plan and provide the answer for that study's objective. Variety in accomplishing that objective is also important. Everyone learns differently. Some are auditory learners, others are visual learners, and still others have to learn by doing. The challenge for the teacher is to match the style of learning to the passage being studied. Wisdom in planning begins with a commitment to the Lord: *Commit to the Lord whatever you do, and your plans will succeed* (Proverbs 16:3).

4. **Praying to invoke the Spirit's leadership.** Since the Holy Spirit is the real teacher, we should always begin a Bible study with a prayer, asking Him to teach us. The human teacher is an instrument in God's hands, but the Spirit of God effects change in the hearts and minds of students. When we invite the Holy Spirit to be our teacher, everyone gathered in the study will know that it is the Holy Spirit convicting them, comforting them, or challenging them to action.

5. **Piloting of the discussion.** Many times during the course of a study, it is possible to experience "topic creep." One of the leader's roles is to keep the group on task and away from rabbit-chasing. This is easier said than done, but establishing that expectation up front will help to foster the right balance of interaction. Certainly we want to encourage participation and questions; this assists in the learning process for the whole group. The key is to make sure we steer the discussion so that it achieves its objective by the end of the session.

6. **Provoking of challenges to paradigms.** A critical key to any Bible study is to allow the Word of God to serve as our authority for both faith and practice. When we stay with what the Bible teaches, regardless of topic, the natural result will include a challenge to a lot of myths and traditions. Jesus challenged the Pharisees with these words: *You have let go of the commands of God and are holding on to human traditions* (Mark 7:8). Paul instructed Timothy about this as well: *If you point these things out to the brothers and sisters, you will be a good minister of Christ Jesus, nourished on the truths of the faith and of the good teaching that you have followed. Have nothing to do with godless myths and old wives' tales; rather, train yourself to be godly* (1 Timothy 4:6–7). Real Bible study should challenge and correct false teachings.

7. **Pointing to the Gospel of Christ.** Every Bible study lesson must point to Christ. The common thread throughout the pages of Scripture is the promise of Christ's coming, the fact of Christ's coming, and the promise of Christ's return. The person and work of Jesus Christ should always be pointed out within the context of the passage, whether we are studying the Old Testament or New Testament. Paul declared: *For I resolved to know nothing while I was with you except Jesus Christ and him crucified* (1 Corinthians 2:2). Too

many preachers and teachers go out of their way to be relevant to their audiences, but there is nothing more relevant than Jesus Christ.

What Are the Seven Steps to Leading a Bible Study?

The seven keys we just reviewed are a great start to understanding how to lead a Bible study. There are some specific steps that we should discuss now before we move on to actually breaking down a passage together.

1. **Choose the right study for your group.** For example, it probably is not wise to lead an in-depth study of the book of Revelation with a group of new believers. That said, all Scripture is useful for teaching, so we should be open to the Holy Spirit's leading about the study, book, and topic.

2. **Determine when and where to conduct the study.** This may seem obvious, but since a Bible study requires a full commitment from all participants, the day and time slots need to be nailed down, agreed to, and held in very high regard. Too many studies begin with a lot of enthusiasm and then lose energy as the distractions of life begin to pull people away. Setting a day, time, and place with the agreement of the whole group gives the study its best chance of completing its task.

3. **Begin with prayer.** It is critical to ask the Holy Spirit to be our ultimate teacher and to open our hearts and minds to the truth of God's Word, which will allow us to effect real change in the lives of the participants. Prayer also serves as a meaningful separation between the group's social interaction and its spiritual engagement, giving the teacher the floor to begin the study.

4. **Read the passage.** This is not something to simply consider: it is imperative! This may seem like an obvious part of Bible study to you, but you may be surprised at how often a teacher/preacher will spend the greater portion of his time trying to introduce, illustrate, and insert his own experiences or opinions about the topic without ever reading the Bible passage aloud. If you are part of a Bible study group or church that does not read the Bible, find another group or church!

5. **Encourage participation.** Two-way communication and group interaction facilitates the learning process for everyone. Asking someone to pray, someone else to read, and someone else to answer a question are all good ways to engage group members. It also provides a mechanism to involve those who are less likely to speak up. One reason many teachers discourage participation is that they are afraid they may not have the answer to a question. The best way to handle a question to which we don't know the answer is to say, "I don't know, but I will do some study this week and get back to you." There is nothing wrong with that, and nothing will propel our study more than striving to answer a specific question. A guideline to use during the study is to ask for volunteers; do not call on others within the group unless you know them all personally and know they can read. We live in an increasingly illiterate society, and, as teachers, we need to be sensitive to that fact. If we do not know for sure that a person can read aloud, we should not call on him or her to do so. A good idea is to ask a couple of folks prior to the study session if they would pray and/or read the passage. This gives them some time to mentally prepare and be ready when asked. It also saves the teacher a little embarrassment if the person were to refuse in front of the group.

6. **Summarize the discussion points for the group after each point is made.** This keeps the big picture in view and allows

for an easy way to review as the study progresses. A good rule of thumb is to read the entire passage for the study, then go back and read each paragraph within the passage, stopping to discuss that paragraph's content. Oftentimes, we will be able to develop the essence of what is being taught in the passage by working paragraph by paragraph and pulling biblical truths and principles out of the text. This method is known as expositional or inductive study. We begin with the Word of God and take out of it God's truth. This is truly the only way to experience transformation of mind, heart, and will. Beware of teachers who begin with a topic and then go to the Bible to find a verse or passage that best aligns with that topic. There is no power in that kind of teaching.

7. **Challenge the group to move along in their faith.** After all, we already know that *faith without deeds is dead,* so learning biblical knowledge is not enough. We must do something with that knowledge (James 2:26). Working out our salvation combines learning with working. Whatever the passage studied, there must be some call to action. The best Bible study leaders offer tangible ways in which the group can put what they learn into practice. As each participant learns how to apply the Word, the spiritual result is increased faith.

What Does Hebrews 12:1–3 Teach?

Now it's time for us to try our hand at preparing to teach a short but powerful passage in the book of Hebrews. Remember the Seven Cs of Bible Study? Do your best to answer those questions after you read Hebrews 12:1-3.

1. Context: Within what setting is the author writing? In other words, why is this passage here?

_____

_____

_____

_____

2. Characters: Who are the main characters?

_____

_____

_____

3. Content: What is the passage about?

_____

_____

_____

4. Central proposition: What is the main spiritual idea being taught?

_____

_____

_____

5. Christ: How is Christ related to this passage?

_____

_____

_____

_____

6. Cross-references: what other verses or similar passages are there in the Bible?

_____

_____

_____

7. Change: How can I apply this scripture to my personal daily life?

_____

_____

_____

_____

We now know what Bible study leadership is, some of the reasons people don't want to be a Bible study leader, seven keys to leading a Bible study, and seven steps to follow when leading a Bible study. We also tried our hand at applying the Seven Cs of Bible Study to a passage in Hebrews. The bottom line is that every Christian can lead or facilitate a Bible study, because the Holy Spirit who authored the Word of God is the same Holy Spirit who lives within us. What about you? Will you pray about taking that step?

We have just over a mile to go! Let's dig deep down inside and complete our race with a strong kick to the finish! As we pass mile marker 25, let's review our next memory verse:

Preach the Word; be prepared in season and out of season; correct, rebuke, and encourage—with great patience and careful instruction.

(2 Timothy 4:2)

Influencing Our World

I will never forget the young lady who was so on fire for Christ that she was literally responsible for seeing dozens of her friends and acquaintances from high school come to faith in Jesus over a weekend revival. She was a relatively new Christian and was so convinced of God's love that it simply poured out of her to everyone within earshot. She wore her faith on her sleeve, and while she was ridiculed by some, countless others were taken by her passion and conviction. I watched with amazement as friend after friend came up to the altar and thanked her for faithfully living out her faith. She had truly influenced her world for Christ. This mile talks about the power of a positive Christian influence on the lives of others.

What Is Christian influence?

When we decide to follow Jesus, we are commissioned to make disciples. The most immediate impact we can make for the Kingdom of God is in our existing relationships—in our home, at school, at work, and in our neighborhood. Christian influence can be defined as putting our faith into practice in such a way that the world takes notice and is compelled to respond to the call of Jesus Christ.

Have you ever met a Christian who had such a contagious enthusiasm for God and His work? This enthusiasm is one aspect of having Christian influence. The word "enthusiasm" is taken from the Greek word, *en-theos*, which means "God within." A great example of enthusiasm is Paul the apostle and his missionary partner Silas. After Paul drove out an evil spirit from a slave girl in the city of Philippi (modern-day Greece), he and Silas were arrested, beaten, severely flogged, and thrown into prison, where their feet were fastened in the stocks. How did they respond? They began to pray and sing hymns to God; all the other prisoners listened to them. When an earthquake shook the prison foundations, causing the shackles to break free and the prison doors to burst open, the jailer was about to kill himself, fearing that he would die for allowing all the prisoners to escape. Paul assured him that they were all still there. As a result, the jailer and his family were saved! (Acts 16)

Years later, Paul would write these words to the church in Philippi from a Roman prison: *Rejoice in the Lord always. I will say it again: Rejoice! Let your gentleness be evident to all. The Lord is near. Do not be anxious about anything, but in every situation, by prayer and petition with thanksgiving, present your requests to God. And the peace of God, which transcends all understanding, will guard your hearts and your minds in Christ Jesus.* (Philippians 4:4–7)

When we trust God in all situations, no matter how dire they may be, then we can have a profound influence on those who God has put into our lives.

Another aspect of Christian influence is promoting a Christian perspective. This is perhaps one of the greatest distinctions between the Christian faith and all other world religions. The reason is that for the Christian, God is transcendent yet immanent. This truth about God gives us joy, peace, and hope. The author of Hebrews, when explaining how God promised to keep His covenant with Abraham, concluded: *God did this so that, by two unchangeable things in which it is impossible for God to lie, we who have fled to take hold of the hope set before us may be greatly encouraged. We have this hope as an anchor for the soul, firm and secure* (Hebrews 6:18–19a). When tragedy hits, this hopeful perspective is very appealing to the non-Christian community. They want that hope. They want that peace. They want that joy. When we allow those attributes of the Spirit within us to shine forth, the world takes notice.

Yet another aspect of Christian influence is persuasion, which involves producing a lasting effect on others. There is an axiom in sales that says, "You can't sell what you don't believe in." In the same way, the Christian who is not convinced about God's power, protection, and provision will never be able to convince anyone else. Are you convinced that God is bigger than any other force in your life? Jesus comforted His apostles with these words: *I have told you these things, so that in me you may have peace. In this world you will have trouble. But take heart! I have overcome the world* (John 16:33). What a bold claim! What a powerful promise!

When Paul wrote his final letter to his young protégé, Timothy, he declared: *That is why I am suffering as I am. Yet this is no cause for shame, because I know whom I have believed, and am convinced that he is able to guard what I have entrusted to him until that day* (2 Timothy 1:12). Paul's life was marked by suffering, and yet, because he knew Jesus, he had no doubt that Jesus was able! Are you so convinced that Jesus is who He claims to be that nothing can keep you from trusting Him? True, powerful Christian influence begins with a resolve to put Jesus on the throne of our life, never to replace Him with anything or anyone else!

What Are the Seven Keys to Influencing Others?

Christian influence is earned. Our culture is increasingly hostile to Christians and Christianity. Let's be honest. Most people who are outside the Christian community believe that Christians are hypocritical, judgmental, and intolerant. And the truth is that many of us are. We say one thing and do another. We tend to see others' faults and not our own. We prefer to speak instead of listen. Yet the mature Christian is ever mindful of how far down into the slimy pit God reached to save him. The psalmist victoriously declared: *He lifted me out of the slimy pit, out of the mud and mire; he set my feet on a rock and gave me a firm place to stand* (Psalm 40:2). When we really understand God's mercy and grace, we will see people the way God sees people, and we will love them the way God loves them. So, we must earn the right to exert our Christian influence on those around us. The seven keys to having a positive influence on our world are:

1. **A godly life.** A godly life does not mean a perfect life. No one is perfect, but all of us must continuously strive to become more like Christ every day. When others see us working out our salvation with fear and trembling, they will be more inclined to have a spiritual conversation with us.

2. **A genuine interest.** Too often, Christians are on such a mission that they miss out on the opportunity to invest in another life. We can come across as disingenuous, because others may think that we're only interested in converting them. Only the Holy Spirit can give us a heart to love people, especially those who are hard to love. When we yield to His leadership, we will be more apt to portray a genuine interest in the lives of others.

3. **A gracious ear.** Grace is defined as unmerited favor. Are you willing to listen to another person's worldview without interruption or disdain? Are you willing to hear how others need prayer or direction or counsel? Being gracious should be the standard operating procedure for Christians. When we listen well, we gain a hearing when it comes our time to share our beliefs.

4. **A good answer.** The Bible offers this encouragement to every follower of Christ: *Even if you should suffer for what is right, you are blessed. "Do not fear what they fear; do not be frightened." But in your hearts, set apart Christ as Lord. Always be prepared to give an answer to everyone who asks you to give the reason for the hope that you have. But do this with gentleness and respect* (1 Peter 3:13–15). We cannot give the reason for our hope without doing so with gentleness and respect. We often miss the command to be gentle and respectful!

5. **A great perspective.** As we mentioned in the previous section, a person's perspective on life changes when he or she becomes a Christian. My father used to be so afraid to die, but when he gave his life to Jesus, his fear went away. Why? He knew his ultimate destiny was certain. He then adopted the following quote as his personal slogan: "It isn't where you start, but where you finish, that matters." No matter the circumstances, mature Christians tend to respond with a quiet confidence in God's sovereignty.

6. **A giving attitude.** This includes giving our time and resources to advance the cause of Christ. When we choose to spend time with others, investing our time and our relational energy in them, they are more apt to listen to our biblical worldview. Most of the time, this does not happen overnight, but it does require an intentional and compassionate spirit. Our compassion breaks down barriers and opens up the lines of communication.

7. **The Gospel message.** Even if we demonstrated the previous six keys, without the Gospel of Jesus Christ, we are just nice people. Jesus said: *I am the vine; you are the branches. If you remain in me and I in you, you will bear much fruit; apart from me you can do nothing* (John 15:5). Jesus is the Gospel and without the message that He is the Savior of the world, our efforts to be influential are meaningless. When we are given the opportunity to share our faith, we must do so unapologetically. To water down the Gospel is a grave error. A weak message produces weak Christians. A strong message produces strong Christians. Salvation is free, but it will cost us everything!

How Should We View the Opportunities We Have?

Believe it or not, God opens up opportunities for influence every day. How can we make the most of those opportunities? First, we should celebrate the fact that God has given us the relationships we have. Whether it is our family, our school, our workplace, or our neighborhood, God has placed us right where we are, and He has commanded us, as Christians, to make disciples. Consider each day a tremendous privilege to act as Jesus to those who do not yet know Him.

Second, we should thank God for putting us in the school or job we currently have. We spend an average of eight hours a day in school or at work. This is a huge mission field for us. If we truly believe that God is sovereign, then it is no accident that you are going to school or working where you do. If you have a secular job, don't fret because your workplace is not a wholesome environment. Your opportunities are that much greater than a person whose schooling or employment is already within a Christian community. Those within the Christian community have to be that much more intentional in developing relationships with nonbelievers.

Third, pray to God for influence at your school or workplace. Prayer aligns us with God and His will. Praying for opportunities to share our faith is in line with what He wants us to do. Obviously, praying must lead to seeing and acting. Therefore, part of our prayers should be to see what God sees, and to have the boldness to act when the Holy Spirit prompts us to act, whether it is to walk across the room and talk with the student we have never met, or to speak up when someone asks a spiritual question in the lunchroom at work.

Fourth, we should respect the rules of our school or workplace. Nothing will serve us worse than behaving as though the rules apply to everyone else but us. Believe it or not, people watch what we do, especially if we have the Christian label imprinted on us. Sadly, some people are only waiting for us to take one misstep so they can justify their refusal to join our ranks. So, we must be diligent to walk with integrity in all areas of life.

Fifth, we should be competent in our job responsibilities. Displaying a strong work ethic and developing our job skills will build our reputation as a valuable asset to our company. Being a valuable asset leads to opportunities for advancement. Advancement exposes us to a greater sphere of influence. A greater sphere of influence brings a greater impact for the Kingdom of God. The message is simple. Followers of Christ are not victims. We are not even survivors. We are thrivers!

Paul talked about the treasure that every Christian possesses:

But we have this treasure in jars of clay to show that this all-surpassing power is from God and not from us. We are hard pressed on every side, but not crushed; perplexed, but not in despair; persecuted, but not abandoned; struck down, but not destroyed. We always carry around in our body the death of Jesus, so that the life of Jesus may also be revealed in our body.

(2 Corinthians 4:7–10)

That treasure is the knowledge of the glory of God found only in Christ.

What Are Ten Creative Ways to Create Influence?

There are a lot of ways to create influence in the workplace. We have discussed the seven keys to being influential, but now let's brainstorm some specific ways to create that influence. Here are ten simple ways we can create influence in our workplace:

1. **Invest** in one of your coworkers. Develop a new friendship with someone in your office. This person could be new to your company or just someone you never had the chance to get to know on a personal basis.

2. **Invite** someone who is struggling in some way to lunch. Be attentive to coworkers who may be experiencing a crisis. Examples might include a death or sickness in their family, a bad performance review, issues with a spouse or children, or problems with addictions, etc. Take them to lunch and serve as a sounding board.

3. **Increase** your accessibility/usefulness to others. When someone moves, offer to help; when someone is raising funds for her children's school, donate; when someone needs a ride, offer one. There are a number of other ways to increase your usefulness.

4. **Initiate** personal or even a group Bible study before work or during your lunch break. Get to work early each day and study your Bible there; just make sure to complete it prior to your shift. Before beginning a group study, make sure to ask management first, but if it is permissible, then begin the process described in the previous mile.

5. **Improve** your value to the company or office. Don't just be a good employee, but take on a mind-set of an owner. When we own something, we go the extra mile to succeed. Always follow company policies and rules, be a model employee, sign up for additional training, and volunteer for the most difficult projects.

6. **Incline** your ear to the needs of others in your office. This does not mean gossip but is instead about showing a genuine interest in the lives of others. We are so often consumed with our own busy lives that we miss the opportunities to be there for someone else. Asking questions and asking people how we can pray for them establishes the basis for learning their needs.

7. **Invent** ways to prompt spiritual conversations with coworkers. In other words, be creative. We serve a creative God, and He wants us to find creative ways to share our faith. In mile 23, we discussed specific ways to prompt spiritual conversations. Review them, and then create a list of ways that are specific to your workplace dynamics.

8. **Institute** strategies to develop faith-based initiatives within your company. Most companies have humanitarian initiatives or partnerships with various nonprofit organizations. Get involved and be a part of your company's face to the community. There may even be opportunities for input into additional initiatives that will make a difference in your community.

9. **Ignore** persecution that may result from others knowing your beliefs. This is becoming an even greater possibility in our world today. Jesus said to *pray for those who persecute you* (Matthew 5:44). Instead of responding to negative comments or jokes, simply ignore them and then go pray for your persecutors. Loving them right where they are is the best way to bear witness for Jesus.

10. **Illustrate** your faith in your interpersonal relationships. Most people relate to a story. Know your story and how Jesus has changed you; then you can be prepared to call up appropriate aspects of your testimony or training in order to make your faith real to other people. When they see that your faith is the root of who you are and not just something you let out on Sundays, then your Christian influence will begin to make a positive impact.

Wow! Mile 26 flew by! We have learned about Christian influence; seven keys to creating it; strategies for making the most of every opportunity God gives us to extend it; and ten practical tips for creating it in our workplace. We have only 0.2 miles to go to finish our race of faith! It has been quite a journey, one that has convicted us, comforted us, and challenged us. Now, as we make our final push to the finish line, let's remember our last memory verse:

So whether you eat or drink or whatever you do, do it all for the glory of God.

(1 Corinthians 10:31)

The Finish Line

You made it! As you cross the finish line, you are tired but fulfilled, exhausted but ecstatic, sore but victorious! The crowds are cheering, and your loved ones embrace you and congratulate you. The moment slows before your eyes, and you are able to take it all in. What a race! What a winner! What a champion of Christ!

You did it. You know what you believe, and you know why you believe it. And you don't merely believe—you know how to live what you believe. You know God, and He knows you. You know His Son as your Savior, Redeemer and Friend. You know the Holy Spirit, and He lives inside of you. The Bible has come to life before your very eyes, and you see the amazing panorama of God's perfect redemption plan like never before. You have connected the scriptural dots, and that has propelled you into action. You know the disciplines of the faith that will strengthen and sustain you throughout your life on Earth. You know what it takes to be saved, and you know what it takes to deliver the message of salvation. You know the purpose of the universal and local church. You know your spiritual gifts, and you know how and where to use them. You know how to invest in the lives of others and invite them into a relationship with Jesus Christ. And you know how to share the Good News about Jesus Christ with your family, work, neighborhood, city, and the world.

Even as Paul announced at the end of his race, we too can claim the truth of his words:

For I am already being poured out like a drink offering, and the time has come for my departure. I have fought the good fight, I have finished the race, I have kept the faith. Now there is in store for me the crown of righteousness, which the Lord, the righteous Judge, will award to me on that day—and not only to me, but also to all who have longed for his appearing

(2 Timothy 4:6–8).

When Paul was near physical death, he recounted his life in Christ with the powerful words: *I have fought the good fight, I have finished the race, I have kept the faith.* Every Christian who finishes his or her race of faith in this life is promised eternal life and the crown of righteousness. We should look forward to that day when we will meet our Savior face-to-face. And your hope should be that when that moment comes, He looks into your eyes and says…

Well done good and faithful servant! You have been faithful with a few things; I will put you in charge of many things. Come and share your master's happiness!

(Matthew 25:23)

To share in our Master's happiness is to share in His inheritance. After all, we are heirs of God and coheirs with Christ. And since we are heirs of God and coheirs with Christ, then we are God's children.

314

As we keep our eyes fixed on Jesus, awaiting the Day when we will see Him face-to-face, God's love letter, the Holy Bible, encourages us to *run with perseverance the race marked out for us.* (Hebrews 12:1)

Keep running!

Afterword

For more information about *The Race of Faith*, please visit my website at www.theraceoffaith.com. This website contains:

- An online workbook for study groups
- The e-version of the Spiritual Gifts Inventory
- *The Race of Faith* blog
- Additional information on how to lead *The Race of Faith* study
- Instructions on how to invite me to speak at your next gathering
- An area to give me your feedback on the book

Please stop by and visit. I would love to hear from you.

Until then, keep running!

> Forever in His Grip,
> Randy

Made in the USA
Charleston, SC
25 July 2013